The Actual Jesus

The Actual Jesus

Tina Pippin

CASCADE *Books* • Eugene, Oregon

THE ACTUAL JESUS

Copyright © 2025 Tina Pippin. All rights reserved. Except for brief quotations in critical publications or reviews, no part of this book may be reproduced in any manner without prior written permission from the publisher. Write: Permissions, Wipf and Stock Publishers, 199 W. 8th Ave., Suite 3, Eugene, OR 97401.

Cascade Books
An Imprint of Wipf and Stock Publishers
199 W. 8th Ave., Suite 3
Eugene, OR 97401

www.wipfandstock.com

PAPERBACK ISBN: 979-8-3852-1741-0
HARDCOVER ISBN: 979-8-3852-1742-7
EBOOK ISBN: 979-8-3852-1743-4

Cataloguing-in-Publication data:

Names: Pippin, Tina, author.

Title: The actual Jesus / by Tina Pippin.

Description: Eugene, OR: Cascade Books, 2025 | Includes bibliographical references.

Identifiers: ISBN 979-8-3852-1741-0 (paperback) | ISBN 979-8-3852-1742-7 (hardcover) | ISBN 979-8-3852-1743-4 (ebook)

Subjects: LCSH: Jesus Christ—Person and offices. | Bible—Hermeneutics. | Jesus Christ—In motion pictures. | Jesus Christ—In literature.

Classification: BT205 P585 2025 (paperback) | BT205 (ebook)

VERSION NUMBER 07/11/25

Chapter 2 appears in a revised form: "Behold the Sons of Man: Fantasy and the Markan Messiahs." In *Simulating Aichele: Essays in Bible, Film, Culture and Theory*, edited by Melissa C. Stewart, 335–45. Sheffield: Sheffield Phoenix, 1025. Used by permission.

Chapter 5 appears in a revised form: "Air Jesus: Fear of Flying in the Gospel of Mark." In *Bible and Theory: Essays in Biblical Interpretation in Honor of Stephen D. Moore*, edited by K. Jason Coker and Scott S. Elliott, 109–126. Minneapolis: Lexington, 2020.

Chapter 6 appears in a revised form: "(Un)holy Saturday." In *T&T Handbook of Jesus and Film*, edited by Richard Walsh, 261–72. New York: T&T Clark, an imprint of Bloomsbury Publishing Plc., 2021. Used by permission.

Chapter 7 appears in a revised form: "Jesus a Fantasy Mother." In *Mother Goose, Mother Jones, Mommie Dearest: Biblical Mothers and Their Children*, edited by Cheryl Kirk-Duggan and Tina Pippin, 141–56. Semeia Studies 61. Atlanta: SBL, 2009. Used by permission.

Chapter 8 appears in a revised form: "The End of Jesus." In *Those Outside: Noncanonical Readings of the Canonical Gospels*, edited by George Aichele and Richard Walsh, 43–64. New York: T&T Clark, an imprint of Bloomsbury Publishing Plc., 2005. Used by permission.

For my daughter Jacy. Our adventures into the imagined, fantastic worlds of stories have made the actual world so much better.

Contents

List of Illustrations

Acknowledgments

My encounter with Jesus scholarship began many years ago in an "Introduction to New Testament" college class with Dr. James L. Blevins. All the criticisms of nineteenth- and twentieth-century scholarship about the canonical Gospels helped to situate these ancient tales in some tentative layout. The contingent nature of what one can certainly say about Jesus led me to easy distraction by the work of people and groups committed to the social justice message they heard in the Gospel texts. The theories only make sense to me in the hands-on work of justice and human rights. I also owe a debt to my graduate school ethics professor, Dr. Glen Stassen, for his modeling of anti-nuclear and anti-death penalty commitments. The open nature of my graduate education allowed me the space to do interdisciplinary work and Marxist feminist literary readings of the Apocalypse of John with Dr. Blevins. There is another Jesus in that last book of the Bible, one that shares an apocalyptic message with the Jesus of the Gospels, yet is more ethically problematic for me. In this book I return to the Gospels in their multiple incarnations: in text, film, art, politics, popular culture, and artificial intelligence. Jesus makes appearances in unexpected places, and my curiosity takes me into many directions, thanks in part to these teachers.

A big motivation to write some of the chapters came with invitations to participate in the Festschrifts for colleagues (George Aichele and Stephen Moore), along with anthologies on film and critical theories of the Bible. I have special appreciation to Richard Walsh for his film expertise, and to the Bible and Film, and also the Reading, Writing, and Theory sections of the Society of Biblical Literature, where I presented some parts of this book. In many ways, I continue to be guided and inspired by the creative scholarship of George Aichele. His readings of the Jesus stories remain revolutionary.

I offer special thanks to the library staff at Agnes Scott College, especially Stephanie Kurth, for locating the hard-to-find materials, and Christopher Bishop for obtaining the obscure films. There have been several supportive sister-scholars along the way as I pulled this book together. Dr. Cheryl Kirk-Duggan is, among her many talents, a "writing whisperer." Dr. Mitzi Smith is a great debate partner on our walks around the local lake. Writing-focus buddies include Dr. Kristyn Sessions, who in weekly Zoom sessions pushed me along in grace-filled ways. And my colleagues, Buddhist scholar Dr. Jan Willis and Islamic studies scholar Dr. Roshan Iqbal, gave much inspiration with helpful comments over years of writing gatherings. I thank Rev. Dr. Anna Pinckney Straight, Dr. John Arrowood, and members of the Rothermel Foundation for their hospitality and for bringing me back to lecture about Jesus in my home territory in eastern North Carolina. The students in my "Jesus in History and Culture" class at Agnes Scott College over many years provided the necessary questions, challenges, and insights.

My wonderful family, Jerry, Jacy, and three (now one) cats were part of the process from the beginning of this book, offering support and love. I dedicate this book to my daughter who provided the excuse over many years to delve into so many books and movies—time well spent.

Introduction: Downloading Jesus

In a recent advertisement for a popular Catholic meditation app for the season of Lent, "Jesus" appears at a couple's bedside as they sleep, casually dressed in jeans and a Henley shirt. The alarm goes off, and a woman awakes, startled to see "Jesus" sitting very close and cross-legged on a side table. "What the?! Who are you?!," she exclaims. "Jesus" replies, "I'm your guide," meaning, a guide on the app. "I don't remember downloading you," she argues, to which "Jesus" replies, "Actually, you downloaded me several months ago," as he goes on to explain the many offerings on the app, ending with, ". . . and best of all, yours truly." The woman makes a connection that continues the conversation: "It's like I'm with the actual Jesus." He counters, "I'm not the actual Jesus. I just play him on TV." The conversation concludes with the woman responding, "I know." And "Jesus"/the actor Jonathan Roumie says, "I know you know."[1]

The woman knows, and yet is she still fantasizing a bit that Jesus is "actually" with her, watching over her as she sleeps. The Jesus she has downloaded and will continue to download multiple times is a virtual Jesus, but yet in this commercial, a flesh and blood actor "playing Jesus" and thus Jesus/not Jesus is in her bedroom, hawking a product. This male actor knows he is not the actual Jesus, that he just plays one in a popular series; he also suspects that people could easily confuse him with Jesus.

1. Hallow commercial, "A Day with Hallow," has changed the ads slightly since I first viewed them in summer 2023. The "actual Jesus" discourse occurs in an added bit with the woman in a business suit at the computer working when Gregorian chant and Jonathan Roumie appear in the hallway in prayer stance. He explains the calming features of the meditation app, with prayers, music, and Bible readings, ending with "And best of all, me." She replies: "Yeah, it's like I'm with the actual Jesus." Then he reminds her, "I'm not the actual Jesus. I just play him on television." The woman is immediately defensive: "Oh I know!," to which he replies, "Oh I know. I know you know."

The woman knows it also, and yet has her mind in two places. In the perpetual period between the biblical ascension and parousia is she substituting the actor for the "actual Jesus"?

Another scene in this meditation app advertising finds the same couple at night, with "Jesus" in his satin pajamas on the end of the bed. Then the ad cuts to the pajamaed Jesus sitting between the sleeping husband and wife, reading from a big Bible. He is reciting the Matthean Beatitudes, in that soft, sexy voice common in meditation apps, but he has switched his accent to a blend of an imagined Middle Eastern English, the accent he uses in the series *The Chosen*. Is this the Jesus-voice she hears when she reads the Gospels? Then he directs the viewer to considering during this Lenten season that instead of giving up chocolate to give a free trial of the app a try, "to help you close your day with God." The ad closes platonically with the sleeping husband turning over to rest his head on "Jesus's" arm. This "Jesus"/actor is an intruder, yet there is no concern about how he broke into and entered a private dwelling to watch this couple sleep and talk about the virtues of the Hallow meditation app.

The effectiveness of these seemingly innocent commercials, and the app, rests on the presence of "Jesus" as the endorser and voice of the meditations. Closing your day with God is the equivalent of being in bed with "Jesus." That is, bringing you in (really) close proximity to Jesus is the promise of this app. Although you know it is not the actual Jesus, it is a fantasy, a fictional representation, a dream of being really close (physically, spiritually, and metaphorically) to "Jesus." The line between the actor Jonathan Roumie, who plays (the character) Jesus in the series *The Chosen*, and the Jesus of the Gospels is blurred in these ads, and also in the series. Jesus is a pitchman, selling a mediation app. His sales tactics are illegal—as in breaking and entering the house—yet such actions are acceptable because he is "Jesus" on an extended series and is rather miraculously appearing in the couple's bedroom. I am placing "Jesus" in scare quotes because I find these views of "Jesus" scary. There is a certain unspoken and unintended (by the ad creators) creepiness to "Jesus" in his pj's in bed with you, certainly mitigated by having a standard "hot Jesus," with light brown skin, long wavy hair, a deep, sexy male voice, plus the chance of a snuggle, and hints of a holy threesome. The second coming can occur every time you download Jesus. Now that is a new Lenten practice! It certainly beats giving up chocolate for Lent.[2]

2. On Jesus as an object of desire, see Graybill, "Rock Me," 195: "Jesus may be 'sexy,' Jesus may have a time machine and 'abs that transcend space and time,' but we are still

As the first episode of *The Chosen* tells us, "*The Chosen* allows us to see Him through the eyes of those who knew Him." The series creator, Dallas Jenkins (son of the *Left Behind* series co-author Jerry Jenkins), proudly offers viewers their vision of the authentic Jesus, told through apparently verifiable eyewitnesses, and he works hard to come as close as possible to the "actual Jesus." The series has high production values, with carefully recreated sets and experienced actors and detailed, plotted back stories, along with honed theological statements. There is a certainty to the series: Jesus believes he is God's son the Messiah (so you should also believe), he fulfills all Jewish messianic prophecy, and faith is all that is needed, especially if you want to be healed and saved. The diverse and imperfect male disciples and the faithful women supporters are examples of how to be a human follower, within certain gender-determined lines.

The series attempts to make an absent Jesus present. Due to the series, "Jesus" is everywhere, all at once. One of the numerous revenue-producing spin-offs of the series is a contemporary *Diatesseron*, "a harmony of the Gospels," divided to be read over forty days.[3] There are numerous "after shows" with the actors and producers, and especially Jonathan Roumie/"Jesus." Of course, we, like the woman in the Hallow app ad, know that Roumie is not the "actual Jesus." Or are we encountering the uncanny? Where is the line between reality and fantasy? All representations of Jesus are fictional, fantasies, made-up stories of the divine incarnate in our world. God had a son, and as an absent father set him on a course for execution. There was no turning back; no ram in the thicket diversion as for Abraham at Isaac's planned execution. The scenario is more Jepthah's daughter (Judg 11:1–12:7) than the binding of Isaac (Gen 22). There is only the return to the ancient practice of sacrifice of the firstborn son (from a god with a human woman). The good news is that this son is immortal. Playing the character of Jesus, Roumie assumes the role of a knowing and obedient son, one who is very close with his father.

Consider another ad for the Roman Catholic meditation app Hallow. The actor Mark Wahlberg joins actor Jonathan Roumie to hawk prayer. (Wahlberg to the camera): ". . . I got Jesus here, and we were wondering if you might want to pray with us." (Roumie): "I'm not the actual Jesus

waiting for a queer messiah after all."

3. Laube, Jenkins, and Jenkins, *Blended Harmony*, 4, states, "The goal of this book is to have the Jesus story told in a seamless form." There is a panopticon effect to this form of narrative control. Even so, the narrative seams and folds persist, and some of those are the spaces I explore in this book.

obviously. But let's spend some time with the real me."[4] Roumie is lending his image as an actor who plays Jesus for the meditation app and his presence muddles what is "actual." Part of Roumie's "real me" is representing Jesus on screen. Spending prayer time with the actor can assist one in being closer to the "actual Jesus," and this message sells the meditation app (and, in turn, supports *The Chosen* series). Of course, I know these are paid actors, even as the "real" remains elusive.

This theme of actuality comes to the forefront in the four-part docuseries *Jonathan and Jesus*, with the actor Roumie commenting on the emotional burden and experience of playing Jesus in *The Chosen*. The cameras follow him through his tour in the US and Europe and his pilgrimages to historic Christian sites, such as the Vatican and Notre Dame cathedral. People who meet Roumie often get slightly confused, calling out, "There he is! There's Jesus!"[5] Throughout the episodes, passersby often cry, want to touch him, or ask him to pray with them. At a meeting on Capitol Hill, someone announces when they see Roumie: "We've been waiting for Jesus."[6] There's a definite reaction to Roumie and "Jesus" and as a Christ figure, and the documentary stresses the actor's deep Roman Catholic faith. Again, the lines are blurred.

For an actor, playing the role of Jesus can be a burden and on occasion mess with their heads. In an appearance on the TV talk show *The View*, Whoopi Goldberg asks Roumie, "Are you finding that people are having a little bit of trouble separating you from the part?" Roumie replies, "Occasionally the line seems a little blurred," with people asking to do confession or otherwise confusing the line between actor and biblical character.[7] I am most interested in this blurred line, the visions of Jesus that are indistinct, indefinite, and incomplete. A complete vision of Jesus troubles me. The Christian right exhorts me to "keep my eyes on Jesus," but their vision of Jesus, with his nationalistic, white supremacist, misogynistic agenda is one I have to oppose. So playing Jesus is not an innocent act; it is politically loaded and calls attention to the "politics of interpretation,"[8] and proposes reading the Gospels

4. In this role Mark Wahlberg and Jonathan Roumie are "Christian influencers." The video appeared on their Facebook feed but is no longer accessible.

5. Stewart, dir., *Jonathan*, episode 1.

6. Stewart, dir., *Jonathan*, episode 2.

7. *The View*, "Jonathan Roumie."

8. See Mitchell, ed., *Politics*.

as an ethical act. But reading and hearing the Gospels is not as easy or contained as the Hallow app depicts.

In this book I am looking at/for "Jesus" in different manifestations in contemporary times and asking questions about what different ethical interpretations entail. Seeking Jesus in texts, material and popular culture, and dreams and visions can lead to new understandings and questions. What I am offering is not an overview of historical Jesus studies and the multiple "quests." I suppose one is always questing to some degree, and in one way or another, but my adventures are not in hunting for "origins," for the orientalist roots of origin hunting are too thick.[9] The multiple old and new quests are about finding "origins" and ultimately, an "original Jesus," or as getting as close as possible through text criticism, sociological criticism, archaeology, and the rest. The Hallow commercials show how close to "Jesus" one can get through an app. Fiction and film reveal different Jesuses spread out over the globe and centuries. Any original may have "existed" but it has long ago dissipated, lost in a multitude of copies and copies of copies of copies, and so on.

There has been and probably will always be an origins project. What did Jesus say, do, and did he even really live? When I read the history of the quests (one, two, three, four, and more),[10] I find multiple "historical Jesus/es" and am made dizzy by the turning of my head this way and that as each one "speaks" in a different way, and each scholar claims to discover (or come as close as possible to) the real words and happenings of this first-century prophet. There is an evolving "Gospel of the year/decade," with recent emphasis on the Gospel of Thomas (the Jesus Seminar) and the Gospel of John (the Fourth Quest). The trajectory of historical Jesus studies seems to me to circle back on itself, with new volumes tracing the theories of the nineteenth- and twentieth-century scholars, the major debates, and the next directions in the field.

The majority of recent Jesus studies is historical-critical, tracing the trajectories from the eighteenth century and Ernest Renan through Albert Schweitzer to Rudolf Bultmann to the various quests for Jesus's words and deeds that followed. The quests morph over time, with the most extreme origins project of the twentieth century the Jesus Seminar's color-coded Bibles of Jesus's sayings and deeds.[11] There

9. See, for example, studies by Said, *Orientalism*, and Masuzawa, *Dreamtime*.

10. In a 1997 article critiquing the quests for the historical Jesus, Marsh, "Quests," 415, counted as many as "nine interlocking quests of the historical Jesus since 1778."

11. Funk et al., *Five Gospels* and *Acts of Jesus*.

is new movement to expand into even newer, more open-ended and diversity-centered "quests," including the "next quest."[12] This quest explores what can be known about the historical Jesus while allowing more space for what cannot be known.

With all these volumes tracing the research on the historical Jesus, the basic questions remain: Did Jesus speak Aramaic? Was he (semi-)literate? What was his profession? How Jewish was he? Did his family know who he was? (Not according to Mark's Gospel). Did Jesus have siblings? Was he "illegitimate"? Was he a miracle worker and healer? Was he short? Dark-skinned? Did he have short hair? Charismatic? Queer? Celibate? Ascetic? Did he really like children? Did he ask his followers to keep his identity a secret? Did he call twelve male disciples? Was he inclusive of women in his movement and inner circle? Was he a peasant or a slave? Was he Palestinian or Judean? A revolutionary or Zealot? How did he feel about the Roman occupation? What were his politics, especially toward Rome? What was his teaching on slavery? Was his teaching apocalyptic? What was his self-understanding, and when did he understand what things about himself? Did he think he was the messiah, and if so, what did that mean for him? Was he a blasphemer? What can outside sources tell us or confirm about Jesus? All the rabbit holes of the Qumran, Josephus, Apollonius of Tyana, Gnostic Gospels, et al. have led me back out the other end. I find these questions intriguing but exhausting. What can we "actually" know about Jesus?

Scholars before and after Ernst Renan and Albert Schweitzer touted a historical Jesus in their different ways. Rudolf Bultmann took form-critical scissors to the Gospels in order to resist the temptation to "quest" for Jesus, since Bultmann did not find much "authentic" in the Gospel stories about Jesus. Bultmann's students resisted him by creating a "new quest," hoping to enlarge that demythologized canon. And then other quests followed, a stream of (mostly male) scholars examining the individual trees of an expanding forest. What I am offering here is not an overview of historical Jesus quests studies. My interests are in examining the ideologies and motivations of the act of questing and not in settling in on a quest of whatever number (old, new, or next) or some definitive statement or view of Jesus. Is not the act of not questing also a quest? Therein lies my dilemma. Even knowing this, I am looking deeper into various glimpses of Jesus, some provided by these quests and some in culture and politics, along with their

12. Crossley and Keith, eds., *Next Quest*; Schröter and Jacobi, eds., *Jesus Handbook*.

influences, effects, etc. Many of the sightings of Jesus in this book come from films. Although I have seen only glimpses of "Jesus" over my years of study, the good news is that new glimpses keep coming.

In exploring various appearances of Jesus and their influences, reception, and affects, I am responding to various representations of "Jesus" as reimagined in fictional retellings (in particular, film, art, novels, advertisements, social media). The journey of exploring and encountering Jesus in stories, histories, (artistic) visions, fiction, film, and popular culture is for me more interesting and engaging than an arrival at some (for me, shaky) historical "certainties." The stories about Jesus, from all the Gospels (canonical and not), rolling through the centuries in text and image, draw me in and provide ways to glimpse "Jesus." I find all the multiple quests also provide only glimpses, even as they intend to provide fuller portraits. With only glimpses, my eyes might deceive me, or maybe deception is the point.

I received much traditional training in questing. The first scholarly book on the Bible I encountered in college in an "Introduction to New Testament" class with James L. Blevins was Rudolf Bultmann's *Primitive Christianity*, followed by *Jesus and the Word*, *Jesus Christ and Mythology*, and the two volumes of *The Theology of the New Testament*, and next the post-Bultmannians who launched the "New Quest." My first impression was that for Bultmann Jesus was more word than actual historical person, and sitting as a nominal Episcopalian in a sea of Southern Baptists I was thrilled by Bultmann's pronouncements. For example: The virgin birth is a myth! The resurrection was a spiritual not physical event in the experience of the disciples! Bultmann's existentialism ruled my reading of the New Testament. My Bultmannian background may be a driving force in the paths I have chosen in biblical interpretation. Ideological criticism, postmodern readings, interdisciplinary wanderings are all part of my approaches. In my first semester of seminary, Leander Keck's "Lives of the Historical Jesus" course provided more historical background to the variety of quests, from exposing the mythological (David F. Strauss) and romanticized autobiographies (Ernst Renan). I continue to be indebted to Bultmann and his students. Narratology and deconstruction and postmodernism followed only later as major influences. Bultmann's existentialist Jesus took these journeys through critical theories with me.

As much as I want to keep these quests at bay, they continue to be embedded in Jesus scholarship. Speaking particularly of the Third Quest, Stephen Moore observes, "Many have joined in the manhunt, many more cheering or yelling obscenities from the sidelines. Startled eyes turn as hysterical Jesus suspects are dragged into the church by the triumphant band of critics. To the dubious congregation in the pews, each Jesus seems more unlikely than the last. 'Did you at any time claim to be the Christ, the Son of the Living God?,' each asked in turn. 'I most certainly did not,' most of them reply.' But if the congregation is in shock, we critics are in our element."[13] Moore is tapping into the motivations behind such quests, along with the many Jesuses who appear in scholarship.

How much of the "actual Jesus" has been discovered? There has been so much emphasis in Jesus scholarship on the existence of a historical Jesus that the Gospels become de facto biographies, or at least approximations of a real, enfleshed, human being. Or it is possible, with the correct assortment of scholarly tools, to sort out the actual Jesus, what he actually said and did and what was said and done to him? The goal seems to be to get as close as possible to something "original," embracing the impossibility of finding a completely restored Jesus, while getting "close enough" with each new attempt. Meanwhile, Jesus keeps replicating, spreading gospels and pieces of himself throughout the visual and digital and political and theological landscapes. Jesus remains elusive.

Playing Jesus

Director Dallas Jenkins and actor Jonathan Roumie provide several "behind the scenes" interviews to explore the inner workings of a professional actor playing the character of Jesus.

Jenkins describes his vision for the character as "masculinity combined with tenderness."[14] In many ways *The Chosen* is a "bro series," focused on the male disciples and the women connected to them and to Jesus, and of course, the male, father deity who sends his only son to be sacrificed for the sins of humanity. Despite a more inclusive focus on the key women characters, they remain tethered to the patriarchal constructs of the first—and the twentieth—centuries. But the series is about "the chosen" one, with all the others, men and women, being supporting cast.

Actors who have played Jesus comment on the heaviness of the role. Roumie talks about approaching "the role of Jesus as an actor versus the deity." In other words, he takes a professional actor's approach

13. Moore, *God's Beauty*, 93.

14. *Chosen*, "Immense Weight."

to the character, with a focus on the humanity of Jesus in the midst of the character's messianic awareness. Roumie relates that he does not feel like he is Jesus, even in the emotional moments on the set, and that his goal is "to try to get the closest possible feeling that Jesus might have had." He talks about how the role has deepened his own faith and led him to focus on the humility it takes to make the character convincing. Both director and actor emphasize "feeling the weight of [the whole project of *The Chosen*]."[15] One way they deal with the weight is through humor and "Jesus jokes," in which Jesus is not perfect, e.g., not athletic, not good with directions, and also able to joke about his own messianic knowledge of himself. Jesus smiles and laughs and weeps, and all these reactions show his humanity.

Jenkins and Roumie admit that sometimes the line between the actor and the character of Jesus can get crossed; a day actor or ensemble actor feels the spirit and shares their story with Roumie/Jesus. Roumie acknowledges, "It could start to cross the line into people thinking 'I feel like I'm looking at Jesus.'" He notes that the distinction can become hazy for fans of the show, "where it gets a little surreal when you meet people outside the set who have seen the show . . . there's this other thing in some people's eyes," that he is actually Jesus.[16]

What does it mean to be/not be actually Jesus? Actors interpret their characters and play a certain role based on multiple resources and direction. Their Jesuses are always interpretations, as is every "Jesus." Also, the weight of the character of Jesus on the page (Gospel or film script) lends itself open to the confusion over whether or not the actor is or is not actually Jesus. Roumie, along with other actors who have played Jesus (e.g., Willem Dafoe, Jim Caviezel, and Ted Neely) are not the actual Jesus, but does an actual Jesus exist? Does each actor get close to something "actual," and if so, what would that even be and how could we ever know what "it" is? We are entering a metaphysical dimension here. Roumie represents Jesus, as his character on screen and as a believing evangelical Roman Catholic. He is a double, a clone, and archetype of a modern evangelical Jesus. The character informs his belief and vice versa. *The Chosen* presents a duality of a possible biblical world and this invention is merged with the an imagined "actual" ancient world. Roumie the actor exists, as Jesus/not-Jesus, even as Jesus

15. *Chosen*, "Immense Weight."

16. *Chosen*, "Immense Weight."

does not exist, except in the distant past of an imagined first century Judea. Or in heaven, in some future parousia, in the hearts of believers, or as the Hallow app ads intimate (in intimate ways), in our beds.

Jesus's actual existence (on earth and eternally) is a necessary component for apocalypse. We fill in the stories of the christological "u-shape" of preexistence, existence, and post-existence. There are so many possibilities in the stories about Jesus, and the stories make Jesus "real," whether they are Gospel or other fiction. The website for *The Chosen* claims: "*The Chosen* allows us to see Him through the eyes of those who knew him."[17] Filmic representations of Jesus give us hints, glimmers of a spiritual leader and the path he set, wrong paths, problematic racial and gendered images, and dangerous traces of anti-Jewish messages. The actual Jesus keeps slipping away, finding the loophole, the gap, the easy getaway.

Jesus Lives!

The back cover of Bart Ehrman's book *Did Jesus Exist?* hawks the book's premise, that it explores "The truth behind the Jesus myth." My first reaction is that truth is not "behind myth" but infused through it, with myth remaining intact. The back cover further summarizes that Ehrman "provides a compelling portrait of the Jesus you may not have hoped to meet—but did exist whether we like it or not." So, "whether we like it or not," Jesus existed, and likely a Jesus some of us would not like. While Ehrman admits there is no proof, "the view that Jesus existed is held by virtually every expert on the planet."[18] He drills down on this argument, as a historian (and former fundamentalist believer): "What I do hope is to convince genuine seekers who really want to know how we know that Jesus did exist, as virtually every scholar of antiquity, of biblical studies, of classics, and of Christian origins in this country and, in fact, the Western world agrees."[19] As I hope to show, philosophers have expanded the concept of "existence," and to claim that Jesus existed as a real, historical, first-century Judean Jew is beside the point in the philosophical debate. Jesus exists, in memory, in imagined retellings, and that is all I can claim with certainty, not that I really want to make any certain claims about Jesus.

17. *Chosen* TV show website.
18. Ehrman, *Did Jesus Exist?*, 4.
19. Ehrman, *Did Jesus Exist?*, 5.

There is no proof of Jesus's existence, and I am not interested in the historical Jesus, even as I imagine a person who lived and taught and died and inspired followers who in turn founded a new religion. I also find studies of the "first-century context" of the Gospels necessary companions, especially in teaching undergraduates. A Marxist/socialist, revolutionary, de-colonial Jesus who causes "good trouble" against the Roman empire is useful to me in my economic justice work. I think all scholars have a "canon-within-a-canon," and that is natural, and many of these interpretations are enlightening. I just do not find the arguments for or against Jesus's existence fruitful. At this point the philosophical debate provides assistance, and I think takes us out of the mythicists or conspiracy theorists or scholarly evidence debate that Ehrman sets up. When I say "Jesus exists," it has a different meaning than finding a person grounded in certain certainties of history. This view is not based in my natural skepticism and questioning nature, but in my entering the portals of the various Gospels and films and novels and other locations of "Jesus" looking to experience an adventure, like Alice, and the siblings of Narnia, and Lyra of Oxford before me. Did Paul, with his nonconcern for most of the story details of the life and teaching of Jesus, not just go all in for the adventure, with his travels and spiritual evolution? The open narrative of the Jesus stories provides many portals to be explored. The search for stability in biblical studies describes my college and seminary education. I am not abandoning the historical-critical methods as I was never able to completely focus on them. To name a few examples of my distractions: films such as *Jesus of Montreal* and *The Life of Brian*, the novel *Lamb*, and the Jesus at the former Holyland Experience. These and many other stories drew my attention away from historical studies. Here I defer to Jacques Rancière: "To restrict oneself to art itself is to forget that art itself exists only as an unstable frontier which, to exist, needs to be crossed incessantly."[20] The interpretive adventure begins at the unstable frontier. Imagination is a primary tool of scholarship, even for those setting out to provide an argument of solid evidence to inch as close to the "real Jesus" as possible.

The Gospels are seeking to free themselves from any "historical Jesus" as scholars from the Enlightenment and after want to present it. It is not my job to free the Gospels from these tethers; they are already in another space-time continuum where they are free from any imagined real Jesus

20. Rancière, *Intervals*, 6.

in the real world. Rancière: "Cinema did not arise *against* theatre, it arose *after* theatre. This does not mean it simply places stories from books onto the screen. Rather, cinema comes after the literary revolution, after the overturning of the relations between signifying and showing that, in the name of literature, it has arrived at the art of telling stories."[21] In this book I am in conversation with several films, primarily *The Last Days in the Desert*, *The New Gospel*, *The Book of Clarence*, and *Us*. And I also show my engagement with other fictional Jesuses in art and fiction. In the conclusion I trace some encounters with Jesus through artificial intelligence. These various media appearances extend my limited imagination.

Every telling about Jesus is a retelling. As with George Aichele's "phantom messiah," I follow Jesus's shadow self in several appearances on the screen, in art, in literature, and through the political ramifications of these stories. There are so many "stand-ins" for Jesus and first-century Roman-occupied Judea: the many actors, the many "Jerusalems" and "Judeas" of Matera, Morocco, Montreal, Palestine, South Africa, "America," the Southern California desert, and Texas, and the sufferings of oppressed peoples through the centuries. A grand animatic of these stories of Jesus keeps moving on, with multiple authors, numerous narrators, and a revolving door of Jesuses.

Aichele brings a fresh honesty to reading the multiple texts and actors—biblical and otherwise—about the signifier "Jesus." Not bound by the false promises of originalism, he shows new ways to engage the dizzying number of appearances of "Jesus." Using critical theory and film studies, Aichele begins in and honors the uncertainties of the Gospel stories, and thereby engages with "reading from the outside."[22] He shows that traditionalists/insiders read theologically; he uses the example of how they read the Gospel of Mark to uncover the "mystery" of the text and of Jesus: "The great majority of theological and biblical scholars, despite their diversity in other ways, attempt to create such disciples, that is, to provide readers with a way inside the text, authoritative and reliable access to the true meaning of the text."[23] Any reader "from the outside, who appears to them as a thief, a violent, barbaric, and illegitimate reader . . . seems like a Judas who betrays the true meaning of the text."[24] The gospel texts (especially canonical) are vulnerable containers

21. Rancière, *Intervals*, 43.

22. Aichele, *Jesus Framed*, 1.

23. Aichele, *Jesus Framed*, 2.

24. Aichele, *Jesus Framed*, 3.

for the stories. Aichele observes: "For traditional biblical exegesis . . . the physical stuff of the text is merely an outer husk to be shattered and penetrated and eventually left behind."[25] Traditionalists often lay claim to "insider" knowledge of the inner workings of the text, using various methods from archaeology, sociology, Roman history, textual and form criticism, and more. When one method reaches an "end," then another is utilized. Those betrayers who read from the "outside" disrupt the "progress" of scholarship. Aichele offers further analysis: "Reading from the outside exposes the fundamental incompleteness and insufficiency of the material text. It reveals that the text is empty of meaning, and thus it uncovers the arbitrariness of the insider's reconstructions."[26] Such pronouncements do not win any academic popularity contests in Jesus studies.[27] Womanist, feminist, and minoritized critical approaches have had to claim their own spaces to expand and reimagine Jesus.

In a similar way, Richard Walsh investigates representations of Jesus in film: "In other words, the Jesus of film is no more innocent than is the Jesus of historical research. If Jesus films are less safe places to construct ideology (and it is not clear that they are), it is only because they are more public than the academy's images of Jesus."[28] Walsh reads the Gospels side by side with film, and in doing so shows how film opens up ways to interpret the Jesus stories. Whatever "meaning" the Gospels have can be opened up to surprising revelations.

The Original Jesus

Searching for the authentic stories of the central figure or founder of a religion is a common action of curious scholars and believers. We all know, generally speaking, how the story is going to end. In all the Gospels Jesus is crucified and dies and the tomb is empty. Resurrection and ascension (see chapter 5) are additions to the base story.

This story gets repeated over and over, such that any "original" is deep in the historical imagination. In her critique of originalism,

25. Aichele, *Jesus Framed*, 2.

26. Aichele, *Jesus Framed*, 4.

27. Consider Clive Marsh's, "New Historicist Perspective," 417, pronouncement, "[Historical Jesus scholarship] has been largely an all-male club of wealthy intellectual Euro-American contributors." For further critique of white, male, Eurocentric scholarship, see, for example, Schüssler Fiorenza, "Ethics," and Smith and Kim, *Decentering*.

28. Walsh, *Reading the Gospels*, 15.

Tomoko Masuzawa offers a reminder that "Repetition veils."[29] Following Mircea Eliade, Masuzawa is questioning the whole search for origins in modern scholarship as impossible to uncover, even as religion is all about origins and creation stories.[30] She turns to postmodern theories, and Walter Benjamin in particular, to address the problem of origins. Reproductions and copies of art "'reactivate' the original. Indeed, we are familiar with such a phenomenon: an artwork worn out and made into a cliché through innumerable reproductions invariably affects our experience of the 'real thing' when we finally encounter it."[31] Masuzawa continues, "In sum the photographic representation partially but significantly moves out of the reach of the original, liberates itself from the economy of origination and dissemination; it circulates on its own terms, and in turn co-opts the original into its own economy." What results also is "an indefinite number of reproductions but no original, save one that is, literally a *negative*."[32] When do we encounter the "real thing," or in Masuzawa's term, the negative, of Jesus?

Edward Said is also helpful with terminology, with "the notion of *beginning* as opposed to *origin*, the latter divine, mythical and privileged, the former secular, humanly produced, and ceaselessly re-examined."[33] The notion of beginning/s brings with it a critical edge in terms of "the critique of domination, the re-examination of suppressed history (feminine, non-white, non-European, etc.), the cross-disciplinary interest in textuality, the notion of counter-memory and archive, the analysis of traditions," and so forth.[34] Said avoids the term *origins* because of its link to an Enlightenment, colonial past. Said connects the desire for origins with colonial, European thought and practices. Said is showing what many modern scholars do, and to revert back to the fantastic legacy of the biblical stories is to ignore the Enlightenment. There are multiple beginnings to the stories about Jesus, with or without genealogy, or birth narrative, or discussion of paternity and family ties, or place of birth. As Said notes

29. Masuzawa, "Original Lost," 324.

30. Masuzawa, "Original Lost," 309.

31. Masuzawa, "Original Lost," 312.

32. Masuzawa, "Original Lost," 313.

33. Said, *Beginnings*, xiii.

34. Said, *Beginnings*, xiii. Said, *Beginnings*, 5, admits: "whether an interest in beginnings is practical or highly theoretical, there is an imperative connection to be observed between the idea of a beginning and an aboriginal human need to point to or locate a beginning."

about Ernst Renan's *Life of Jesus*, "The authority of a text, according to Renan, is tied to the realization that a text has outlived whomever participated in its original making."[35] Of Renan's project Said observes: "The text leaves behind its origin (which in this case of the New Testament is Jesus), for the text is the beginning of a series of substitutions which altogether comprise the formal object we call a text."[36] A text immediately becomes many texts, "since there is really no such thing as an absolutely primal text, each act of composition involves other texts, and so each writing transmits itself, receives other writing, in an interpretation of other writing, *reconstitutes* (by displacement) other writing," with each iteration a positive "affirmation" of the textual possibilities.[37] The Gospels are templates for both scholarly and fictional/filmic interpretations and reimaginings of Jesus, even as these templates have been imagined from other visions of Jesus. Quests for origins become just another way to continue the myths, fictions, fantasies about Jesus. Film and fictional reimaginings of the Jesus story re-immerse the reader in the alterity, loosening (hopefully) the hegemonic hold on the "actual" Jesus.

The Actuality of Jesus

To speak of the actuality of Jesus invokes the philosophical concept of actualism. The basic debate in philosophy is between "possibilism" and "actualism." Philosopher Chris Menzel defines possibilism as "what could have been," while actualism's concern is with what is already actual. He states that "for the actualist, there is no realm of reality, or being, beyond actual existence; to be is to exist, and to exist is to be actual."[38] Following Willard Van Orman Quine, Menzel relates the dominant view in the debate, that abstract, fictional, or fantastic objects exist and are fully actual.

Most helpful in clarifying this debate are the concrete examples from philosophy in the study of fiction and mythology. In her study of the connection of fiction and metaphysics, Aime Thomasson argues that fictional characters are not theoretical[39] or imaginary;[40] rather, "fic-

35. Said, *Beginnings*, 217; emphasis his.
36. Said, *Beginnings*, 218; emphasis his.
37. Said, *Beginnings*, 218; emphasis his.
38. Menzel, "Possibilism-Actualism."
39. Thomasson, *Fiction*, 20.
40. Thomasson, *Fiction*, 22.

tional characters are ordinarily maintained in existence by the existence of some copy or copies of the literary work containing them. . . . They exist as long as literary works regarding them remain."[41] André Leclerc also outlines the notion of fictional characters being "actual." Simply put, "To exist, it is enough to have been introduced at some moment in the history of the world."[42] Leclerc uses the example of Conan Doyle's famous fictional detective Sherlock Holmes, and declares "that it is just a plain fact that Sherlock Holmes, the fictional character, exists."[43] What he means by this existence is that the "material base" of the character can be changed and adapted so that there can be different iterations of the character in different time periods.[44] For example, Holmes can have a variety of "accidental properties" of hats, pipes, love interests, and violins; for Leclerc, "This is enough to determine Holmes's identity *as long as there is no radical change in the material basis*."[45] He clarifies further, "Even if we could find a single candidate possible detective to identify with Sherlock Holmes, this would be a possible man with the property of being born in the nineteenth century, not of being created by Arthur Conan Doyle."[46] Likewise, even if we could locate a first-century Judean Jew who fit the description of Jesus, he would not be the same Jesus/es created by the Gospel writers. What the philosophers show us is that the quests for the historical Jesus are futile, and unnecessary. The actual Jesus cannot be nailed down, so to speak.

Is Jesus a fictional character? Yes, and stating this does not mean he did or does not exist. Jesus may or may not have been a person, as created by the Gospel writers (with commonalities and differences) who lived in first-century Judea, yet he is dependent on these texts for his existence. Leclerc finds kernels of truth in characters, stating succinctly: "But there are true sentences about fictional characters and their truth must be explained."[47] For Leclerc, Holmes exists, as "there is no merely possible Holmes."[48] This existence of Holmes is based upon this truth: "*having been created or introduced at some moment in the history of the*

41. Thomasson, *Fiction*, 23.
42. Leclerc, "Actualism," 80n2.
43. Leclerc, "Actualism," 62.
44. Leclerc, "Actualism," 67.
45. Leclerc, "Actualism," 73; his emphasis. See the discussion of Thomasson, 44–46.
46. Thomasson, *Fiction*, 18.
47. Leclerc, "Actualism," 71.
48. Leclerc, "Actualism," 68.

world is more fundamental than to be concrete."[49] Thomasson adds to this understanding: "there is no *real* (spatiotemporal) thing to which the term 'Holmes' refers, even if someone happens to match those descriptions. Moreover, there is no possible man to whom it refers. But this does not show that 'Holmes' cannot possibly refer."[50] In other words, "If we give up the idea that fictional names refer to actual or possible people and turn to the idea that they instead refer to a kind of abstract artifact," then we can let the character breathe. For Thomasson these artifacts are fictional objects that have been "baptized" in a "chain of reference."[51] This chain extends from the text to different manifestations and sites.

The character name "Jesus" is a signifier. This signifier "Jesus" refers to many "Jesuses" who appear in a variety of different literary and visual forms. Nicholas Wolterstorff describes the signification process: "the heart of representation, no matter in which of the arts it occurs, lies not in composing a copy of the actual world but rather in using some artefact to project a world distinct from our actual world. Representation, or mimesis, is world projection."[52] He continues: "Though the fictional projection of a world is an activity distinct from that of making claims about our actual world, yet one can make a claim about our actual world by fictionally projecting a work's world. . . . by approaching worlds from the side of fiction we will avoid getting hung up on actuality."[53] Wolterstorff believes that "projected worlds are always *anchored* to entities existing in the actual world."[54] He goes on to assert: "Projected worlds, in the first place, exist—that is, they actually exist."[55] He emphasizes that art can be "true" or "false" and has the potential "for altering our convictions and for confirming us in the ones we already have."[56] The representations of Jesus we are drawn to in Gospel, art, film, and the rest can upset us (thinking as an example of the pickets by protestors of *The Life of Brian* and *The Last Temptation of Christ* when these films were first in theaters) or draw us in with its affirmation of the Jesus we imagine. But true or false to our reality, we connect to the fantasy most of all. Fiction can be true,

49. Leclerc, "Actualism," 64; emphasis his.
50. Thomasson, *Fiction*, 46–7; emphasis hers.
51. Thomasson, *Fiction*, 46–7.
52. Wolterstorff, *Works and Worlds*, v.
53. Wolterstorff, *Works and Worlds*, 107.
54. Wolterstorff, *Works and Worlds*, 356; emphasis his.
55. Wolterstorff, *Works and Worlds*, 356.
56. Wolterstorff, *Works and Worlds*, 363.

or false, but it is the emotional power of it that matters to Wolterstorff.[57] All we have are copies, and copies of those copies and on and on, and some of those copies lead us to fantastic (and not actual, or rather, actual as fantasy) worlds, where the sick are healed, the dead are miraculously resurrected, and the disciples and the Roman authorities have detailed backstories (e.g., *The Life of Brian*, *Behold the Man*, and also *The Chosen*). The text (or artwork or film) is a portal into other worlds. I think every story about Jesus is an escape into another, imagined world. With what objective certainties do we return? Works of art, from the canonical Gospels to contemporary representations, have emotional power as they perform the (imagined) past. Films and theme parks such as the Holyland Experience in Orlando (no longer in existence) or the passion play in Eureka, Arkansas, attempt to recreate first-century Judea; the latter examples were complete with a living (actor) Jesus. A popular line of Jesus scholarship is to dig deep (pun intended) to excavate the actual world of Jesus's time. If I say, "The historical Jesus actually exists," what am I saying? Is it like saying Sherlock Holmes exists?

Like the famous literary detective, Jesus has been written, re- and overwritten, expanded, and understated. There are so many versions of "Jesus" that, as Thomasson observes about multiple accounts of a character, "A problem arises here: On what basis is a literary work to be counted as part of the same series as another work?"[58] Standard Jesus films and novels privilege the Jesus(es) of the Gospels, and those films and fictions that make the most up-front "commitment to authenticity" are commended for their attention to historical and scholarly details. Still, what ultimately remains on screen is a characterization of Jesus. Thomasson suggests a loose set of "identity conditions" for a character in different literary spaces.[59] She explains, "The moral here is plain: Similar characters do not the same characters make (nor do dissimilar characters different characters make). . . . Instead of treating them as ideal abstracta distinguished solely by their properties, we may get farther by treating fictional characters as historical entities individuated at least in part by the circumstances of their creation."[60] In a similar vein Mieke Bal reveals some inner workings of characters: "Characters give the most pleasure when they are allowed to resist their readers instead of being overruled and forced to

57. Wolterstorff, *Works and Worlds*, 234.

58. Thomasson, *Fiction*, 61.

59. Thomasson, *Fiction*, 63.

60. Thomasson, *Fiction*, 62.

conform to readers' expectations."[61] The Jesuses I am most drawn to are the ones who resist climbing into my mental box.

In a similar way, the character/s of Jesus from the four Gospels "exist." We can visit Holmes's home on Baker Street in the same way we can visit Jesus sites: the birth site in the Church of the Holy Sepulchre, the two locations for baptism and for the empty tomb, etc., as well as the reproductions of these sites. We cannot visit the underworld or heaven, as tradition tells Jesus did, except in stories. The difference is that "Jesus sites" belong to the realm of the deities and have a different authority and meaning. In addition, deities are seen as historical, as having concretely walked the earth in their divine or semidivine forms at determinable moments in history; plus they have superhuman powers. The brilliant but still human detective Sherlock Holmes is fictional, even as the context of his narrative is set in different historical time periods, depending on the version of the story. Leclerc argues that we believe the differently embodied Holmeses (from Clive Brook in 1929 to Benedict Cumberbatch to Johnny Lee Miller in *Elementary*, the latter two set in contemporary times) because the material basis of the character's phenomenal crime-solving expertise is pretty much the same. In a similar way perhaps the different Jesuses embody a set of material bases that are expanded and reimagined by the actors and the screenplays. Based on this philosophical line of thought, Jesus films that play too fast and loose with the material base become controversial; I am thinking of Martin Scorcese's *The Last Temptation of Christ* (based on Kazantzakis's reinterpretation of Jesus in his novel) and *Jesus Christ Superstar*. (*Corpus Christi*, *Ultra Christ*, *Jesus Christ Vampire Slayer*, *Black Jesus*, José Saramago's novel *The Gospel According to Jesus Christ*, and the bronze sculpture of *Christa* are different matters). Terry Gilliam's *Life of Brian* still has a traditional movie Jesus in the background scenes, although in a distance, difficult to hear clearly. Representations that stray too far (and that border is certainly variable) become scenes of controversy and protest. *The Chosen* presents an acceptable and affable and also actual Jesus, as it claims a close reading of the four Gospels. The Gospel writers believed that Jesus existed, and filmic interpretations draw from this belief. They also extend the fictional character.

61. Bal, *Narratology*, 106. She further relates, 108, what can happen when fictional characters are given flesh and blood: "Aspects of the anthropomorphism of characters can play nasty tricks. Characters are attacked or defended as if they were people that the critics like or dislike."

Leclerc points out that there are internal and external perspectives of these existing characters.[62] Internally, as with Sherlock Holmes novels and films, when we read the Gospels or watch a Jesus film, "We collude, so to speak, with the author. There is no other way to *enjoy* the novel."[63] As a New Testament scholar and a fan of (many) Jesus movies, I am colluding, each time, as I add to my interpretation of "Jesus." In this collusion, am I not admitting that I am discovering, even in small hints and glimpses, an "actual Jesus"?

Leclerc points out the external perspective in which "we refer to Holmes as a fictional character, as an abstract artefact, not as a (feigned) person." Following philosopher Saul Kripke, Leclerc states that fictional characters are not ghosts, rather, "They are inhabitants of our world."[64] They exist. The character of "Jesus" exists—in the Gospels, in fiction and film, in the hearts of believers, and in the bed/room of the couple in the Hallow app ads. What I mean by the actual Jesus is very different from the debates of the century-plus of questers. The terms *myth, fiction*, and *fantasy* are essential for me in understanding these Jesus stories and characters.

The actuality of "Jesus" is present whether there was a historical person or not. Gianni Vattimo draws from Michel Foucault's concept of "the ontology of actuality." The translator of Vattimo's work adds a note to trace the etymology of the word *actuality*: "Like the French term actualite, the Italian term 'attualita' means 'current events,' 'current affairs,' or 'the state of the world.'" The translation to "actuality" is "due to the connection maintained between actuality, activity, act, and action, that is, with the ethico-practical sphere."[65] The movement and essence of actuality is in the realm of the metaphysical for philosophers. The metaphysical nature of actuality makes it difficult to deny the existence of Jesus, but it allows for Jesus to exist as a fluid, morphing being. Following this philosophical line of thought, it is possible for Jesus to exist, in the past (even "preexistent") and in the current time. By this logic, those waiting and hoping for Jesus to appear in some future "second coming" could be told that Jesus already exists in that future time. All this time-sliding thought is mind-spinning and comes with a warning: every appearance may not be an ethical one. Here I am thinking of Jesus's role in the apocalypse

62. Leclerc, "Actualism," 69–71.

63. Leclerc, "Actualism," 69.

64. Leclerc, "Actualism," 70.

65. Vattimo, "Actuality," 105n4.

and destruction of the planet and most of humanity. Or, to bring it to the actuality of current events, to the rise of Christian nationalism in the US and neofascism.[66] The appearance of Jesus in the rationale for book bans in Florida, for instance, is not a moral appearance. As I write this chapter, Faith in Florida activists in churches are resisting this whitewashing of history by developing a "Black Lives Matter" curriculum to fill in the gap created by the right-wing politicians.[67] The Jesus in these black churches is different in body and being than the one of the conservative politicians, and he (they?) stands with the marginalized against the dangers of historical revision and erasure.

A likely argument from Ehrman and other historians in reply to this philosophical understanding of actuality and existence would be that Sherlock Holmes is a fictional character and Jesus is not. If the Gospel writers had invented Jesus as a fictional character, like say, Odysseus, Jesus exists in a different way as a divine/human being. My response is that "Jesus" as a referent has been baptized in multiple times and ways, rising up from the Jordan and wandering on. The imagined and enlarged "biblical" scenes are fictional and authentic at the same time. There exist pieces of Jesus, like holy relics, along with various whole Jesuses around in and outside the biblical text. And then the "Jesus/Christ figures" in fiction provide yet another layer on the existence of Jesus. Jesus/Christ has lives and afterlives. Unlike Sherlock Holmes, Odysseus, or Pegasus the winged horse, Jesus as an actual person is a possibility. But even if he was not a possibility, the "actual Jesus" continues to appear in our world.

How do I feel about Jesus? This project has left me emptier, more confused, and more amazed at the proliferation of images and appearances of Jesus. The actual Jesus is a manifestation of many imaginations. A flesh-and-blood actor one can reach out and touch or have pray with them, even virtually, makes Jesus "real," and knowing that he is not really the "actual Jesus" is a bit beside the point.

This volume represents encounters of various kinds and across numerous disciplines with the actual Jesus. The framework that initially emerged was ecological, guided by the main elements of water (baptism and ecological crisis), earth (desert wandering and food worker justice), air (the ascension and descent into hell), and fire (apocalyptic teachings and threats). Philosopher Gaston Bachelard is my guide for some of the

66. See Eco's definition and discussion of "eternal facism" in "Ur-Facism."

67. Faith in Florida, "Black History."

thinking through the different elemental and ecological spaces. I am applying a structure to the book (elements) that I have invented. As this project developed, and new Jesus appearances continued to distract me, it is these distractions that convince me to stay distracted. These paths provide ethical challenges. I conclude with some of the apocalyptic threats, Jesus in "the cloud" of artificial intelligence and virtual reality. I am drawn more to the uncanny cracks and crevices of the narrative, portals to explore alternative and adjacent worlds to the "official" version, whatever that is.

Framing Jesus

The elemental framing of the chapters allows for some deeper investigation of parts of "the actual Jesus." As Festschrifts and handbooks I contributed to increased over time, so did this structure expand. This introductory chapter contextualizes the title of the book, "the actual Jesus." The next section, water, explores the baptism of Jesus, and the geopolitics of the Jordan River. The "earth" section looks to the wilderness wanderings of Jesus through the film *Last Days in the Desert*, filmed in the US borderlands. The second earth offering explores tomato farmers in Matera, Italy and Immokalee, Florida, and the fair food and worker-driven social responsibility through the hybrid documentary film *The New Gospel*. Both earth chapters deal with issues of immigrants, refugees, and asylum seekers. The "air" section is about the ascension of Jesus in the excessive text of the longer ending in Mark through art and film. The second piece in this section is on the spaces of the empty tomb and hell, or where Jesus went on "Holy Saturday." I use Jordan Peele's film *Us* and horror theories as conversation partners. Next I explore the element of "fire" through some of the apocalyptic teachings and images of Jesus. I conclude with a return to the concept of an "actual Jesus" through an investigation of Jesuses in artificial intelligence bots and racialized imaging. Through all these elements, the "actual Jesus" appears, many times and in multiple ways, actually.

2

Wade in the Water: Swimming with the Markan Jesuses

The Fantastic Baptism in Mark 1:9–11

THE JESUS STORIES DEFY reason. The general premise is as follows: a male god has a son by a virginal earth-woman, and this son grows up in poverty in a Roman-occupied village to become a prophetic teacher and messiah. This son gathers a variety of followers and breaks all sorts of social and cultural rules and treks across his country for either a year (the Synoptic Gospels) or three years (John's Gospel). He works miracles and heals people. Then he gets into trouble with authorities and is eventually executed by the Roman government in occupied Palestine. There are a lot of missing years, and even more missing information about the politics and personality of Jesus. And there are a variety of different retellings of these stories, with lots of gaps and exaggerations and inventions and starting points. Each of the four canonical Gospels begins differently, with Mark introducing an adult Jesus entering the story through his baptism by John the Baptist. From here the narrative flies toward the gaping hole of its open ending in Mark 16:8. There is an infinite loop to this Jesus story and the event of the baptism returns and has afterlives. The placement and movement of this story through time is what interests me. Mark pulls the reader into the water with John and Jesus, warning: "Prepare to get wet."

The baptism of Jesus defies reason, or at least any definitive version. The baptism of Jesus in Mark is a marker, a starting point, a watery gate into Mark's story. John the Baptist dunks Jesus not once, but again and again—in Mark and in the subsequent Gospels and beyond. Jesus films (and fiction) portray this scene in multiple ways, from gritty prophetic space (*The Last Temptation of Christ*) to holy water (*The Greatest Story Ever Told* and most other films). I want to trace the Markan baptism/s through the thin spaces of heaven and earth, in other words, as texts of fantasy. I want to return to the scene, wade in the water. What happens when Jesus goes under, when the heavens are torn apart, when the heavenly voice speaks? I do not assume that this story is "historical," for that would be a diversion away from the text. And I do not suppose I will ever have a definitive answer, or a definitive version of the story. If Mark's baptism story is an invention,[1] then it serves to immerse (pun intended) the reader in the slip between worlds and into a world where messiahs are born and work miracles, die and are resurrected from the dead (or at least are missing from their tombs, as in Mark). This split—in the Jordan Valley Rift in which the river flows, in the text of Mark, and in the heavens—provides spaces for interpretation and multiple retellings of this story and also for multiple Jesuses and endless baptisms.

Mark keeps the baptism story, like most of his stories, brief:

> 9In those days Jesus came from Nazareth of Galilee and was baptized by John in the Jordan. 10And just as he was coming out of the water, he saw the heavens torn apart and the Spirit descending like a dove on him. 11And a voice came from heaven, "You are my Son, my beloved; with you I am well pleased." (Mark 1:9–11)

How do you imagine this scene: John as a wild prophet in the wilderness, preaching an existential message mixed with doom and hope? John as pacifist, or as Zealot? John pronouncing certainty about Jesus as the messiah or as conflicted? Is Jesus confident about his (non) calling and mission? Who hears the voice: John, Jesus, an unacknowledged crowd, or only the narrator? Mark tells us Jesus sees the heavens open. Certainly, we the reader see the water, watch the dove descend, and hear the voice. Robert Fowler sets the stage for the reader/s of Mark to take charge. "Mark's Gospel exploits the rhetorical possibilities of a variety of kinds of gaps and places of indeterminacy, all of which help to make

1. See Vaage, "Bird Watching."

it open and indeterminate."[2] Mark's gospel puts the reader in the front row for the action. What Mark has figured out, according to Fowler, is the importance of not settling for a singular truth or meaning—in other words, for not being able to step in the same river twice.

We will never know a lot of things about this short scene of baptism, especially about the relation of John and Jesus and the meaning of the baptism: what kind of baptism it was (proselyte? repentance to be marked as saved in the future reign of God? an "adoption" ritual? a one-time event? or a multiple ritual of cleansing?). Neither will we ever know for certain what John thought of Jesus (a prophet? madman? coming messiah?). Did Jesus linger with John, or dash to the desert? John as the forerunner of Jesus sets the stage, and the two men have some commonalities. According to Günther Bornkamm, John and Jesus had an eschatological message in common, but different ministries. The message Jesus got from John provided the basis of his teaching: "Clearly, this baptism has the meaning of an eschatological sacrament, not, however, acting as magic without regard to the preparedness of the baptized, but as a 'baptism of repentance' (Mark 1:4), it is the last preparation and sealing of the baptized for the coming 'baptism' of the Messiah, and preserves them from the day of wrath to come."[3] John and Jesus go their separate ways after the baptism in Mark; they do not confer or have further eschatological chats. John meets his eschatological ending a bit sooner than Jesus, and Mark weaves a longer tale about John's end than the baptism.

Unlike Mark, who understands the baptism is a ritual of repentance, subsequent retellings of the story shy away from this approach. Josephus understands this act of John not as a repentance but as a purifying rite that is preceded by just acts: "They must not employ it [baptism] to gain pardon for whatever sins they committed, but as a consecration of the body implying that the soul was already thoroughly cleansed by right behavior."[4] The baptism in Mark is of water (John) and the Holy Spirit (by Jesus). John tells those gathered at the river, "'I have baptized you with water; but he will baptize you with the Holy Spirit'" (Mark 1:8). The addition of fire to baptism comes in Matthew (3:11–12) and Luke (3:16–17)

2. Fowler, *Let the Reader*, 153.

3. Bornkamm, *Jesus*, 47.

4. Josephus, *Antiquities* 18.116–119. See the discussion in Crossan, *Jesus*, 33–34. Of John's arrest and execution, Crossan asks the question, 34, "how did ritual piety get misinterpreted as potential revolt?" Crossan, 43, believes Josephus "sanitized John for Jewish and Roman consumption."

and adds a layer of a final eschatological judgment. Justin Martyr, in his *Dialogue with Trypho*, goes further, and sets the river Jordan on fire:

> And then, when Jesus had gone to the river Jordan, where John was baptizing, and when He had stepped into the water, a fire was kindled in the Jordan; and when He came out of the water, the Holy Ghost lighted on Him like a dove, the apostles of this very Christ of ours wrote.[5]

Epiphanius of Salamis relates in his examinations of various heretical groups that the Gospel of the Ebionites mentions a great light at the baptism (13:7): "And straightaway a great light shone round about the place," thus pumping up the supernatural tone of the baptism.[6] A kind of fireworks lends a celebratory tone to these revisionary tales. Overall, this baptized Jesus is the One who will resurrect and rule forever, or in Mark, at least go permanently missing.

Even so, traditional scholarship wants to know the definite details, often claiming the baptism as a story that can be assumed historical. David Rhoads, Joanna Dewey, and Donald Michie relate that "Jesus'[s] whole character, in a sense, evolves from [the] formative experience [of his baptism]."[7] Jesus is in the line of a tradition of Moses, Joshua, and David crossing water (Josh 3:1–5:1). Jesus becomes "the beloved" son of the voice from heaven, which Mary Ann Beavis suggests translating *agapetos*, "dearest" or "darling," declaring an intimate relationship.[8] According to Jeremy Hutton, Mark's Gospel makes a literary (not historical) claim that Jesus is "a new king of Israel."[9] Jesus gives no response to the heavens except to leave.

Mark starts his story by opening the prophetic book of Isaiah, then heading straight to this mysterious tearing of heaven. There are cracks everywhere in this text: the crack of the scroll or codex pages at their seams, the crack in the earth formed by the river Jordan, the crack formed by John's preaching against the political hegemony of Herod and the Roman imperialism that propped him up, and the crack in the very cosmos, between worlds and times and spaces between God and humans. Eve sought

5. Justin Martyr, *Dialogue with Trypho*, 137.

6. Epiphanius of Salamis, *Panarion of Epiphanius*, 142. The mention of Justin Martyr and Epiphanius come from Strauss, *Life of Jesus*, 239.

7. Rhoads, Dewey, and Michie, *Mark as Story*, 84.

8. Beavis, *Mark*, 38.

9. Hutton, "Topography," 177.

this cosmic crack, deemed a sin by patriarchal interpretations and retellings. Babel tower reached for it too. And Moses, asking to see God's face, saw the backside of God (yet another crack; Exod 33:18–23).

What comes through this biblical opening of heaven? Here are a few examples of the stuff that passes through: flood water (Gen 7:11); "sulfur and fire" (Gen 19:24; fire: 2 Kgs 1:10–12; Apoc 13:1; 20:9); God's (or an angel's) voice (Gen 21:17; Mark 10:10 and par.; Apoc 10:4; 18:4); angels to mate with human women (Gen 6:1–4); a ladder (Gen 29:12); several of the plagues of the exodus story (especially hail, Exod 9:22–23; see Josh 10:11; Apoc 16:21); visions (Ezek 1.:1; 8:3; Dan 4:13, 23); angels and bird spirits (Mark 1:10; Apoc 10:1; 20:1); ascending prophets (Elijah: 2 Kgs 2:1, 11; Jesus: Mark 16:9); a great star/stars (Apoc 8:10; 9:1; 12:4); a dragon and his angels (Apoc 12:10); the new Jerusalem (Apoc 3:12; 21:2, 10). The smoke of burnt sacrifices goes up (Gen 8:20–21); the pole of the goddess Asherah attempts to bridge the distance between heaven and earth (2 Kgs 17:10). There is quite a bit of action between heaven and earth. Heaven is leaky and never completely sealed up. This tear is a rupture in reality, a fantastic moment in (narrative) time.

Again, the story of baptism provides a bridge not only between heaven and earth, but also from the past, present, and future in Mark and in the early church. One major event in this passage—this image of rending, of tearing—joins disparate parts of Mark's Gospel. Mary Ann Tolbert observes, "The rending of heavens and the rending of the temple curtain may describe similar transportations from realm to realm, one literally and the other symbolically."[10] Stephen Moore continues this thought in saying the ripping of the veil in the temple at the crucifixion reveals the absence of God: "But when at Jesus'[s] death the veil of the temple is torn in two, it reveals the presence of God—as absence . . . You undo the bands, unfurl the cloth or shroud, pull back the veil—endlessly. You wait endlessly for apocalypse."[11] Not all openings are created equal, and some of the current day warning signs in the river (Danger! Don't enter or drink the water!) apply across centuries. What is in the little "holy water from the Holy Land" containers pilgrims bring back from the Jordan? These vials are, in fact, vile. The water is contaminated—by the ideology of the Gospel writers, by the endless occupation forces and wars, and by the vague prophecies at the baptisms—of Jesus and into the future.

10. Tolbert, *Sowing the Gospel*, 281.

11. Moore, *Mark and Luke*, 38.

Jacques Derrida is drawn to the baptism too. He notices the differences in the four Gospels and that in John and in Mark, the fire in Luke and (Matthew) disappears.[12] Derrida's focus is on the splitting of heaven: "Jesus has finally chosen (*wählte*) the split, but this gesture cannot be simple. In breaking in two and in fleeing, he has declared war in the name of reconciliation; he is divided in his own proper split, hardened [*tendu*] against division itself, multiplying it and raising it thus to infinity."[13] Jesus leaves a place of water for one with no water, the desert. The voice from heaven gives no instruction. The slit/split in the sky is the mouth of someone/thing that claims Jesus as a son. What is the nature of this relationship? Is it healthy? Is this a voice Jesus obeys or respects? The river, heaven, the desert—these all serve as some of the many portals in Mark's Gospel. With the Markan rhetoric of "immediately," these spatial doors become openings into a different sense of time.

Portals into Other Worlds, with Other Jesuses

The baptismal water provides the entry into the Jesus story, giving it wild guidance and dousing it with a (non)sense of purpose. Such is the nature of the fantastic, to steer and veer into strange lands and plots. Mark begins with prophecy, followed by John's and then Jesus's eschatological message. Fantasy theorist Brian Atterbery notes, "Prophecy has always been a major channel for magic's infringement on narrative time."[14] Thus John's prophetic message is eschatological and beginnings and endings converge in his message and ritual action at the baptism. Magic happens, especially in the magic water of the magic river Jordan. The river is a portal, as is the ripped-open heaven, like the wardrobe in Lewis' Narnia or the bridge into other worlds created by the magic knife in Pullman's *His Dark Materials* series or Alice's rabbit hole or looking glass. These portals between multiverses enable characters to enter fantastic lands. Thus the fantastic enables a broader reading of Mark's story.

George Aichele reads Mark's Gospel alongside fantasy literature, such as Lewis Carroll's *Through the Looking Glass*. Aichele notes that when Alice tells the White Queen she is "exactly" seven and a half years

12. Derrida, *Glas*, 89a. I am mostly using the left column of Derrida's text that is his commentary on Hegel; the right column is Derrida's riff on Jean Genet.

13. Derrida, *Glas*, 93a.

14. Atterbery, *Strategies of Fantasy*, 58.

old, it is neither possible that Alice knows this definite time nor that the time stands still. But the distinction is trickier in Mark 1:9. Aichele discovered a split reference in this verse to a truth of Jesus's baptism that occurs "in those days": "The reference of the words in . . . Mk 1–9, is no more directly to the action of some actual, extra-terrestrial Jesus or John than is the reference of Carroll's words to the words of an actual, extra-textual Alice."[15] Thus the Jesus of Mark 1:9 is not the same character as the other Jesuses that roam other Gospels or fiction or film, and to equate these Jesuses "requires metaphysical postulates as well as religious beliefs that go far beyond any message provided by the Gospel of Mark alone."[16] Aichele raises the question of the historicity of narrative, including Mark's mention of geographic places. "'Galilee" is just as fictitious as the rabbit hole in Carroll's story. The references are split because of the existence of real places.[17] But these (possibly or even probably) real, geographic locations—and characters—have been colonized by the text. Aichele points out that the existence of "Nazareth" in the first century CE is questionable. Mark calls Jesus as one from Nazareth, not a Nazarene, as Matthew and Luke prefer. Jesus arrives in Mark 1:9 as "from Nazareth" and departs in 16:6 as "the Nazarene," and these locating words "form a structure through which Mark's fictionality is made explicit."[18] Aichele finds these descriptors empty and ambiguous in Mark, linking John to Jesus "in an iconic rather than indexical way . . . Mark 1:9 can have no truth value, apart from its reference to the story that is the Gospel of Mark."[19]

So too does Aichele dispute the origins of the voice from heaven and the Spirit: "A spirit descends on Jesus at the moment of his baptism (Mk 1:10), but it is not described as God's spirit (as it is in Mt 3:16 and Lk 3:22), and the voice from the sky or cloud that calls Jesus 'my beloved son' in 1:11 and 9:7 is not identified as coming from God."[20] In fact, "it is never clear who the father of Mark's Jesus simulacrum is."[21] Furthermore, the spirit that descends is also ambiguous. Is it the Holy Spirit? The spirit comes upon, or literally into (*eis*) Jesus in Mark's Gospel. "Whether Jesus is spirit-possessed is not a question in Mark

15. Aichele, *Sign*, 79.
16. Aichele, *Sign*, 80.
17. Aichele, *Sign*, 80.
18. Aichele, *Sign*, 84. See also Aichele, *Phantom Messiah*, 151.
19. Aichele, *Sign*, 85.
20. Aichele, *Simulating Jesus*, 82.
21. Aichele, *Simulating Jesus*, 83.

but rather whether the spirit in him is good or evil, from God or Satan (Mark 3:20–35)."[22] Could this spirit be a demonic spirit? Aichele comments, "Because the voice from the sky that identifies Jesus as 'my beloved son' at his baptism (1:11) is not identified, this leaves open the possibility that the scribes may be right: perhaps Jesus is possessed by an evil spirit!"[23] Mark shows uncertainty about the origins and identity of Jesus even as he writes "Nazareth" and "spirit" and "Jesus."

This uncertainty about the supernatural shows up even more clearly in contemporary lives of Jesus. In his novel *Lamb: The Gospel According to Biff, Christ's Childhood Pal*, Christopher Moore presents a teenage Jesus (Joshua) on a search to understand his mission. "'You are not the anointed one,' John said to Joshua. 'Gabriel came to my father. Your angel didn't even have a name' . . . 'Fine, I want nothing more than for you to be the Messiah, John.'" During a visit to Joshua's cousin John, Biff tells of Joshua's miracle healings and resurrections. John replies, "'I am so relieved. I didn't know what I would do. I don't know how to be the Messiah.' 'Neither do I,' said Joshua."[24] After a seventeen-year journey to the East to try to find the Magi who were present at his birth, Joshua and Biff return to Palestine and join John the Baptist's group of followers. They are baptized multiple times, but one day Joshua wakes up Biff to tell him that day will be special:

> At the river, John preached to a small gathering as he lowered Joshua into the water. As soon as Joshua went under the water a rift opened across the desert sky, which was still pink with the dawn, and out of the rift came a bird that looked to be fashioned from pure light. And everyone on the riverbank said "ooh" and "ahh," and a big voice boomed out of the heavens, saying, "This is my beloved son, with whom I am well pleased." And as quickly as it had come the spirit was gone. But the gatherers at the riverbank stood with their mouths open in amazement, staring yet into the sky.
>
> And John came to his senses then, and remembered what he was doing, and lifted Joshua out of the water. And Joshua wiped

22. Fowler, *Let the Reader*, 16.

23. Aichele, *Phantom Messiah*, 142–43; 56. See also Aichele, *Tales of Posthumanity*, 112: "Perhaps these voices come from an implied author attempting to address the reader, as in Mk 13:14, or more specifically to reinforce the phrase 'son of God' in 1:1."

24. Moore, *Lamb*, 89.

> the water out of his eyes, looked at the crowd who stood stunned with mouths hanging open, and he said unto them: "What?"[25]

In this retelling, different from Mark's gospel, everyone heard the voice from heaven, of God the Father, except for Joshua, who was underwater. A direct call eludes this messiah.

In the science fiction classic about Jesus by Michael Moorcock, *Behold the Man*, the time traveler named Karl Glogauer from 1970 lands in Roman Palestine in the year 28 CE, the year before the crucifixion of Jesus. His time machine lands close to where John the Baptist and his followers have their encampment. "The Essenes had seen stranger things than his time machine. They had seen men walk on water and angels descend to and from heaven; they had heard the voice of God and His archangels as well as the tempting voice of Satan and his minions."[26] As the time traveler heals from his 2,000-year trip through time, he slowly joins the community, even though at first they were unsure whether he was "a devil or a messenger from Adonai." Karl Glogauer replies, "I am neither."[27] Glogauer decides he cannot warn John of the dangers he remembers the Gospels telling about; he was not certain the Gospels were historical. "He realized dimly that the reason for this was because he wanted the events to be true. He wanted the New Testament to be right."[28] An avowed atheist, Karl begins to engage John in debates about religion and the belief systems of the group of followers.

Initially John intends to be baptized by Glogauer, but the latter refuses. As they enter the water John has an epiphany: "'Emmanuel!' John cried suddenly. 'The spirit of Adonai is within you!'"[29] In the river, a panicked Glogauer gets a migraine and becomes dizzy and nauseated, vomiting into the water.[30] He then takes to the wilderness and heads toward Nazareth, in search of Jesus.

When Glogauer finds Jesus in Nazareth, instead of a wise, charismatic prophet he finds a mentally damaged and confused man, a "'good-for-nothing'" according to his father, Joseph.[31] Jesus looks nothing like

25. Moore, *Lamb*, 324.
26. Moorcock, *Behold the Man*, 27.
27. Moorcock, *Behold*, 31.
28. Moorcock, *Behold*, 36.
29. Moorcock, *Behold*, 43.
30. Moorcock, *Behold*, 43–4.
31. Moorcock, *Behold*, 63.

the reverent pictures in European art: "The figure was misshapen. It had a pronounced hunched back and a cast in its left eye. The face was vacant and foolish. There was a little spittle on the lips. It giggled as its name was repeated. It took a crooked step forward. 'Jesus,' it said."[32] Glogauer wonders, "'Could he be in some other dimension of time where Christ had never been?'"[33] This twentieth-century time traveler who goes back in time to find Jesus finds instead a mentally disabled peasant who is a burden to his family. His search results in his becoming that which he seeks: the Christ, the Anointed One.

If we could go back in time, and assume, for the sake of this argument, that this baptism event of Jesus in Mark did take place, what would we see? Would we see the heavens rip, hear the voice from heaven proclaim? If we could step into the book/s (think, e.g., of *Inkheart*[34]) of Matthew and Luke or John, we would witness a fantastic event. Stepping into Mark, heaven is not silent, but the Secret remains intact. Nothing would happen, except the internal rumblings of religious experience. The laws of physics are not violated. If, according to some versions of string (M) theory, there are multiverses, there has been no documented experience of any alternate universes imposing themselves on ours. If it is possible for multiple universes parallel to our own, could there not be the possibility for multiple Jesuses? As in the film *Another Earth* and the novel *Jesus Christs*, the one Truth or Reality or Messiah is disrupted, and multiple.[35] There are an infinite number of possible lives of Jesus. For example, what if Jesus emerges from the water and immediately goes into the wilderness (as in Mark's Gospel), but after a month of fasting and deprivation, he dies of starvation?[36]

In a similar way Aichele uses China Miéville's fantasy novel *Un Lun Dun* as a way of exploring an "ungospel" of John the Baptist in which John the Baptist is really the messiah and Jesus his trusty sidekick.[37] In this ungospel a different baptism occurs: "When John baptizes him, a dove flies down, and Jesus hears a voice proclaiming John to be the chosen one, as in Mk 1:9–11, where thanks to an ambiguous

32. Moorcock, *Behold*, 64.

33. Moorcock, *Behold*, p. 65.

34. Funke, *Inkheart*.

35. Cahill, dir., *Another Earth*; Langguth, *Jesus Christs*.

36. Jesus's wandering and eventual starvation in the wilderness is the subject of Crace, *Quarantine*.

37. Aichele, *Posthumanity*, 172; Miéville, *Lun Dun*.

pronoun, 'him' (*auton*), it is not clear upon whom the spirit-dove descends or to whom the voice speaks." Thus Jesus becomes the "Christ" only after John's arrest and death, as he carries on John's apocalyptic message. Aichele explains, "In the ungospel of John the Baptist, Jesus keeps no 'messianic secret' because there is no messianic secret to be kept. The messiah is simply someone else."[38] There are many sons of man, many baptisms, many apocalyptic proclamations.

Swimming Hole

The site of the baptism, the river Jordan, is the geographical and political border of Palestine, Jordan, and Israel. The river, winding its way down the valley, provides a certain verticality to the story, as it descends from the mountains north of the Sea of Kinnereth to the Dead Sea. There is also a horizontal vein, not just of tributary rivers, but of the countries and religions that cross the Jordan. Even though threatened today with years of drought, the spaces of the river are flooded with political meaning. Elizabeth Malbon points to three types of relations of space in Mark's Gospel: topographical, architectural, and geopolitical.[39] Malbon notes the "porous boundaries" caused by Galilee's location.[40] Eric Stewart observes, "Boundaries, then, were (and are) primarily sites for negotiation of identities. This fact is due in large part to the absence of 'normal' patterns of behavior, as they are defined by centers of civilization, in boundary territories."[41] Stewart reads Mark as creating "a depopulated Judea/Jerusalem" and replacing the temple sacrifice with baptism. The wilderness is the site of baptism, not the city or a religious institution. He summarizes, "The space of the wilderness in the opening verses of Mark is a borderland. It is a contestation of identities and the forging of a new identity for the people of God."[42] In fact, Stewart posits that the "geographic center" in

38. Aichele, *Posthumanity*, 173.

39. Malbon, *Narrative Space*, 8. For Collins, *Mark*, 142, the Jordan River is a central locator of history: "It was and is the primary river in the land of Israel, a perennial stream . . . This foundational significance apparently gave rise to eschatological expectations in the late Second Temple period."

40. Malbon, *Narrative Space*, 15. Freyne, *Galilee*, 63, notes that the "divine presence . . . is no longer to be localized, and hence knows no boundaries."

41. Stewart, *Gathered Around Jesus*, 145.

42. Stewart, *Gathered Around Jesus*, 206.

Mark is Jesus.[43] Jesus travels to see John for the baptism, and then others travel to and with him throughout the rest of Mark.

This river is full of gods: Baal, Pan, Jesus, to name a few. The shape of the river is serpentine—the symbol of the goddess wisdom. There is something in the water; in the rite of Christian baptism it becomes "living water" and even blood ("washed in the blood of Jesus"). Mark 1:9–11 is when we first see Jesus, his body exposed in the ritual washing. The river offers miracle cures, even of the enemy (of the Syrian general Naaman, of leprosy, in 2 Kgs 5:1–14). Divination rituals in the water can open heaven. The water is magic.

The river is also a place of dreams and of passage into a dream world. Birth and death collide; the river provides both, as does baptism. Is Sheol skirting the edge with the baptism? When John immersed Jesus in the river, he goes (waist?) deep, but not too deep. Does the Hydra lie beneath the waters, guarding the gates of the Underworld? Or is Tiamat, another serpent goddess of chaos, ready to claim him? Easing into the face of the deep, slipping, descending into the deep. Is there a voice of the deep that speaks that those above the water cannot hear? The baptism is a place of vulnerability—for the divine, but for demons too. Gaston Bachelard argues that water is the primeval feminine. He asks, "what, then, is the sexual function of the river? It is to evoke feminine nudity."[44] The masculine Jesus, Markan strong man, enters the river to the embrace of the primordial goddess of wisdom.

Or Jesus rewinds creation, and becomes a fish in a sort of reverse evolution. Stephen Moore imagines Jesus as a fish in the water:

> It is in such a habitat that Jesus-Ichthus dwells: the gospel of Mark, God's pool of muck. Dragged from the muddy river in 1:10 . . . Jesus slithers across the surface of the text. Who can ever grasp him? Mark itself comes closest. Mark's plotlines are fishing lines, as are the line of its page. And its genre is that of the fishing manual: "I will make you fishers of men" (1:17). Caught and taught by these fishermen, Jesus's followers will be a school of fish.[45]

43. Stewart, *Gathered Around Jesus*, 210.

44. Bachelard, *Water and Dreams*, 33. Bachelard, 34, notes that "For certain reveries, everything which is reflected in water has feminine traits."

45. Moore, *Mark and Luke*, 56.

Moore is playing in the water here, and playing with words in French: *pêcher* (to fish) and *pécher* (to sin).[46] The baptism sets the plotline for the Christian symbols of the fish, and the cross.

And what of the return to the Father (assuming the voice is a patriarchal voice), the ascension to the shore and dry land? Derrida comments on the opening of heaven and the speaking voice out of this portal:

> But this split, like Jesus' death, which is analogous to it, permits the return to childhood and to the water element. . . . He leaves the water in order to let himself be penetrated by the spirit of one greater than he . . . the emergence uproots the body from the natural element, the water or the mother, only in order to immerse the spirit in the paternal element. The father penetrates the spirit—the metaphor of the father then is the metaphor of the mother—on condition the body has broken with the mother, that is, on condition of its death. That is of its birth, its erection, its resurrection. Birth upsurges *as such* only in resurrection. So death is this equal inequality of the father and the mother—the spiritual metaphor, Christianity, nomination, baptism, and so on. . . . In the glory, with the erection of the dead-born [*mort-ré*] anointed one, the equal inequality of the father and the mother has just appeared . . . But what is stated, in the voice, as a play of liquid and solid.[47]

In such dialectic exuberance Derrida further marginalizes the feminine. The ultimate return is to the father. But what Derrida highlights is how the Markan story of the baptism is a time capsule; break it open and the contents of the whole Jesus story spill out: birth, death, uncertainty, the raw edges of the river and the wilderness, the outlier spaces of Galilee, the wandering message of the peasant prophet. Out of the chaos of the water comes a genesis; once again as in Genesis 1, the/a spirit appears to breathe and brood. Out of the womb of water emerges the one who will have power over the water, a primordial fish. What pleases the spirit? When Jesus comes back on the riverbank, the Spirit, and Satan, and wild beasts await. The next time we see water in Mark is at the lake, the sea of Galilee. A lot of action happens at and on the lake: Jesus's teaching (4:1), pig genocide (5:13), miraculous walking on water (6:48–49). The presence of water in the story alerts the reader to a magical event. Water is to be feared, but it is also essential for life, and for all things disruptive.

46. Moore, *Mark and Luke*, 56n109; here Moore is using Taylor, *Altarity*, 295n52.

47. Derrida, *Glas*, 90a–1a.

Bachelard offers a study of water as part of his larger project on the elements, which Joanne Stroud, in her foreword to his book on water, calls "hormones of the imagination." Water is both inner and outer, bodies of water and also internal to human bodies.[48] The 60 percent of water in Jesus comes in contact with the river. Stroud explains that for Bachelard, "Water calls for a seeing in depth and a seeing beyond."[49] In this way the watery depths are spaces of dreams. Bachelard traces the idea and representation of water from the ancient cosmologies to the present. He finds water to be "an element more feminine and uniform than fire, a more constant one which symbolizes human powers that are more hidden, simple, and simplifying."[50] Water is "a type of intimacy" and leads to a special imagining; it "is also a *type of destiny* that is no longer simply the vain destiny of fleeting images and a never-ending dream but an essential destiny, that endlessly changes the substance of the being."[51] The baptism provided Jesus with his destiny, already told to us as readers in Mark 1:1, but verified by the voice.

Bachelard further explains, "A being dedicated to water is a being in flux. He dies every minute; something of his substance is constantly falling away . . . daily death is the death of water. Water always flows, always falls, always ends in horizontal death . . . death associated with water is more dream like than death associated with earth: the pain of water is infinite."[52] According to Bachelard, water is "a form of anger" because of its tendency toward violence.[53] Jesus enters the narrative water, a calmer remnant from the angry flood of Genesis (complete with the appearance at the end of a dove). He emerges with water in his words: "human language has a *liquid quality*, a flow in its overall effect, water in its consonants."[54] Bachelard develops a "poetics of water," a dreamy world of being.[55] Water reflects the sky, heaven.[56]

48. Stroud, "Foreword," vii (vii–x).

49. Stroud, "Foreword," ix.

50. Bachelard, *Water and Dreams*, 5.

51. Bachelard, *Water and Dreams*, 6; emphasis his.

52. Bachelard, *Water and Dreams*, 6.

53. Bachelard, *Water and Dreams*, 15.

54. Bachelard, *Water and Dreams*, 15; emphasis his.

55. Bachelard, *Water and Dreams*, 20. Further, 189, he states that "the river is speech, with no punctuation," and, 195, "The stream will teach you to speak."

56. Bachelard, *Water and Dreams*, 48.

So too for Derrida is water a chain of signifiers. The *point d/eau* can mean "both 'source of water' and 'no water at all.' . . . As the French *source* makes plain in its double meaning (it can be translated as either origin or spring, fountain) contradictory movement is always found."[57] The *point d'eau* is the place of water, or not. Derrida notes that the *point d'eau* is a departure, "locations which are all very near to veering off, in a wax that is not fortuitous, toward the figures of drought, the negative, and separation."[58] After the baptism is Jesus on the edge of veering off? He veers toward death, fasting in the wilderness, and onward to Jerusalem and the cross.

There are many layers of history at the river: conquest, return, nation. Hutton notes, "The demythologized—but nonetheless symbolic—conception of the Jordan River existed simultaneously and, apparently, unproblematically beside the more mythologized one."[59] As there are multiple versions, there are multiple Jordan Rivers. The present-day diversions of the river (to kibbutz or to power plant) continue the multiplicity of the river.

The Jordan is also a portal from and into heaven. The voice and the bird peek through; Jesus eventually ascends, but only after a descent into water. According to Rachel Havrelock, in the baptism stories of Jesus, "Redemption no longer transpires on a spatial plane, but rather on a temporal axis kept aloft by the perpetual tension of heaven and hell."[60] Thus is the baptism at a crossroads—X marks the spot—and quite an imaginary spot it is, but loaded with signifiers.

Conclusion: Baptism by Fire in the Borderlands

Today there is an official holy site on the Jordan River of Jesus's baptism by John for tourists. At the Yardenit Visitors' Center Christian pilgrims don white robes and experience the baptism in the Jordan. Videos on YouTube show tour groups lining up to participate in the ritual cleansing, and for many, the act is one of repentance, as John the Baptist preached in Mark. The act of "going biblical" is meaningful; it opens the imagination to participate in a (probably harmonized) version of

57. Wolfreys, "Justifying the Unjustifiable," 36.

58. Derrida, *Margins*, 280.

59. Hutton, "Topography," 172.

60. Havrelock, *River Jordan*, 168.

the baptism story. At the same time, the river is a chain of signifiers, although in this case a chain of constrained (by the Israeli military) signifiers. The relatively small area is cordoned off; pilgrims cannot "cross over" the Jordan as Joshua and company did.

But there are two other "authentic" sites. The first is Al-Maghtas in Jordan near Jericho and close to the Dead Sea. It opened in 2000.[61] Israel responded by building a baptism site about six feet away on the opposite bank in 2008.[62] These sites are more Johannine (based on a baptism near Bethany), but they have much support for authentication, and papal visits (Pope Benedict XVI in 2009 and Pope Francis in 2014). Regardless, these baptism sites are hotly contested political spaces. Havrelock points out that "the tourists are unknowing players in the baptism business and its role in political competition" and that these baptisms "no matter the point of entry, are initiations into a state of globalized pollution for which nations, not to mention industry, refuse to accept responsibility."[63]

The Jordan River is a border, a boundary. Today it is the border between Israel and Jordan. More specifically, the country to the east is Jordan, and to the west Israel (in the north, the Golan Heights) and Palestine (the West Bank). Havrelock states that "Christian visitors tacitly support the Jordan River as the eastern border of the country, if only along its northern course."[64] Each site has its own political importance, but Yardenit's proximity to the Sea of Galilee and other important (and able to be visited in the same day) Jesus sites makes it the prominent site. The baptism site is a crossroads (both environmentally and politically) all the way down. Who controls the river? Who owns the water? The Christian claim for authentic (or close enough) sites is an eschatological claim of an eschatological event. The messianic age is at hand, always and in every age, and at every bend in the river.

Writing in 1943, Nelson Glueck noted that the Jordan "has deserved the name of Wilderness. Three main reasons . . . (1) the intolerable heat and malaria, (2) the wild beasts, and (3) the wild men."[65] There is now another wildness on the river—of political conflict, of competing water claims, and of rampant pollution. Instead of malaria there is "the

61. Havrelock, *Jordan*, 280.

62. Havrelock, *Jordan*, 281.

63. Havrelock, *Jordan*, 283.

64. Havrelock, *Jordan*, 278.

65. Glueck, "Jordan," 62.

transmission of viruses from the untreated wastewater in the Jordan."[66] The environmental group Friends of the Earth Middle East (FoEME), established in 1994, works on a Jordan River Rehabilitation project. They summarize the current environmental context: "The Jordan River is unique in its natural and cultural wealth, but is threatened by excessive water diversion and pollution, threatened as a backyard dumping ground." On top of all this, the Jordan is drying up due to drought and the evaporation of the Dead Sea. And the river is used as a channel for untreated sewage and also for trash. FoEME estimates that 96 to 98 percent of the Jordan's water flow is gone—diverted for irrigation for farming or for power plants.[67] Whitney Bauman further observes, "By any environmental assessment, the Jordan River is dying."[68] An even stronger pronouncement is made by Michael Schwartz: "The Jordan today is a shallow sewage canal, its shore a stinking sludge pile" from the Alumot Dam to the Dead Sea.[69] The environmental importance of the river has been trumped by water wars and other conflicts.

The river of life and purification has become a place of death, even as it represents rebirth for the (mostly clueless) Christian pilgrims coming to be baptized. In order to build all these baptism sites, the governments had to remove land mines.[70] Not all have been removed; therefore, it is not safe to cross over, for stray mines still exist. Crossing over the Jordan in Christian hymns means either entering the promised land from the exodus, or dying and going into heaven. The Jordan is thus a place of death, a watery tomb. There is the potential of land mines, of a real baptism by fire.

There is also hope in the plans for a Peace Park by FoEME. Their efforts to "save the Jordan" across environmental and political lines, from their river clean-up efforts to their peacemaking work, such as the "Big Jump Event" of local (Palestinian, Jordanian and Israeli) mayors into the river.[71] As Jesus discovered, entering the river is a dangerous, political act. If Jesus returned today and reentered the Jordan, he would need a visa (and a passport) to enter the Jordanian site. He would have to get in

66. Havrelock, *Jordan*, 282.

67. Friends of the Earth Middle East.

68. Bauman, "Jordan River," 113.

69. Schwartz, "River Revival," 22.

70. Schwartz, "River Revival," 23; see Religion News Service, "Landmines," 19, on the land mines from the 1970s Jordanian threat to Israel.

71. Friends of the Earth Middle East.

line behind all the Christian tourists. If he went to a place not sanctioned as a "holy site" (where no fresh water is pumped in), he would likely be pushing trash aside and risking a skin rash. But he might also step on a stray mine. Jesus might be blown to bits.

Of all the Jesus stories, the scene of the baptism is traditionally foundational and one of the pillars of truth for the Jesus story. Since there is no clear call narrative, or training in a prophetic school, or especially clear origins for this Jesus of the common name, the baptism substitutes for all these, providing a sense of certainty. Aichele reminds us that we are in uncertain territory, and the maps in our Bibles are of little use for locating these mythical places. And the Gospels are also of little help in identifying the "historical John" and the "historical Jesus." These pillars of truth in the Gospels only look sturdy from afar; lean against one and it begins to sway and crumble, giving way to other truths and exposing other Gospels, other worlds, and other messiahs. For the Christian pilgrims who trek to the River Jordan to reenact the baptism, this story in Mark 1:9–11 provides a portal, a way of entering the faith, but not of crossing over. Barriers exist; the crossing is too dangerous, for there are still land mines in the water. For the believer to cross over means risking their certainty about Jesus, and also their faith. What Aichele reminds us is that this land, this "Jesus spot" of the baptism, is all an imagined world. He invites us to welcome Mark's ambiguity and uncertainty and revel in the story world. When we go down to the river with Mark, what do we discover? A great many things: the stories of exodus and crossing into Canaan, the politics of water, the polluted sludge, the undiscovered land mines, but also the hope of another (story) world.

3

Desert Tales: Mark and *Last Days in the Desert*

Introduction: Where the Wild Things Are

> And the spirit immediately drove him out into the wilderness. He was in the wilderness forty days, tempted by Satan; and he was with the wild beasts; and the angels waited on him. (Mark 1:12–13)

THE VOICE-OVER IN THE trailer for the film *Last Days in the Desert* pronounces, "A holy man . . . an endless desert." With this simple premise director Rodrigo García reimagines the temptation story of Jesus. In his story Jesus is not alone; he encounters a Bedouin family that disrupts his solitude and exposes the limits of any idealized retelling of the gospel story. Jesus experiences continual interruptions on his way. The world is full of dysfunction and grace. Mark's Gospel, unencumbered by the additions of Luke and Matthew, provides an easier portal. The sparse details spark dreams.

In fiction and film Mark's plot does not provide the necessary drama, or character development, or excitement. Does the "not said" need to be left unsaid? If there were only Mark's Gospel, we would still be left with temptations, the multiple versions that speak from the other Synoptic Gospels. The temptation to edit and add to Mark's story is really an obligation. Mark extends an offer, one that traditional historical critical readings are unable to fulfill. Mark agitates for a creative response, as in his open-ended "ending" in 16:8. Even stuck between and overshadowed by Matthew and Luke in Gospel parallels, Mark wriggles free, first in flight.

A film and a novel occupy my time in this conversation with Mark's version of the wilderness adventure: Rodrigo García's *Last Days in the Desert* and Jim Crace's *Quarantine*. Since I had read the novel many years before, it echoed in my head, so I hear both fictions in conversation with and against each other. In both adaptations the desert is a main character. Michael Welland summarizes that the desert is a powerful image in the Bible, from the expulsion from Eden onward: "Thus the desert became a place of testing, judgment, punishment, purification, self-denial and sacrifice, a theme dramatically continued through the New Testament."[1] There is a lot of this action in the stillness of the desert. Jesus is not the only human in the stories. There are other seekers: Bedouins, bandits, prophets, and false prophets. And everyone dreams in the desert—dreams of violence, of healing, of the future, of gods and demons. The desert is also where wild tales are told, and where the wild things are, and where the wild gods roam.

A Desert Tale

The temptation falls early in Mark; a dripping-wet Jesus steps into the wilderness for his shamanistic vision quest. In Mark there is no time to tarry, or to banter further with John the Baptist over a meal of locusts and honey about theology or messianic models. In Mark it is as if Jesus steps into a wormhole and out the other side; the forty days fly by. As a reader I want to tarry; there is a hesitation in the text, a sure sign of the fantastic. Satan, wild beasts, and angels all amount to a magical gathering in the desert. The down-to-earth assumptions of such a bare-bones spiritual journey for a grueling forty days becomes suddenly complicated. There is danger (Satan, beasts, the wilderness place); what was the nature of this tempting? There is also support by angels. What does it mean that they "waited on him?" Were they assistants during his journey? Or did they wait until he finished? Was Jesus triumphant? Mark's sudden fiction leaves the reader to fill in the gaps in the story, as Luke and Matthew did with their renditions of a conversation between Jesus and Satan/the devil. Mark's silence is too great for many readers. We do not get a story of Jesus as a lion tamer (in the mode of the prophet Daniel). Or as a tortured soul

1. Welland, *Desert*, 188.

(like Job or Jesus in *The Last Temptation of Christ,* 1988). Or as a holy man holding deep certainty (like Jesus in *The Greatest Story Ever Told,* 1965. What we get in the beginning of Mark is a Jesus we hardly know; the introduction and the resume ("Christ, the Son of God"—Mark 1:1 and "my Son, the Beloved"—Mark 1:11) are bold but sparse descriptors. And by the time of his desert adventure Jesus has not spoken a word.

Both the baptism and the days in the desert serve as a sort of pre-passion narrative; they are passages to the passion. Jesus faces death in order to face death. He goes to the depths of earth (a forty-day quest in the wilderness) and emerges intact and ready to start a movement. The "forty days" (the Exodus template) is the extent of Jesus's messianic training, as far as Mark and the other Gospels relate. Regardless of the outcome of his encounter with Satan, Jesus comes out of the experience raring to go, preaching the good news proclaimed by John the Baptist (Mark 1:14–15) and immediately calling disciples, healing and preaching—all in the first chapter. The sparse details of Mark's temptation telling tempt the reader to invent, to wander/wonder with/at Jesus. Satan is (sort of) left behind as Jesus moves on, but we do not know what passed between the two.

The wilderness is the receptacle of barrenness, but one that is teeming with life. Jesus emerges from water to arid vastness. Mark does not mention fasting (food or water) or whether or not Jesus had other provisions or shelter, only luring the reader into a brief glimpse of desert dangers. Mark's short text lends itself to tinkering, adding stories onto stories. The temptation story is thus open to much tampering, as Luke and Matthew have done through their extended conversation between Jesus and Satan. So pick any of the main nouns: *wilderness, Satan, wild beasts, angels,* and there is a portal into other possible worlds.

This desert tale in Mark has holes, and a lot of wind blowing around and through it. To linger in the story we have to do more than read between the lines. We must go deep, burrow underneath the words, dropping from the printed letters to the interior of the text, to a desert place. The interiority of the text is a desert, a blankness that purports a nothingness. But there is room to roam and imagine new speech acts and characters—interiors upon interiors. In this space we may discover that Mark does not tell the end (or beginning) of his tales. Jesus is not born of a god-impregnated Mary. Jesus is not triumphant over Satan. Jesus does not resurrect from the tomb. The women do not tell anyone of the empty tomb. Jesus does not fix the world; the Romans are still the imperial power; Satan and his minions still live in the desert and in the sick. Jesus is sent into the story (and the desert) as a sacrificial goat. In the end he is forsaken by his absent, silent father, and by his disciples. Others must embellish the story.

The Place of Light and Shadows

> "How far can a man walk into the desert? Only halfway, and then he's walking out." (The Father tells a riddle to the Son in *Last Days in the Desert*)

In *Last Days in the Desert* Yeshua's (Jesus's) first line is, "Father, where are you?" Yeshua wanders the desert beseeching his father, whom he has never seen, to speak to him. There are only hot days, bitterly cold nights, sandstorms, and silence in Jesus's vision quest. In preparation for his mission, Jesus makes this vision quest. This white, blue-eyed holy man, equipped with an inner and outer robe, a scarf-blanket, sandals, a bedroll, bag, and water bladder, makes his way in a hilly wilderness of grand vistas and demons. Yeshua hallucinates an encounter with a demon (snake?) woman. He gives her water, only to have her hiss in return before disappearing. Gaston Bachelard adds context, "The serpent is one of the most important archetypes of the human soul. It is the most *earthen* of animals. It is truly an animalized root and, where images are concerned, the link between the vegetable and animal kingdom."[2] The image of the serpent is also sexual—both phallic and female. In his rendition of Jesus's temptations, Scorcese envisions the serpent, with the voice of Mary Magdalene, accompanied by the sound of her bracelets, as sexual seductress. Encased in his shaman circle of protection, Jesus looks out into the dark desert night into moments of emptiness and demons. This circle is the womb that births him into consciousness. Is Jesus dreaming of Eden? Or is he dreaming of defeating the great apocalyptic dragon? The river Jordan, the wadis of the desert landscape, the serpent (real and of dreams) are all earthly shapes. Bachelard outlines the literary uses of the serpent; he notes, "Everything becomes animate when our pens dream, be it festoon, creeper, or serpent, or even life that is intertwined, twisted, and coiled up."[3] The serpent is cosmic, is soul, is earth. "An image that ranks as a fundamental image becomes the fundamental matter of our imagination.

2. Bachelard, *Earth and Reveries of Repose*, 192.
3. Bachelard, *Earth and Reveries of Repose*, 199.

This is true of each of the four elements."[4] The serpent as earth is naked desire, good and evil, beginning and end.

In García's film Jesus is his own Satan; he avenges himself with his twin image. Satan knows God and knows who Yeshua is, and follows him on his trek in order to torment him and undermine his confidence. Yeshua and the desert Satan debate, often face to face. Satan asks him to name one thing he learned in the desert and Yeshua replies, "Man makes do, anywhere." Satan counters with a multiverse theory that God is always creating new worlds and possible destinies: "You think you're his only child. There are others." Yeshua disagrees, "No. There is only me." Yeshua then wants to know, "Is there a face?" Satan replies, "No. There is no face." And in response to Yeshua's reaction, Satan adds, "What anger! You are your father's son." Satan has more intimate knowledge of God than Yeshua does, and makes a wager (mirroring the Satan in Job) with Yeshua. Satan represents Jesus's interior struggle with the silence and absence of God. The desert is the place for this struggle between fathers and sons, and for encountering the convergence of inner and outer hostility. Satan can only go so far though:

> Satan: "This is it for me. You didn't think I was going to walk you all the way, did you?"
>
> Yeshua: "Why here?"
>
> Satan: "My feet hurt." (Jesus chuckles.) "I'll come to you in the end."

The desert is a place for dreaming. Jesus goes to the earth to dream, to descend and face the serpent. The images in the film—cross, stones, thorns, serpent, sky, desert—all the images are potential threats. Yeshua lays down on the earth and dreams of death. In the end, men lay him in his desert tomb. Jesus returns to the desert, to the earth.

Gaston Bachelard, with his Jungian framework, calls such dreaming "the Jonah complex"; the descent is always into the past.[5] Yeshua dreams on the margins of existence, with the constant threat of being swallowed up—by the river, by the earth, by the demons, by empire. In his nightmares he drowns and is chased by wolves; he levitates over the desert canyons. Each dream is rooted in the landscape. For Bachelard there is will and it is accompanied by "the dynamic existence

4. Bachelard, *Earth and Reveries of Repose*, 202.

5. Bachelard, *Earth and Reveries of Repose*, 90.

of the resistant world."[6] The wilderness aggressively resists: extreme temperatures, steep cliffs, dangerous wildlife, and the presence of evil (real and imagined). The dream of the possibilities—of continued life and of death—calls everything into question. Bachelard notes that "the struggles of earth and water, the marriage of earth and water, their endless sadomasochistic exchanges, provide countless case studies for a psychoanalysis of material and dynamic imagery."[7] For Yeshua's nightmares in the film: "The monsters we encounter are but the externalized projections of our inner torments."[8]

Northrop Frye also finds parallels with the temptation stories but more so with Job. He examines the themes of John Milton's interest in the temptation of Jesus in *Paradise Regained* (1671). Milton is reading Luke's version, but calls out the Satan figure with its ties to the Leviathan, the dragon, the sea monster, and finally, the serpent in the Eden story. Frye sees a parallel between the Gospel stories and the book of Job; Satan makes a grand bet on Job's life, and as in Job, Satan disappears as a character in the story frame. By emerging victorious from the wilderness, Jesus becomes a dragon killer.[9] So Jesus, stripped of all possessions and family, is in the desert as part of a grand bet between Satan and God—this time over the life of God's son. Jesus descends first into water, and then into desert; this ascent/descent/ascent theme provides the structure for Jesus's preparation for ministry. The serpent of the watery chaos is also the serpent of the dry wilderness. These images are present in the film as well, as Yeshua becomes more entangled with the family dynamics, and Satan hurls taunts and triggers Yeshua's self-doubt.

Yeshua's confrontations with Satan are also with himself. In the film Yeshua's revelation comes with the relationship with the family he encounters in the desert. He wants to help the family and does so with his carpentry skills—and his compassion. He is unable to heal or work miracles. The relationships, like the rocks and the house the father is building for his son, are unstable. With such abundance of sky, air and wind, there is a shortness of breath: the sick mother, the elderly father, those who carry heavy corpses (Yeshua and later his pallbearers).

By the late fourth and early fifth centuries the desert in Judea became a place of pilgrimage and asceticism. "At the height of monastic life

6. Bachelard, *Earth and Reveries of Will*, 13.

7. Bachelard, *Earth and Reveries of Will*, 57.

8. Bachelard, *Earth and Reveries of Will*, 307.

9. Frye, "Return to Eden," 116.

in the Judean desert there were approximately sixty-five monasteries,"[10] and "the number of monks who lived in the Judean desert was approximately three thousand."[11] Jesus (and Abraham, Moses, and Elijah before him) started a desert movement. Wilken observes, "Almost imperceptibly Christians were beginning to use the biblical language and images of Jerusalem and Judea to speak about the Christian communities living in the land. Which is to say, Christians were beginning to give the biblical promises a political or historical interpretation."[12] Reading backwards from the desert fathers to the biblical desert stories, G. G. Harpham notes: "The desert to which the aesetic is called is a complex geography, a binary grammar of temptation. Under one aspect the desert is a scene of primal rectitude in which man and beast exist without disharmony. . . . But in an equally accepted trope the desert is the allotted domain of demons. As such the desert brings sin to man."[13]

Jacques Derrida speaks of "desertification."[14] John Caputo draws on the Derridian concept of *khôra*, "the placeless place of absolute spacing."[15] Caputo calls Derrida an "an-khôra-ite, a postmodern desert father." He elaborates: "The desert is a kind of placeless, displacing place—or the place for the displaced—that gets us past the politics of place and the wars over place, not a *Heimat*, but an *open* place, without borders or immigration laws, a kind of postgeographical meta-country."[16] Negative theology is found here, for God is but a trace on the landscape.[17] Following Derrida into the deconstructive desert, Caputo finds "the traces of invisible tracks left in the desert: the *messianic* and *khôra*."[18] Jesus in this desert also makes invisible tracks, toward this God and Satan, demons and angels. What draws us to this desert?

10. Wilken, *Land Called Holy*, 312n28.

11. Wilken, *Land Called Holy*, 165.

12. Wilken, *Land Called Holy*, 164.

13. Harpham, *Ascetic Imperative*, 69.

14. Derrida, "Faith and Knowledge," 21; see the discussion in Branch, "Desert," 813–14.

15. Caputo, *Prayers and Tears*, 156.

16. Caputo, *Prayers and Tears*, 154.

17. Caputo, *Prayers and Tears*, 37.

18. Caputo, *Prayers and Tears*, 155.

The Time of Quarantine

John Updike makes a grand pronouncement: "The original Gospels evince a flinty terseness, a refusal, or inability, to provide the close focus and cinematic highlighting that the modern mind expects."[19] Yet the Gospels have provided the terrain for such big screen, and big novel, drama. Updike speaks here of Jim Crace's novel *Quarantine*, which is about Jesus's forty-day wilderness experience and temptation. Jesus, and separately, a group of four pilgrims seeking healing, enter the wilderness to fast and pray. Crace reimagines the Gospels' imagined stories of this uncanny and humanly impossible feat, as he acknowledges in his opening quote to the novel. A human would simply not survive for forty days with no food or water. Crace then pauses these stories of Jesus in the wilderness and steps boldly inside to take a look around. What he finds is a trading caravan with an abusive merchant, Musa, and his pregnant wife, Miri. The novel opens with Musa sick with fever, near death. "Her husband, Musa, was being baked alive. Good news."[20] Musa's death would bring liberation for Miri. The caravan continues on, and Miri is left to tend to her dying husband. As she prepares his grave, a band of five pilgrims arrive to do a forty-day quarantine in the caves, fasting all day and eating only at night. "This was the season of the lunatics: the first new moon of spring was summoning those men—for lunatics are mostly men. . . . Mad enough to think that forty days of discomfort could put their world in order."[21] Three men and one woman with various ailments were together; a fifth "was bare-footed, and without a staff. No water-skin, or bag of clothes. No food. A slow, painstaking figure, made thin and watery by the rising, mirage heat."[22] Crace describes the dangers in this wilderness: "There were robbers in the hills, army deserters, lepers, devils, animals, avalanches of dry scree and a threatening conspiracy of ricks, wind and heat which made the landscape treacherous and unpredictable."[23] The fifth, a bruised and weary pilgrim, moved like a leopard: "He was a traveller called Jesus, from the cooler, farming valleys in the north, a Galilean, and not one used to deprivations of this kind."[24]

19. Updike, "Stones into Bread," 331.
20. Crace, *Quarantine*, 1.
21. Crace, *Quarantine*, 12.
22. Crace, *Quarantine*, 13.
23. Crace, *Quarantine*, 13.
24. Crace, *Quarantine*, 21–22.

Crace relates pieces of Jesus's childhood. He was prayerful to the point of parental concern. He eventually began to hear God's call in everyday sounds. "Jesus was an optimist" and answered God's call to him to go to the desert: "Creation was unfinished here. This was where the world was not complete. What better place to find his god at work."[25] There is no mention of the baptism by John the Baptist, or any other contact with John. Nor does Jesus follow John's example: "Now John was clothed with camel's hair, with a leather belt around his waist, and he ate locusts and wild honey" (Mark 1:6). Jesus goes to extremes, barefoot and without any food or water, intently believing his God will provide.

Before following God's lead to find a cave in which to complete the forty-day deprivation, Jesus heads for the merchant Musa's tent to get water and food. Musa can vaguely make out his presence in the tent: "A Jewish face, young and long and womanly. A Galilean face. A peasant face. A robber's face, for sure, because the man had helped himself to water and was standing with their water-skin in his hand."[26] Crace further describes Jesus: "He was as skittish, pale and narrow-shouldered as a goose. The neighbours called him Gally, a common nickname for a Galilean boy whose accent was strong, but ideal for Jesus. He was like a gally fly. He could not rest."[27] As Jesus sets off toward his quarantine, he inadvertently heals Musa with a sprinkle of water and a common blessing for the sick, "So, here, be well again."[28] When Musa awakens, he declares, "Here was a man who was in the mood to divine grand meanings in the simplest acts."[29] Musa believes Jesus must be a healer and prophet, and seeks him out for what might become a profitable business.

The other pilgrims also pick caves, but gather in the evening to break the fast and meet together. Jesus goes off alone and is unresponsive to the growing, concerned calls from the group. "He only understood that he should choose a way that was more punishing. The worst it was, the better it would be. That, surely, was the purpose of the wilderness. He knew the scriptures and the stories of the prophets. Triumph over hardship was their proof of holiness."[30] In the cave Jesus could dwell

25. Crace, *Quarantine*, 22.
26. Crace, *Quarantine*, 25.
27. Crace, *Quarantine*, 72.
28. Crace, *Quarantine*, 26.
29. Crace, *Quarantine*, 128.
30. Crace, *Quarantine*, 71.

with God: "He could tuck himself into the folds of God."[31] "Why else had Jesus come into the wilderness? To be the chosen one. To be eased to freedom from the devil's grasp."[32] Instead, Jesus finds that his God is mostly absent, or indiscernible from the devil.

Jesus enters the wilderness without bag or outer coat or sandals, putting total trust in God to provide; "God's unfinished landscape would provide a way, he thought."[33] Eventually, he throws his tunic and undergarment off the cliff.[34] But the desert is unforgiving and full of demons: Jesus observes, "Perhaps this was the devil's realm."[35] Jesus seeks enlightenment from God, but all he gets is more confusion: "Jesus knew that angels and demons could not be told apart just by their looks."[36]

Satan does not have Jesus's face and voice, mirroring some inner monster. But Satan is a real monster. The abusive Musa serves as the tempter,[37] asking Jesus to come out of his cave to the group of pilgrims and heal them all. "Indeed the devil was living proof of god, for everything that god had made was weak and blemished and imperfect by design. . . . To deny the presence of the devil was to turn against the perfect blemishes of god."[38]

Like Anthony and the desert fathers after him, Jesus dreams of temptations, and considers the folly of his fast, but it is too late to change course because he is too weak to move and too stubborn to accept the food and drink from the pilgrims.[39] The wilderness experience is a proleptic event: "Quarantine had been the perfect preparation for his death."[40] For Crace the quarantine is also the preparation for the invention of Jesus, as healer, teacher, and eventually, savior. This message becomes the invention (and property) of Musa. Like Luke/Paul, and the Gospel writers, Musa elaborates on an experience. One difference is that

31. Crace, *Quarantine*, 72.

32. Crace, *Quarantine*, 150.

33. Crace, *Quarantine*, 75–76.

34. Crace, *Quarantine*, 131.

35. Crace, *Quarantine*, 77.

36. Crace, *Quarantine*, 112.

37. Crace, *Quarantine*, 147–68.

38. Crace, *Quarantine*, 149. David Jasper claims Pasolini's Satan is a "Musa," "a grubby, ordinary man who catches people foolish enough to travel in desolation at their weakest and most dependent," *Sacred Desert*, 102.

39. Crace, *Quarantine*, 154–64.

40. Crace, *Quarantine*, 191.

Musa is an eyewitness. In the unreliability of the eyewitness testimony Crace is revealing the fictional roots of the Gospel messages.

Eventually the quarantine and basic biological facts intervene. Jesus dies after thirty days. There is no cowherd woman to bring him milk or middle way (as with the Buddha), or God to save him. Crace's narrator describes this tragic ending:

> Jesus was a voyager, at last, between the heavens and the earth. There was a light, deep in the middle of the night. He tried to swim to it. He tried to fly. He held his hands up to the light. His hands were bluey-shite like glass. The light passed through. The mountain shivered from afar. He felt the cold of nothing there. He heard the cold of no one there. No god, no gardens, just the wind.[41]

Marta and Miri bury Jesus, and Marta discloses her dream: "'I know his face from dreams. If it was dreaming,'" in which Jesus touches her stomach and makes her pregnant with her husband's child.[42] Jesus's death makes Musa even more determined; he decides to trade in Jesus; "He'd 'trade the word' and tell tales of how Jesus healed him."[43] Musa sees Jesus in a mirage.[44] Jasper asks, "Is this just mirage upon mirage—a double mirage of desert seeing?"[45] The entire Gospel erupts from one sentence spoken by Jesus.

Crace says that his initial intent in writing the novel was to eviscerate Christianity:

> It would be a simple matter. Take a venerated Bible story (Christ's Judean fast), add a pinch of hard-nosed fact (nobody going without food and drink could survive for anything like forty days) and watch the scripture take a beating. *Quarantine* with Science its sword would kill Christ after only thirty days in the wilderness. There'd be no ministry or Crucifixion. The novel would erase two thousand years of Christianity. This would be my party-pooper of the millennium. . . . Jesus does not let me kill him off entirely.[46]

41. Crace, *Quarantine*, 193.
42. Crace, *Quarantine*, 225.
43. Crace, *Quarantine*, 242.
44. Crace, "Finding Jesus," 243.
45. Jasper, *Sacred Desert*, 103.
46. Crace, "Crace on *Quarantine*."

Crace cites his inspiration as a facility for mental health patients in Moseley, England, a result of "the Thatcherite money-snatching policy of 'Care in Community,' that produces a building of bleak cells and suspect care." Crace relates the starting question for the novel, "how does a community of people, all living on the edge, secure some comfort, resolution and transcendence in what I considered to be a godless universe?"[47] Many readers saw the novel as inspired; a priest commented that Crace had the Holy Ghost beside him as he wrote. Crace replied: "No, not the Holy Ghost, I said, but the Imp of Storytelling, celebrated for its mischievousness, its cunning, and its generosity."[48] Could it be also this Imp of Storytelling at Mark's shoulder?

Updike compares Crace's story to that of the Mailer's first-person account as/of Jesus: "Jesus' forty days in the wilderness are dramatized with an archeological command of the texture of life in Herod's Palestine and with a troubling heterodoxy."[49] Crace's investigation of the wilderness story evokes the mysterious silence of Mark's version: "Such an assaultive retelling, far from smoothing the rough spots in the Gospel account, raises new ones. Crace is a writer of hallucinatory skill and considerable cruelty."[50] Mark certainly has rough spots, many smoothed over or ignored by Luke and Matthew (who each have their own rough spots). Do Mark and Crace share a similar cruelty? Mark's rough Jesus, emerges an adult at John the Baptist's river revival, only to have the Spirit immediately roughly place Jesus in a rough place. Translations of course differ: the Spirit "drove him out into the wilderness" (NRSV, NEV, KJV "driveth"), "sent him" (NIV and Phillips), "impelled him" (New American Standard Bible), "made him" (Good News), "drove him out" (Sarah Ruden),[51] or "urged him" (The Living Bible)—all these translations confirm the discomfort of Mark's rough words. The Spirit tosses Jesus out.

Crace has written an apocalyptic text; he places Jesus's bones in the dry valley of Ezekiel. Crace leaves us with an undiscoverable grave and little trace of Jesus. Jasper links the desert experience to the empty tomb in Mark; "the tomb must remain empty . . . the hidden body . . . there is no signified, for there is nothing outside the signifier that is the Word,

47. Crace, "Finding Jesus."

48. Crace, "Finding Jesus."

49. Updike, "Stones into Bread," 331.

50. Updike, "Stones into Bread," 331.

51. Ruden, *Gospels*, 4.

and the flesh made word," (sliding from Mark into John's prologue).[52] There is an emptiness in Mark's telling, a cave/tomb into which we peer, hopeful, knowing already of the emptiness. For Jasper, "The desert is insistently *there*, and yet it is also inside us and our imaginations, a no place, a utopia, the land to which we are led back, as their God let the erring Israelites back into the desert as a 'door of hope' in Hosea."[53] The desert is a "meeting point,"[54] the place we have to go to start our quest for Jesus. But he has already left, moved on in the dream.

Jasper surveys Crace's differentiation of the inner and outer desert: "Crace's novel, like the desert itself, as always, confuses interior and exterior."[55] For Jasper, "When Crace's Jesus dies there is nothing, or almost nothing, that is dreamed in the desert—'no god, no garden, just the wind.'"[56] Only the dream of a certain made-up messiah remains.

Jasper further observes that like the Gospels, Crace makes things up: "But in this place, in the desert, that is all you can do, and only then can it become a place of vision from which all else flows."[57] Does Jesus invite us to follow him into the desert? We cannot access Jesus in the desert; he is off limits. Only desert tales (like the one from Musa or Garcia) remain. And all the stories are made up.

Borderlands

Although not directly on the border with Mexico, the Anza-Borrego Desert, the filming location of *Last Days in the Desert*, is close, between San Diego and the Salton Sea. The border lies just to the south, a mostly invisible line in the sand except for the areas of border fence and border patrol. The proposed extension of the border wall between the US and Mexico (totaling 700 miles or about a third of the border distance) will also divide indigenous land (is not all of it indigenous land?). Gloria Anzaldúa explores the space of having a home in these borderlands:

> The U.S.-Mexican border *es una herida abierta* where the Third World grates against the first and bleeds. . . . Borders are set

52. Jasper, *Sacred Desert*, 51.
53. Jasper, *Sacred Desert*, xviii; emphasis his.
54. Jasper, *Sacred Desert*, xviii.
55. Jasper, *Sacred Desert*, 100.
56. Jasper, *Sacred Desert*, 100–101; Crace, *Quarantine*, 93.
57. Jasper, *Sacred Desert*, 175.

> up to define the places that are safe and unsafe, to distinguish *us* from *them*. A border is a dividing line, a narrow strip along a steep edge. A borderland is a vague and undetermined place created by the emotional residue of an unnatural boundary. It is in a constant state of transition. The prohibited and forbidden are its inhabitants.[58]

The border designates a line of power for Anzaldúa: "Do not enter, trespassers will be raped, maimed, strangled, gassed, shot. The only legitimate inhabitants are those in power, the whites and those who align themselves with power. Tension grips the inhabitants of the borderlands like a virus. Ambivalence and unrest reside there and death is no stranger."[59] Jesus in the multiple deserts is surrounded by borders in the form of fences and patrols (from the Roman army to the present). As Jesus travels in the Gospels and beyond, he puts himself at risk.

Miguel De La Torre puts Jesus's crossings into the present US/Mexico border context: "And while most border crossers today do so as an act of desperation, Jesús, theologically speaking, chose to be a border crosser as an act of solidarity with the least of these. The biblical text reminds us that, although divine, Jesús became human, assuming the condition of the alienated."[60] Jesús is a migrant laborer, undocumented, an "illegal."[61] Like Yeshua in Garcia's film, Jesús is poor and homeless as he emerges from the desert.

Jesus's trek into the wilderness is into contested territory. The landscape was and is a space of contention and contestation. W. J. T. Mitchell attempts a different approach to surveying landscapes. "Landscape" is a verb ". . . not an object to be seen or a pretext to be read, but as a process by which social and structural identities are formed."[62] Landscape is also about power: "it is an instrument of cultural power, perhaps even an agent of power that is (or frequently represents itself as) independent of human intentions."[63] Landscape as a cultural practice reveals the ideology of space. In terms of the landscape in which we find Jesus in Mark, this wilderness is contested space, under continual control by imperial powers. In other words, there is no unified landscape, only

58. Anzaldúa, *Borderlands*, 3; emphasis hers.

59. Anzaldúa, *Borderlands*, 3–4.

60. De La Torre, *Politics of Jesús*, 33.

61. De La Torre, *Politics of Jesús*, 33–35.

62. Mitchell, "Introduction," 1.

63. Mitchell, "Introduction," 1–2.

multiple landscapes within. Mitchell observes landscape in its complex historical contexts: "The marks of imperial conquest in Israel/Palestine . . . would seem to be absolutely unavoidable. The face of the Holy Landscape is so scarred by war, excavation, and displacement that no illusion of innocent original nature can be sustained for a moment."[64] No matter how much tourists idealize the Holy Landscape, with postcards of Bedouins on camels beside palm trees, with desert filling the frame, this vision collapses under the weight of its own orientalism.[65] And the myth of the empty land also does not apply even to this desert tale of Jesus. He walks on scarred land, one full of ghosts.

Filmmakers search for this landscape in their films about Jesus. There are often stand-ins for Israel/Palestine: for example, Morocco (*Last Temptation of Christ*), Tunisia (*Life of Brian),* and the American Southwest (*The Greatest Story Ever Told* and *Last Days in the Desert).*[66] George Stevens chose Death Valley for Jesus's forty-day ordeal. Pier Paolo Pasolini went on perhaps the most famous location search for his film *The Gospel According to St. Matthew* (1964). He documents the search in the accompanying film, *Sopralluoghi in Palestina (On Location in Palestine*, 1965). After driving around "Palestine," Pasolini decided there is too much modernity. So he returned to southern Italy in the district of Basilicata and the capital Matera (later copied by Mel Gibson in his *The Passion of the Christ*, 2004, and Jemyes Samuel in *The Book of Clarence*, 2023). Italy is a stand in for ancient Palestine. Rodrigo García chose the Anza-Borrego Desert, a state park 100 miles east of San Diego, in Southern California.

Even if Israel/Palestine is too modern or difficultly divided, what is represented on screen is "Israel/Judea/Palestine," at least an ancient mythic vision of it, no matter the location. The land is always occupied, and freedom is at stake. The desert is an ambiguous place of freedom, for gods and demons follow whoever enters.

The desert is a dangerous place, so why not add layers to the dangers? Rebecca Solnit wanders into deserts and discovers their uncanny beauty and "spectacular desert light, the freedom of open space, and the stirring sight of thousands who shared our belief that nuclear bombs were the wrong instrument with which to write the history of the world.

64. Mitchell, "Imperial Landscape," 27.

65. Mitchell, "Imperial Landscape," 27.

66. One example of a film that uses Israel as a location is Jewison, dir., *Jesus Christ Superstar* (1973).

We bore a kind of bodily witness to our convictions, to the fierce beauty of the desert, and to the apocalypses being prepared nearby."[67] Solnit is speaking of (nuclear) weapons of mass destruction that were tested in the Nevada desert, but in some sense she is walking with the apocalyptic Jesus in this desert. What wild territory, of beginnings and endings. "The desert of the real" as Morpheus reveals to Neo in *The Matrix* (1999), exposing the grid imposed by their oppressors. In the desert of the real, past collides with the present, armies upon armies, wars upon wars, walls upon walls.

Conclusion: Desert, Desertion, Delirium, Destruction, Delight

Mark invites us into his earthly dream. But he curtails his dream, and we are left to consider hidden fragments. Mark is telling a desert tale, but not in the fullness of such adventures. He feigns from entering Jesus's desert dreams, standing a safe distance away. We stand with Mark and share his view of the action. What do we *see* in this story? Wild beasts and angels and Satan and Jesus as opaque as mirages in the distant desert. These images become stories. Bachelard calls this "imagination of terrestrial matter" the "dreams of will"[68] as opposed to dreams of reverie or repose. Bachelard is working on two fronts at once: the extroverted dreams of will and the introverted dreams of repose: "The loveliest of images are often hotbeds of ambivalence."[69] The idealized image of Jesus holding steady and defeating Satan in the process of his shamanistic training creates a model for moral competence.

Further, images of immensity, like the desert, reflect depths of imagination within. Bachelard examines this dreamscape of desert: "In analyzing images of immensity, we should realize within ourselves the pure being of pure imagination. . . . Immensity is within ourselves," connected with daydreaming.[70] The vast desert expanses—Bachelard shows how this word ("desert," following Baudelaire) "brings calm and unity; it

67. Solnit, *Wanderlust*, 8.

68. Bachelard, *Earth and Reveries of Will*, 2–3.

69. Bachelard, *Earth and Reveries of Will*, 7.

70. Bachelard, *Poetics of Space*, 184.

opens up unlimited space."[71] This desert dreamscape is under threat of division, with roads and checkpoints and walls.

In pursuing dreamlike space, visual artist Bill Viola went into the desert to film and the results are *Chott el-Djerid (A Portrait in Light and Heat,* 1979) and *Déserts* with composer Edgar Vargèse (1994). About filming in the Sahara desert in Tunisia, Viola says, "It was like being in someone else's dream."[72] Viola plays on the image of the desert mirage—images of people and buildings dancing in the sun that dwell in the space between reality and fantasy. The Jesus of Mark's temptation is also mirage. Stories are made up; there are no eye-witnesses, and even if there were, their testimonies would be suspect. We will never see clearly into this desert, for the gods, like the demons, are tricksters.

Playing with current political and peace and justice themes, the artist Banksy built a hotel in Bethlehem and named it "The Walled Off Hotel" because of its proximity to the security wall and watchtowers built by Israel in the West Bank. It opened March 11, 2017, to commemorate the 100-year anniversary of the Balfour Declaration. Each room has original Banksy art, such as an Israeli soldier and a Palestinian protestor pillow fighting, a masked sculpture enveloped in tear gas, and angels flying around drop-down airline oxygen masks. So what is the wall exactly? It divides the nation of Palestine from the state of Israel and restricts movement between the two for citizens of both sides. Depending on who you talk to it is either a vital security measure or an instrument of apartheid. Its route is highly controversial and it has a dramatic impact on the daily lives of a lot of people. The one thing beyond dispute is that everything here is under dispute. Adjacent to the hotel is a "Wal*Mart": "the graffiti supplies store which stocks everything you need to make your mark and offers expert advice and guidance." Art provides necessary social and political commentary, and guests can make their own statements on the wall. Banksy keeps returning to this wall dividing Israel and the West Bank: "This place is the center of the universe—every time God comes to earth it seems to happen near here."[73]As Banksy illustrates, the landscape is ideological, open always to reinterpretation.

Elbit Systems, the Israeli contractor for this wall that is Banksy's canvas, was awarded a $145 million contract with the US Department

71. Bachelard, *Poetics of Space*, 197.

72. Viola, *Reasons for Knocking*, 55; see Jasper, *Sacred Desert*, 116.

73. Banksy, "Questions."

of Homeland Security to build the additional border wall between the US and Mexico. The Trump administration saw the Israeli wall as a proven security wall, although there is no proof for this declaration. There are mentions of concrete, barbed wire, and even an electric fence to shock any crossers.

In this journey into Mark's temptation narrative I have been wandering in deserts in different locations: (1) in Palestine and (2) in California. Were Jesus to wander today, what would he encounter: (1) security wall, Israeli Defense troops, wild beasts, hunger, thirst; (2) security wall, US Border Patrol, wild beasts, hunger, thirst, detention, deportation? In *Last Days in the Desert*, when Yeshua ends his wilderness time, he sees Jerusalem in the distance. Dirty and smelly, undocumented and bearing a wild message from a wild landscape and the wild prophets before him, Yeshua is at the moment of his journey into the rest of his story. In today's world he would be more than suspect, and great expense and violence would be put forth to forever relegate him to the margins and to bar him entrance to paradise.

4

The Revolutionary Jesus of Matera and Immokalee

THE GLOBAL REFUGEE CRISIS is a humanitarian disaster. An estimated 82.4 million people (according to the United Nations High Commissioner for Refugees) have fled their homes to escape violence or economic deprivation. Many fleeing African countries make the dangerous crossing over the Mediterranean Sea to Italy seeking freedom, safety, and a better economic future. A Swiss filmmaker and theater director, Milo Rau, accepted an invitation from the city of Matera, in southern Italy, to make a film for their celebration as the 2019 European Cultural Capital. He set out to do a contemporary remake of his favorite Jesus film that was done in this city, Pier Paolo Pasolini's *The Gospel According to Matthew* (1964), and where Mel Gibson also filmed *The Passion of the Christ* (2004). Rau took the cue from Pasolini to hire mostly local actors for his Jesus film. What he encountered in Matera surprised him—African asylum seekers who worked for sub-poverty wages on Mafia-run farms. As he toured their ghetto and spoke to the migrants about their work picking tomatoes, olives, or oranges, he learned of the abuse: inhumane living conditions without water or electricity, evictions, long hours in extreme heat, no health care, disrespect, and an impossibly bureaucratic immigration system. From these encounters Rau changed the focus of his film; he mixed fiction and documentary so that the teaching and life of Jesus is side by side with the life and teaching of the

African migrant farmworker and organizer Yvan Sagnet, who plays and embodies a black Jesus. Rau entitles his film *The New Gospel* (*Das neue Evangelium*; release date September 1, 2020) in order to draw attention to the humanitarian crisis, and of Jesus's and the refugees' worlds under different eras of "Roman" oppression. Like Pasolini's Jesus, Rau's activist Jesus is a Marxist, as well as a human rights organizer. Sagnet is Roman Catholic, but the majority of the actors who play the disciples are Muslim. There are many convergences in this film of religion and migration and "Jesus" is in the center of the stories.

Sagnet, as himself and as Jesus, is an activist who is organizing a campaign against a Mafia-controlled farm industry (known as the Agromafia). He organizes the farmworkers to change their situation in an extended political campaign, The Revolt of Dignity (Revolte der Würde). This campaign began with a two-week strike in 2011 to draw attention to the system of "modern or semi-slavery," and its extended days of farm labor, subpoverty wages, wage theft, and slum accommodations. Sagnet describes his experience as enslavement and likens it to "being in the cotton fields of America."[1] The strike led to changes in Italian law, along with drawing international attention to the issue of farmworkers in Italy. Sagnet asks, "If corporals [caporalato] are there, who are the generals? . . . The tomato I'm about to buy, where does is come from? Who picked it?"[2]

The rights of migrants are central in this film. Rau finds the "actual Jesus" in the abusive tomato fields. In this chapter I intend to draw comparisons between the asylum seeker farmworkers in Italy and the immigrant activists in the Coalition of Immokalee Workers in Florida, and their fight for human dignity through their Fair Food Program. Both groups represent worker-driven social change movements. And both groups have experienced trauma: dangerous border crossings and deaths, long working hours in extreme heat, unfair wages, inadequate

1. For a detailed description of the conditions in terms of human rights and environmental issues, see Taylor, "Modern Slavery," and the NOCap (Caporalato) report, *People Before Profit*, from 2020, for "human, social, and environmental rights." The NOCap ethical seal has six raised hands, each hand representing a criterion ("work ethic, short [supply] chain, waste, energy, added value, produce and animal welfare"). Each figure represents an indicator for each worker and environmental justice issue.

2. Sagnet, in *Illegal Gangmastering*, is asking Italians to trace the global supply chain. He details his field work of sixteen-hour days to make enough to pay for services from the corporal of transportation, water, and a sandwich, resulting in about $5 left over each day. Sagnet focuses on the exploitation of workers: "I found a system that trampled on people's dignity." See also Ferrando, "Gangmastering," 529, who states that the caporali can extract up to one-third of a worker's wages.

housing, sexual abuse of women, abuse by immigration police, and racism and xenophobia. I will use border studies, trauma theory, ideological criticism, and liberation hermeneutics to engage the film with the issues it confronts. This film makes the Jesus story explicit for our time and places, in Italy and the US and beyond. Rau presents a "new" Jesus and a "new" gospel of liberation.

Tomato Jesus

Director Milo Rau went on a quest for Jesus in southern Italy and found him not in a cathedral but in a tomato field. He did not find a white Jesus, although Romanian and Bulgarian and other eastern European (and some Punjabi) migrants work in the fields; rather he chose from the majority of black African asylum seekers. These Italian fields are much like the fields all over the world that support what is known as "the new slavery." Here as elsewhere the list of human rights abuses is long. And "Jesus" speaks out against these abuses and pushes for just wages and conditions, along with environmentally conscious farming practices. I think Rau is telling the viewers that if you want to hear the actual Jesus and the gospel message, you have to hear the biblical stories translated in these fields and in these movements.

The pomo-d'oro, the tomato, the golden apple, descended directly from Eden to these fields. These are the fruits of desire, of safety, of a better life, of a future fulfillment of dreams. Where the "apple" of Eden gave life for a humanity bursting out the gates of paradise with possibilities, these Italian fruits are toxic, full of capitalist bile. In their study of the agricultural migrant labor force in Italy, Giovanna Lerner and Elena Past put the tomato in context: "Why is the tomato, a staple of Italian cuisine, beloved around the world, at the heart of a system of forced labor? What forces give a fragile fruit like the tomato the power to create indifferent and hostile zones of exclusion?"[3] Lerner and Past note that the tomato itself is also a migrant to Italy, arriving in the mid-sixteenth century from Latin America: "migration, toxicity, isolation, and hybridity can be connected in compelling ways to the tomato itself and to the legal and illegal practices surrounding its cultivation in Italy."[4] They further point out the cultural importance of the tomato:

3. Lerner and Past, "Toxic Fruits," 593.
4. Lerner and Past, "Toxic Fruits," 594.

"In Italy, tomatoes exist at the intersection of national-cultural culinary pride, Mediterranean petro-politics, contested agro-environmental policy, and even gender politics, to name just a few. They occupy such an important place in the Italian imaginary, and in the world's imaginary of Italy, that their cultural and culinary stature seem to obscure the often deplorable conditions of their cultivation and production and silence the voices of those whose labour delivers them to the global table."[5] Origins and supply chains converge in the fields.

Instead of focusing on the caporalato, "gangmastering," or Mafia[6] food systems, scholar Tomaso Ferrando outlines a network of responsibility: the "passata chain" of "owners, traders, processors, retailers, and consumers."[7] The owners are only one link in a chain from owners to processors to corporations that protect the markets and profits, not the workers.[8]

In its comprehensive study of the human rights context of Italy's migrant farmworkers, Amnesty International calls these chains part of the "labour exploitation spectrum."[9] The human rights organization points to the "Italian 'flows decree' system" that relegates irregular

5. Lerner and Past, "Toxic Fruits," 592.

6. A comprehensive study from Open Society/European Policy Institute, "Italian Agriculture," 14, details the agricultural situation from migration and asylum to exploitation and trafficking summarizes how the caporalato recruit, manage, and control the farmworkers. They continue their explanation, 13: "The caporalato is historically and socially rooted in the southern countryside as a form of irregular and anomalous organisation of the agricultural labour market, in which some social brokers—not necessarily linked to organised crime—act as a link between agricultural entrepreneurs and labourers." Ferrando, "Gangmastering," 525, defines gangmastering: "the phenomenon of caporalato (gangmastering) [is] a diffused practice aimed at extracting value from workers taking advantage of their state of need and inferior bargaining power."

7. Ferrando, "Gangmastering," 537.

8. Ferrando, "Gangmastering," 532. Where is the line to abuse? In our institutions of higher education we pay poverty wages to many hourly staff, creating systems of surveillance and control, denying them democratic voice and power in their work conditions. Abuses are more subtle; there can still be exposure to toxic chemicals, the health effects of working additional jobs, etc. Can we call these poverty wage jobs "the new slavery"? There are no beatings, confinement, accruing debt to the farm/company. Often there is camaraderie and the formation of relationships across class lines. Still, the wages are oppressive, and these workers are most often invisible, with their stories untold and unknown. Those of us who are not higher in the passata chain, whether in Italy or Florida, are still players in the chain. What to call it in higher education—"the facilities chain"?

9. Amnesty International, *Exploited Labour*, 5.

migrants to perpetual illegal status.[10] Without recourse to legal visas and contracts, the work status of farmworkers remains tenuous, putting them at the mercy of their employers and opening them to abuse. Amnesty International notes that migrants in Italy have no access to basic rights: to fair wages, health care, decent living conditions, or legal services to address their exploitation. "Irregular migrants" are criminalized, further removing them from access to their human rights under the United Nations. They state: "Under the International Labour Organization (ILO) Migrant Workers (Supplementary Provisions) Convention of 1975 (No. 143), which Italy ratified in 1981, migrant workers in an irregular situation have the right to equality of treatment in respect of rights arising out of past employment as regards remuneration, social security and other benefits."[11] Human rights law reflects an ideal situation; the reality is governed by neoliberal strategies of highest profit, no matter the human costs. In the midst of these abusive systems, Yves Sagnet created an Italian "fair trade" label on tomatoes, "NO Cap," No to caporalato, and this labeling provides a call to a more just economic and environmental system.[12] Sagnet and other farmworkers want to shift the traditional capitalist narrative in the focus of tomato production to the farmworkers and the farmworkers' telling of their own story.

Ultimately, it is all about the chain of abuses. Ferrando further explains the chain from field to shelf, one that leaves the migrant farmworker with few options because it reinforces "the legal construction of the migrant worker as an invisible, exploitable, available, and disposable means of production. More importantly, they are interconnected: the existence of power asymmetries along the chain and the attempt to reduce costs to increase margins go hand in hand with the search for cheaper labor."[13] Ferrando critiques the need for radical intervention from outside groups, especially responses that focus on the agromafia. All links of the chain are interconnected.[14] Neil Howard and Roberto Forin agree with this broader approach and critique "modern abolitionists" of the new slavery who depict an Italy full of slaves and their gangster overlords: they claim that this approach "both re-inscribes the (neo)liberal paradigm

10. Amnesty International, *Exploited Labour*, 14.

11. Amnesty International, *Exploited Labour*, 30.

12. Lerner and Past, "Toxic Fruits," 612.

13. Ferrando, "Gangmastering," 537.

14. Ferrando, "Gangmastering," 540–41.

that is foundational to the exploitation it claims to wish to overcome and alienates many of the people it purports to depict."[15]

In a similar vein, in their article on the "refugeeization" of migrant workers in southern Italy, Nick Dines and Enrica Rigo point to the nebulous areas in the depiction of the situation of migrant workers in Italy. They object to the use of the language of slavery by popular media; they claim it "depoliticizes the question of migrant labor, by absolving the responsibilities of the state and removing the calculated choices made by migrants when deciding to work in the fields."[16] Dines and Rigo want "to illustrate how discourses that reproduce the representation of migrants as victims (be it during crossings of the Mediterranean Sea or in the various "ghettos" spread across the southern Italian countryside) and institutional and normative practices governing migration find their common ground in the removal of relations of production, in which migrant workers are protagonists."[17] They argue that a more comprehensive look at labor relations, along with human rights issues, is needed to include the agency of migrants in their various statuses regarding legality and citizenship.

Along with citizenship, race is of course a factor. Dominica Perrotta provides a study of the situation of day laborers in southern Italian tomato fields with several discoveries. There is a hierarchy in terms of country of origin, race, and refugee or immigrant status; seasonal workers from eastern Europe are certainly exploited in this system but are temporary and usually not seeking permanent status in Italy. Racism, in an institutional sense as much as in a more general one, is a key factor in managing the labor market. *Caporali* derive their power (and profit) from this segregation because it allows them to monopolize communication between the *forestieri* and the locals and control the labor market."[18] Factors such as race and immigration status have led to the description of this labor system as "the new slavery." This term is not exact since the abuses are not "new" except in terms of the modern iterations of migration and systemic causes of poverty. Still, the experience of the farmworkers exposes the lack of freedom and human rights.

Modern slavery expert Kevin Bales points out that today slavery is technically illegal; people are not owned but controlled. "Slavery" is a

15. Howard and Forin, "Migrant Workers," 580.

16. Dines and Rigo, "Postcolonial Citizenships," 156.

17. Dines and Rigo. "Postcolonial Citizenships," 165–66.

18. Perrotta, "Day Laborers," 200.

strong term that he insists upon to draw attention to the real issues; a term Bales uses in his research questionnaire is "slavery/unfree laborers."[19] Instead of the old term "slaveowners," he prefers the term "slaveholder," and he defines the new slavery as "the total control of one person by another for the purpose of economic exploitation."[20] More strongly, Bales contends: "Slavery is an obscenity. It is not just stealing someone's labor; it is the theft of an entire life. It is more closely related to the concentration camp than questions of bad working conditions."[21] His solutions to the multiplicity of human rights abuses in new slavery include building awareness of consumers, as Rau is doing in his film, and activist movements, as Sagnet and the Immokalee workers have created.

Discussing the word *slavery*, Lerner and Past make an important observation focused on the farmworker, exposing the issues of mainstream media and academic studies of the situation:

> [We argue] that the counter-hegemonic pushback against this fetishization is itself also highly problematic. Although undoubtedly well-intentioned, it remains simplistic, alienating, depoliticizing, and at times damaging. . . . Because the word "slave" is typically associated with shame and its accompanying tales of victimhood deny people their humanity, it reduces the complexity of their lives to one-dimensional accounts of suffering. In this respect, the humanitarian, modern abolitionist gaze should itself be seen as a form of fetishization, constructed by looking at people rather than with them, and abstracting them from the messiness of their contexts. Here is where the worker-initiated justice movement comes in.[22]

What would Jesus say about the passata chain? Rau and Sagnet answer this. Rau made a decision in *The New Gospel* to have the farmworkers tell the story of Jesus through their own asylum and labor stories. The "actual Jesus" walks through their fields and works alongside them. Jesus is a migrant seeking a new "home." Jesus also organizes with them for concrete social change, raising awareness of the situation, building coalitions with religious and human rights groups, and getting better, more ethically sourced products on grocery shelves for consumers. A farmworker

19. E.g., Bales, *Disposable People*, 435.

20. Bales, *Disposable People*, 59. He outlines three types of new slavery: chattel, debt, and contract, 77–79.

21. Bales, *Disposable People*, 60.

22. Lerner and Past, "Toxic Fruits," 594–95.

action in another tomato field in another Naples (not Italy, but Florida) reveals their own similar and distinctive stories.

"I am not a tractor": The Coalition of Immokalee Workers

Farmworkers have typically been referred to with derogatory terms. In the documentary *The Invisibles: Inhumane Conditions of Italy's Migrant Farmworkers*, migrant workers in Italy are called "braccianti," "a pair of arms." Union organizer, filmmaker, and former migrant farmworker from the Ivory Coast Aboubakar Soumahahoro coined the phrase, "I am not a commodity," and the rallying chant, "We are human beings, not arms!"[23] In a similar manner, a rallying cry of the Coalition of Immokalee Workers is, "I am not a tractor." The dehumanization of work and workers is the context of both worker justice movements.

Like their Italian counterparts, the Coalition of Immokalee Workers uses the term "modern-day slavery." CIW farmworker and organizer Geraldo Reyes Chavez names the situation: "Working in the fields, our work is essential, but people are treated as disposable."[24] Like their Italian counterparts, the Florida farmworkers lack decent accommodations of breaks, availability of water and food, bathroom facilities, and just wages. The bloody T-shirt in the Immokalee museum display is a cross symbol for these farmworkers. Sixteen-year-old Edgar was beaten by a supervisor for asking for water. His story helped spark the movement.[25]

In her detailed history of the movement, Susan Marquis explains the use of the term *slavery* in this US context:

> Whether described as debt peonage or human trafficking, there is both evidence and acknowledgment that the word "slavery" is neither a metaphor nor an exaggeration. In this case, the Reverend Noelle Damico, the Presbyterian Church USA's lead for work with the CIW, explained, "Rather it is a new form of slavery in which people are held against their will and forced to labor through force, fraud, or coercion." Importantly, human trafficking is not human smuggling. "Human trafficking involves coercion. [And] you do not have to cross a border to be

23. Doha Debates, *Invisibles*.
24. Robledo and Kenner, dirs., *Food Inc. 2*.
25. Coalition of Immokalee Workers, "Worker Beaten."

> trafficked: people can be and have been trafficked within their own country and state.[26]

The CIW uses a range of strategies to draw attention to the human rights abuses, from performance art, to theater of the oppressed, boycotts, well-organized and advertised public marches, and the "Farmworker Freedom Festival" in March 2024. Leadership is from within, and as Marquis describes: "Led from the inside, by the farmworkers and their community, the CIW and its Campaign for Fair Food and the resulting Fair Food Program have succeeded not only in transforming tomato fields, but in how we view the relationship between workers, producers, corporate buyers, and consumers."[27] These campaigns educate about the exploitation of farmworkers. Susan Haedicke observes that through worker-led workshops, CIW is able to educate and teach about the issues in the lives of the farmworkers. She explains, "The performative protest art that accompanies the CIW's human rights campaigns, I think, often manages to successfully combine aesthetic shock and dialogic collaboration."[28] Through drama and art and music, CIW is able to spread their message.

Farmworker Jesus

Agro-ecologist and activist Gary Paul Nabhan finds much inspiration for his borderlands work in Patagonia, Arizona in Jesus's parables. He has worked as a farmworker in many countries, including Italy (grape vineyards), and describes the typical situation: "farmworkers are typically paid at the 'piece rate,' with wages based not on how many hours are worked, but on how many buckets or bags they pick of whatever crop they harvest."[29] Nabhan makes comparisons between the agrarian situation in Jesus's time and our current time, and this connection works to promote his focus on food and agrarian justice, as it is also a bit of a stretch to make such grand historical claims. Using the work of Ellen Davis, John Dominic Crossan, and others, Nabhan finds a revolutionary kernel in the agrarian images of Jesus's parables. He explains further the subversive rhetoric of these parables: "Rather than merely raging at the machine, Jesus offered game-changing principles that he sensed could

26. Marquis, *Not a Tractor*, 40.

27. Marquis, *Not a Tractor*, 225.

28. Haedicke, "Immokalee Workers," 217.

29. Nabhan, *Jesus for Farmers*, 106.

avert further conflict and help people regain their dignity. He focused more upon strengthening a sense of justice, dignity, hope, and resilience through stories that continue to have staying power centuries after they were first told."[30] There is a gritty reality to the descriptions that evokes emotional reactions to grain, bread, soil, seed, weeds, wheat, sheep, poverty wages. Nabhan rightly shows that Jesus's focus was more on those in the fields, and not the colonial owners: "Could it be that Jesus's heart reached out to farmers and fishers in a dramatic way, not because he romanticized them as the 'salt of the earth' but for another, more troubling reason? *Was it because they had recently joined the ranks of the most oppressed and dispossessed in his society?*"[31] Jesus threatened the political system due to his "feeling the humanity of the poor."[32]

Overall, Nabhan observes that Jesus advocated "spiritual defiance that was grounded in a sense of contemplative action and restorative justice."[33] Is this focus enough to make real change with and for the twenty-first-century farmworker? Do any of the parables upend the system of oppression, and do we ever hear the collective voices of the farmworkers? Are we expecting too much for a first-century peasant carpenter? Jesus was certainly politically engaged and was crucified by the Romans for his teaching and actions, although not in the ways of our more modern activist leaders such as Dolores Huerte, Gandhi, Malcolm X, Fanny Lou Hamer, or M. L. King Jr., Nabhan reminds us that "what was happening then [in Jesus's time] is happening now."[34]

In her search for the enslaved "ghostwriters" of the New Testament, Candida Moss rereads the story of Jesus. She asks, "How might thinking with the interests and experiences of enslaved collaborators broaden our view? . . . Jesus does not seem to have been enslaved, but his story resonated with and drew upon the experiences of those who were. Enslaved coauthors were not in a position to change the whole story, but in their selection of language, and in their omission of certain details and the emphasis they place on others, fragments of enslaved interests might persist."[35] Moss notes that Jesus's identification as a carpenter's

30. Nabhan, *Jesus for Farmers*, 7.

31. Nabhan, *Jesus for Farmers*, 10, emphasis his.

32. Nabhan, *Jesus for Farmers*, 138.

33. Nabhan, *Jesus for Farmers*, 167.

34. Nabhan, *Jesus for Farmers*, 17.

35. Moss, *God's Ghostwriters*, 92–93. This view is debated by Mitzi Smith in her study of Mary's designation in Luke as slave (*doulé*). Smith, "Abolitionist Messiah,"

son points to a marginalized class who worked in smelly materials like manure in the building process. She clarifies: "But carpenters, or more accurately 'construction workers' (the Greek noun *tekton* refers equally to stonemasons and bricklayers), were part of a class of marginalized workers who were often the subject of scorn and derision. Low-level subsistence workers (*penetes*), they struggled to make ends meet and did not always have more legal rights than enslaved workers."[36] The line between this class of worker and the enslaved is thin.

Combining a materialist, Marxist analysis with historical Jesus studies, James Crossley and Robert Myles investigate Jesus in light of class conflict and his role as a social change organizer. They view Jesus in light of "agrarian realism," that is, "The predominant conception in pre-feudal societies that the agrarian mode of production, including its corresponding social relations, was the only viable political and economic system."[37] They utilize the debated term, *peasantry*, "to denote a broad and internally diverse category of rural workers and non-elite actors closely associated with agricultural production of land and water."[38] From fishermen and day-laborers to bandits, the imagery in Jesus's stories and also represented in his followers shows how he was able to build a movement around class conflict and shared antagonism toward Roman occupation. Crossley and Myles are embedded in the historical Jesus Quests, seeking to start a(nother) new quest as they "seek to uncover the collective 'Jesus movement' he was a part of and which, in turn, formed him as a leader."[39] In their quest they seek to cut through the centuries of Christian empire to return to the revolutionary message of Jesus: "For this reason, understanding the life of Jesus as a life in class conflict is inescapable to appreciating the class struggles of today."[40] Their Jesus, and his movement, is relatable to the organizer farmworkers of Matera. Roman Catholic and Muslim, the movement builders in and around *The New Gospel* seek to create new spaces for returning

finds it probable that Jesus was born a slave to a slave mother and began his teaching ministry at age thirty when he was free. Moss, *God's Ghostwriters*, 96–97, thinks Mary might have been a slave and/or sex worker, since no father is present. In any event, this debate has only started.

36. Moss, *God's Ghostwriters*, 95–96.

37. Crossley and Myles, *Jesus*, 279.

38. Crossley and Myles, *Jesus*, 3.

39. Crossley and Myles, *Jesus*, 21.

40. Crossley and Myles, *Jesus*, 263.

their religions to an egalitarian base of social change in the midst of capitalist ideology and occupation. In any "questing" for a "historical Jesus," I believe a gap remains. In one way, the Jesus of *The New Gospel* fills in this gap, telling a continuation of the story in different fields, in a larger, more complex globalized system. And race matters.

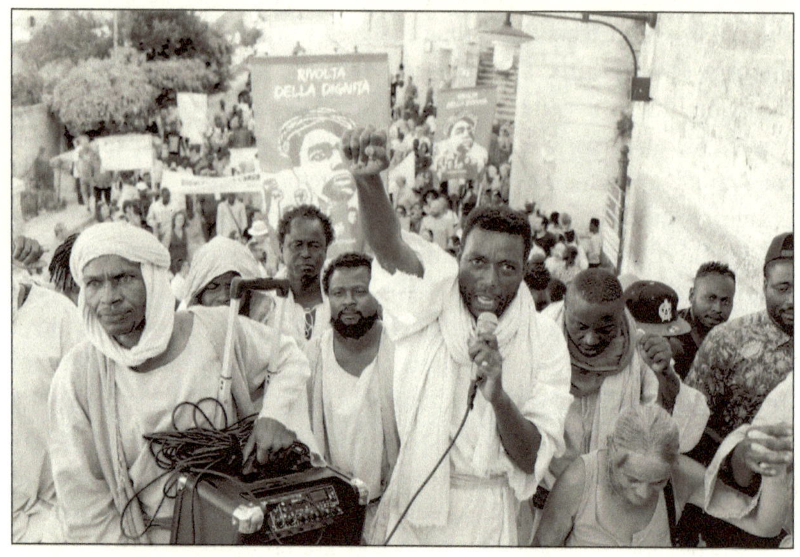

Farmwork and activist Yves Sagnet as Jesus in *The New Gospel*. THE NEW GOSPEL 1 ©Fruitmarket/Langfilm/IIPM/Armin Smailovic 01.jpg

Black Jesuses of Fields and Film

Only a black Jesus can be truly revolutionary. But the black Jesus of *The New Gospel* goes beyond race and into the intersections of class, nationality, and religion of the globalized economy. In an interview at the Venice Film Festival Rau indicates that *The New Gospel* is "the first black Jesus film in European film history."[41] For Rau Jesus has come to fulfill the law (as in Matthew) and the same with existing Italian (and European) law regarding migrants. Rau wants to tell the story from the point of view of "the people Jesus would fight for."[42] Rau points out the failure of government, of nonprofits, of religious organizations to effect

41. Scarpa, "Milo Rau."
42. Scarpa, "Milo Rau."

change in the farmworkers' situation or in the inclusion of asylum seekers in Italy. During the filming police closed a refugee camp outside of Matera, evicting the residents. One outcome of the film, and even more the Revolt of Dignity organized by the farmworkers, was the creation of Houses of Dignity, with the help of the Roman Catholic Church, for the migrants. In Rau's words, "We made a revolt."[43] With this hybrid fiction/documentary, migrants tell their Jesus story, across time, while keeping the focus on the current time of the work in the tomato fields. Like Passolini before him, Rau uses a mix of professional actors and local citizens. For example, Pasolini's Jesus, Enrique Irazoqui, plays John the Baptist (so "Jesus" is baptizing "Jesus" in a way), and Gibson's Saint Mary, Maia Morgenstern, returns in the same role. Rau auditions local Italians for the roles of the Romans, Jewish authorities, and crowd, although some tourists happen by some scenes as themselves, cell phones in hand. For example, the mayor of Matera plays Simon of Cyrene, after refusing the role of Pontius Pilate because he does not think it would be prudent for him as a politician. At eighty-six years old, the mayor opted to carry Jesus's cross through the streets of his city, making the case that this role was more appropriate for a politician.

In addition, local police, including one who evicted the asylum seekers, play Roman soldiers. One policeman is especially enthusiastic and asks to play a Roman soldier and torturer so that he can participate in "Killing. Massacring God himself." The auditions take place in a church sanctuary, with the altar and flowers behind the auditioners. In one long and disturbing audition scene that shocked the director and his assistant, this policeman reenacts the beating of Jesus by hitting a plastic chair with the mop-shaped whip prop and shouting abuses and racist, xenophobic hate: "What's it like on the boats? . . . . In all my life I've never seen a black man who could swim. And that's why so many of you drown. Right? That's it. . . . But I like you. You're a different kind of black. More . . . more . . . dirty black." He closes his audition by kicking and spitting on the chair and making ape sounds and movements. Later, after the filming of the trial scene, the policeman embraces Jesus/Sagnet.

Echoing the policeman's audition, when Pontius Pilate asks the crowd whom he should release, Barabbas or Jesus, and the crowd follows the script to shout the latter, accusing him of blaspheming. But they also add: "The filthy black must be crucified! Kill the filthy black!

43. Scarpa, "Milo Rau."

He must die! . . . . Nail the filthy black to the cross! Crucify the filthy black!" The repetition of the phrase "filthy black" reveals the racism and anti-immigrant part of Italian society. The crowd, comprised of both local actors, a few professional actors, other locals, and tourists, signals the social and cultural issues the uphold the oppressive farming system and food chain. And interestingly, Pilate, representing the political authority, washes his hands of the verdict. As the actor makes his way through the crowd to begin the trial scene, he jokes with the crowd, "You are the true culprits!" It is a way to set the tone, but also to stir up some harsh, xenophobic realities.

Yvan Sagnet's Jesus does not want to overthrow Rome. He wants to be a free citizen and treated as a full human being, and with these things to enjoy full human rights of fair pay, adequate living conditions, a path to fully participate in the nation. Through a nonviolent movement and protest, his Jesus represents M. L. King Jr.'s more than Albert Cleage's Jesus: a liberator who addresses particular oppression and the systemic roots and wider implications of the human rights abuses in the fields. Sagnet's activist message mirrors Jesus in the Gospels as he addresses a rally: "The enemy is not the one who is desperate, but those who throw people into despair. The enemy is not the one who flees, but the society who forces humans to flee." The Gospel according to Sagnet continues, "You say, it's not worth fighting because the situation will never change. The world will always be this way. You're wrong. These are the enemies." His message is one of the exposure of the systemic wrongs, laced with the hope of building coalitions to dismantle that system.

With all the harsh realities of the lives of the asylum seeker-tomato farmers in this film, Rau finds humanity in their stories and their agency. In his review in *The Guardian*, Mark Fisher comments on the positive ending in the film: "It's about what it means to tell the story as much as it is about the story itself. As Jesus, he is passive, wise and accepting; as a campaigner, he is the voice of righteous anger. That he is also a rare black Jesus in European film history brings to notice another layer of injustice in a story that, 2,000 years on, has yet to lose its radical edge."[44] Seeking the "radical edge" of the Jesus story is at the core of liberation hermeneutics. How far does this black Jesus take the viewer and the farmworkers to liberation?

44. Fisher, "New Gospel Review."

Homo Sacer

Jesus is represented in both Pasolini's and Rau's films, and arguably as he is in the Gospels, what Giorgio Agamben terms a *homo sacer*, a man who lives on the margins and is ultimately doomed to death, also termed the sub-proletariat. The connections here are a bit complex; as a young university student Agamben played the disciple Philip in Pasolini's *The Gospel According to St. Matthew*. For Agamben his *homo sacer* is best represented in the refugee. Drawing on the philosophy of Hannah Arendt, Agamben adopts the phrase "bare life" to describe the biopolitical status of the refugee who is always in a "state of exception," as evidenced by under-documentation and detention camps.[45] Agamben, and also Rau, put refugees at the center of the human story.

In his investigation of Pasolini films, Fabio Vighi finds this theme of exclusion in the portrayal of beggars (cf. also Pasolini's *Accetone*) and links to the modern situation of refugees and asylum seekers in Europe. Vighi notes Pasolini's "lifelong attachment to the underprivileged, from the Roman sub-proletariat to the African peasants."[46] In a similar way Rau shares these political concerns. The starting place for Pasolini and Rau is with the excluded, and here is where politics begins. The sub-proletariat is thus a "'shameful' remainder of the country's late-capitalist modernization."[47] Capitalism demands a remainder, an excluded group of the poor and socially and politically marginalized, and the African refugee and asylum seeker fits the role perfectly. Vighi's discussion of Agamben in reading Pasolini is helpful in understanding Rau, for the refugee has no rights because they are not seen as fully human. The connection with Agamben's political thought is through his concept of the *homo sacer*, or the sacredness of human beings. Vighi elaborates on Agamben's notion of the *homo sacer* as "doomed to death" because they are not citizens and thus full members of a nation or society.[48] Vighi describes the historical space further: "In the context of 1960s Italy, Pasolini 'bets' on the sub-proletariat as he believes that the latter is the anthropological breaking-point (the symptom) that can cause the short-circuit of capitalist ideology."[49] The

45. Agamben, *Homo Sacer*.

46. Vighi, "Pasolini," 99.

47. Vighi, "Pasolini," 102.

48. Vighi, "Pasolini," 107; Agamben, *Means without End*, 22.

49. Vighi, "Pasolini," 116.

homo sacer, for Pasolini and for Rau, is sacred and as such provides the starting place for any transformative politics.

Agamben is further useful in reading Rau's film since the focus is on the immigrant farmworkers from Africa, with a starting point in the fields and their sub-standard living conditions.[50] Agamben relates: "If the refugee represents such a disquieting element in the order of the nation-state, this is so primarily because, by breaking the identity between the human and the citizen and that between nativity and nationality, it brings the originary fiction of sovereignty to crisis."[51] As for Pasolini, the dispossessed is the starting point for political change, but also for a reevaluation of the concept of "rights" and "human rights":

> The concept of refugee must be resolutely separated from the concept of the "human rights," and the right of asylum (which in any case is by now in the process of being drastically restricted in the legislation of the European states) must no longer be considered as the conceptual category in which to inscribe the phenomenon of refugees. (One needs only to look at Agnes Heller's recent Theses on the Right of Asylum to realize that this cannot but lead today to awkward confusions.) The refugee should be considered for what it is, namely, nothing less than a limit-concept that at once brings a radical crisis to the principles of the nation-state and clears the way for a renewal of categories that can no longer be delayed.[52]

The Jesus/Sagnet in Rau's film blurs the figure of Jesus: from African asylum seeker and tomato farmworker and union organizer in twenty-first-century southern Italy opposing the political power of modern-day Rome, to the Marxist/socialist first-century Judean opposing the imperialism and oppression of ancient Rome. The stand-in for Jerusalem and Galilee is Matera, used by Pasolini, Gibson, and Rau, and the city takes on specific political meaning in Rau's film. Jesus is a leader in a farmworker movement, and in this role he addresses the poor working and living conditions, the agromafia system, and the global capital connections of the Italian tomato industry.

50. In a section entitled "The Camp," Agamben, *Means without End*, 39, traces the concept from the concentration camps of World War II to the present detention center and exclusionary spaces for the dispossessed: "The camp is the space that opens up when the state of exception starts to become the *rule*" (his emphasis).

51. Agamben, *Means without End*, 21.

52. Agamben, *Means without End*, 22–23.

Rau's film blurs the boundaries between the farmworkers and Jesus and his disciples by using the black African asylum seekers as embodying the Gospel stories. In similar ways in the film and real life, there is xenophobia. The distinction is that in the Gospels Jesus and his Palestinian Jewish cohorts were colonized by Rome and desired to free themselves from this occupying force; in present they are played by asylum seekers seeking safety and economic security in "Rome."

The message of Jesus in this film is nonetheless revolutionary. Writing in the last century, James Cone found the heart of Jesus's revolutionary message: "Black power, even in its most radical expression, is not the antithesis of Christianity, nor is it a heretical idea to be tolerated with painful forbearance. It is rather, Christ's central message to twentieth-century America."[53] "Unless we can articulate clearly an image of Christ that is consistent with the essence of the biblical message and at the same time relate it to the struggle for black liberation, Black Theology loses its reason for being."[54] By a black Christ Cone does not (necessarily) intend a literal color,[55] but a repositioning of a stance with the oppressed: "The definition of Christ as black means that he is the complete opposite of the values of white culture."[56] But Cone is also not separating Christ and Jesus, for both are black. Cone's central question, "Who is Jesus Christ for us today?," is the question Pasolini and Rau dealt with. The black Jesus and Christ are found in the freedom struggles across the centuries. Whether in Palestine of the first century or Memphis of 1968 or Matera or Immokalee of the twenty-first century, the black Jesus stands in solidarity with those on the margins. Cone continues, "Christ is black, therefore, not because of some cultural or psychological need of black people, but because and only because Christ *really* enters into our world where the poor, the despised, and the black are, disclosing that he is with them, enduring their humiliation and pain and transforming oppressed slaves into liberated servants. Indeed, if Christ is not truly black, then the historical Jesus lied. . . . the gospel is not good news to the oppressed."[57] The identity of Jesus is bound up with the struggles of the oppressed. Cone echoes the black Jesus of *The New Gospel*: "When connected with the person of Jesus, hope is not an intellectual idea; rather, it is the praxis of freedom

53. Cone, *Black Power*, 1.

54. Cone, *Black Theology*, 203.

55. Cone, *Black Theology*, 218; Cone, *God of the Oppressed*, 136.

56. Cone, *Black Theology*, 215.

57. Cone, *God of the Oppressed*, 136.

in the oppressed community."[58] Freedom praxis is worker-driven, fueled and inspired by the migrant, farmworker Jesus.

Kelly Brown Douglas summarizes the turn to the black Christ in black theology of the 1960s: "Essentially, the black Christ was such a thorough response to the 1960s freedom struggles that it was impotent in dealing with concerns beyond racism. It, like the movement that called it forth, was grounded in a social analysis focused on race. The black Christ signaled a one-dimensional understanding of social oppression."[59] Brown is reminding us that the struggle continues and oppressions are plural and specific. Films like *Son of Man* (2006) and *The New Gospel* address the tradition in film of a white European Jesus and show how race matters when black and brown people are at the center of oppressive systems. Howard Thurman comes to mind here: "The masses of men live with their backs constantly against the wall. They are the poor, the disinherited, the dispossessed."[60]

Like James Cone, Kelly Brown Douglas makes the connection of contemporary lynchings (in particular, of Emmett Till and Trayvon Martin) to the crucifixion of Jesus. The tragedy of the cross is retold in the murders of black bodies, as these bodies are part of "a crucified class."[61] The Immokalee workers read the story of the crucifixion in a similar way; to see Jesus, you only have to look in the face of this crucified class of black and brown bodies; thus, Jesus is in the face of Trayvon and of George Floyd, Sandra Bland, and too many others.[62] The resurrection is the telling of the stories by the farmworkers, as it is for the Black Lives Matter movement. Jesus lives in these workers and their work for human rights.

Conclusion: Blood in the Soil

The "temple cleansing" in the film takes place in a supermarket, with Jesus and his disciples alarming fellow shoppers as they upend tomato bins and smash the tomatoes under their sandals. In another scene a smiling Jesus/Yves Sagnat poses with the fair food label, NoCap, they have created, to

58. Cone, *God of the Oppressed*, 129. Robert P. Jones relates the problem some white evangelical Christians have with a black or brown Jesus, *White Too Long*, 101: "Whites simply couldn't conceive of owing their salvation to a representative of what they considered an inferior race."

59. Douglas, *Black Christ*, 98.

60. Thurman, *Disinherited*, 3.

61. Douglas, *Stand Your Ground*, 173–74.

62. Douglas, *Stand Your Ground*, 174–76.

raise awareness about the violent harvests in Italy. Rau is on a quest: for Pasolini's Jesus, for human rights, for human dignity. In what ways does Rau's Jesus in "the new Gospel" correspond to the Jesus and his teachings on agriculture and farm work/ers in "the old Gospels?"

Jesus uses agricultural imagery and metaphors in his parables, but does he really address the systems of oppression in first-century Roman Palestine? How does the past (the Jesus of the first century, who is superimposed on the current agromafia situation) influence or translate the present and give us guidance for the future? The Jesus of *The New Gospel* is the Jesus of the Revolt of Dignity and No Cap Association is the Jesus of the Coalition of Immokalee Workers and Fair Food Program. History is lived in the now, in conversation with the past, and with imagination and commitment to concrete social change. But first, as Rau shows us, one has to enter the fictional worlds of the stories of Jesus.

The New Gospel joins several recent Jesus films dealing with social justice issues, and the setting is also Matera, Italy. An example with another black Jesus, *The Book of Clarence* (2023), uses the framework of white supremacy (represented by the all-white Romans) and their imperialist abuse (echoing contemporary police brutality) of the all-black Judeans. Black Lives Matter and Black Power infuse the narrative as the grifter twin brother of the apostle Thomas subverts the white supremacist systems, in particular of slavery. However, in this film Jesus appears only a few times; he is a wise, inspiring, and mystical teacher, but there is no activist social agenda in his dialogue. It is the slacker Clarence, on his journey to become a better person, who sacrifices himself to confront the institution of slavery (for a group of slaves who are gladiator combatants). The director Jeymes Samuel puts these themes of racism and slavery (past and present) to the fore.

In a similar way, Milo Rau fronts the refugee/immigrant crisis in Europe, and the treacherous trip from Africa across the Mediterranean to face poverty and xenophobic systems. The climax of the film exposes the depths of the issues. In the midst of such hopelessness is the worker movement, led by Sagnet/Jesus. As the trial scene is being set up, a Roman Catholic priest embraces Sagnet as Jesus around his knees in a compliant, worshipful move, announcing to the gathering, "Jesus is here now!" The priest knows that Sagnet is playing a role, that he is not the actual Jesus. But as his eyes tear up and he also becomes a spectator of the trial, it becomes a liminal space. In this space the viewer is called upon to act.

5

Air Jesus: Fear of Flying in The Gospel of Mark

"So then the Lord Jesus, after he had spoken to them, was taken up into heaven and sat down at the right hand of God." (Mark 16:19)

Introduction: Looking Up

THE SIGN OUTSIDE THE small, urban church at Easter read simply, "He got up." I checked back on Ascension Sunday, but the sign had not changed. I was expecting, "He was taken up," "he flew up," or something similar that emphasized the direction upward, finishing the action. Is the direction of the ascension necessarily "up"? There is no map of the ascension, although in the Gospels (Luke/Acts and Longer Ending Mark) Jesus went up and the disciples looked up. The sky and the air (sometimes with clouds) provide the path. Jesus had no wings, and no horse, and no angels to lift or carry him up. He just let go and flew, or entered some heavenly transit line, in any event defying the laws of physics. For those on the ground (including the reader), Jesus flew upward. Was Jesus following the same path as Moses, Elijah, Enoch, and later, Mohammed?[1] Jesus was not first in

1. In one of several versions of his death, Romulus also ascended in a fog and disappeared, according to Livy (59 BCE–17 CE) in his *History of Rome* 1:16. See the discussion in Ehrman, *How Jesus Became God*, 25–27.

flight, for the spaces/corridors between heaven and earth had been traveled before by God and angels and by a few special humans.

The ascension is a major-minor story, and Luke is the first Gospel to record it (Luke 24:50–53; Acts 1:1–2, 19; 7:55–56). Luke is also the only Gospel to record the miraculous flight, outside of the Longer Ending (LE) in Mark. LE Mark has Jesus make a proper exit—giving notice and rising upward in the sight of the disciples. The verb is *analambanesthai*, "to be taken up" (Mark 16:19). It is the same verb used to describe Elijah's ascension in 2 Kings 2:1–12 (LXX).[2] Elijah hitches a ride on "a chariot of fire and horses of fire" (2 Kgs 2:11).[3] Jesus's exit is much less dramatic, for he is taken up with only the clothes on his back.

The space of the ascension is vast but also limited. The disciples can only see Jesus rise so far before he disappears. Jesus rises in the air and seconds (?) later there is emptiness? According to Matthew Sleeman, there is an "ascension geography,"[4] an imaginary map of an imaginary journey.[5] The ascension is anticipatory geography in mapping the future end time path for believers. Mark's longer ending reorganizes space in the Gospel. No longer is Galilee the ending destination. Sleeman's interest is in how the ascension in Acts organizes space: "Given that the account is told from the spatial vantage point of the disciples who remain on earth, the *settings of other characters* are also repositioned by Jesus' ascension."[6] In Mark there is quick narration of the event, and as in Luke-Acts the narrator leaves the reader on the ground, looking up to the ultimately desired destination. On earth there remains the cycle of suffering, of life and death. The escape route is "up," in/to the clouds, heaven, eternal life, and immortality.

Studies in the ascension of Jesus usually focus on Luke and Acts. The scholarly consensus is that the short version of the ascension in Mark's longer ending is a second-century retelling of the Lukan story, offering no new take on the story. But what kind of story is this? The stories of the gods tend to be competitive stories, full of drama, with items like

2. Yarbro Collins, *Mark*, 816.

3. In Mark Elijah makes another appearance—and exit—in the story of the transfiguration in 9:2–8. Here Moses and Elijah simply disappear in thin air; there is no flight.

4. Sleeman, *Geography and Ascension*, 22.

5. See Edward Soja's *Thirdspace*, 53–82. He defines thirdspace as an extension of first (real) and second (imagined) space into a radically open and new geographic experience.

6. Sleeman, *Geography and Ascension*, 8.

miraculous births and miracles and eternal life after death. Myths fall to earth from above (heaven, mountains) and return—or desire to return. The gods of Olympus return to the mountain (and Zeus to his throne), and God returns from a walk in the garden to the heavenly realm. It is as if the gods have a homing device. The Genesis people attempt to occupy heaven by building the Tower of Babel, and Jacob dreams of a ladder from heaven, angels coming and going. But entry into "up" is restricted. Presumably, true believers can go "up" after death, following in Jesus's path. Of course, premillennial rapture believers imagine a mass movement "up," creating a grand (naked) spectacle. The Gospels leave an unfulfilled promise of a trip to eternity to the throne room to sit with Jesus and God. Even the additional endings of Mark leave the reader looking upward, anchored to the ground, but dreaming of flying.

Why the desire to go "up"? The end focus of all four Gospels is the resurrection, even though the empty tomb in Mark causes the response of fear and silence, not hope. Matthew and Luke may have needed to tack on traditions of a birth narrative (complete with genealogical chart) in order to compete with the narratives of other gods, but only Luke had Jesus complete a full competition ending with the rising to heaven and the spirit descending. The so-called "U-shaped Christology" meets its fulfillment here. Second-century editors of Mark presumably added stories of Jesus appearing to Mary Magdalene and the disciples after his resurrection, eating with them and then suddenly flying upward into the pantheon of heroes, God, and angels. Jesus has a disappearing act in the Gospels—not only from the tomb and after his resurrection appearances, but also after his birth (in Matthew and Luke, only appearing once at age twelve in the latter). And in Mark, Jesus disappears several times to escape the crowds and be alone. Thus the need for an ascension is as spotty as the need for a birth narrative. Mark had no need for either, perhaps because he saw no need for Jesus to compete after the cross and empty tomb. There is so much we can never know. We may stop reading Mark at 16:8, but the story of the ascension hangs on as Jesus flies off the page.

The Dangling Ending in Mark 16:8

The standard take on the ending of Mark in 16:8 is with the women leaving the tomb in fear, telling nobody nothing (a double negative, for emphasis, in the Greek). This abrupt end to Mark's short story of Jesus leaves the reader with a choice of how to fill in the rest of what they know of the story. The suspense of this suspended ending was too much for some believers.[7] Jesus had to go somewhere (from resurrection appearances in Galilee and Jerusalem), and heaven (the home where he came from—at some point presumably) was the logical place to deposit him. Sometime in the second century redactors completed the picture in different ways. Bridgit Upton states that "regardless, [Mark 16:]9–20 has become part of the 'textus receptus.'"[8] We can ignore, overlook, mark through, bad mouth, or declare heretical these other endings in 16:9–20, but we cannot rip them out (unless we also take out the beginning of Luke in most Bibles). To say that the ascension is not authentic to, and does not belong in, Mark has been a well-fought battle. But with every reasoned argument stand the unwanted guests in these tacked-on endings—ascension—joined by miracle working, including drinking poison and handling poisonous snakes—crashing the party and threatening to ruin the Markan performance. The additional endings reposition everything in Mark, calling attention to their strange behaviors. With their different vocabulary and syntax, these endings sound like foreigners and they do not belong. Plus they came late, and not fashionably late. Yet these strangers get the last word in Mark, no matter how many times the scholarly majority cuts them off. Their rowdiness spreads: to snake handlers and poison drinkers and healings and beyond to believers in the rapture. Things got out of hand, and "Mark," long gone, had no control over the production of his story.

Why did some second-century editors focus on the ending and not the beginning of Mark? What makes resurrection appearances and ascension more important than a birth or origin story? Why not have Jesus give more detailed instructions to the early Christian community? Why stop with adding on at the end? These are questions with no clear answers, but if tampering with a text is done, then why only add new, but odd, endings? There are so many places in Mark to soften the rhetoric, add a miracle or parable, take out a redundant feeding story, make a clearer statement on Roman occupation, pronounce the evils of slavery, etc. The incompleteness of Mark's story of Jesus allows for many possibilities. Is an ascension really necessary? Does it produce the happy ending that Mark 16:8 fails to deliver?

7. On Mark 16:8 as a suspended ending, see Magness, *Marking the End*.

8. Upton, *Hearing Mark's Endings*, 155.

George Aichele observes this open-ended question of the endings of Mark: "How do the various conclusions of Mark disguise and resolve the inadequacies of Mark's story—or do they?"[9] He concludes that the additional endings shore up the narrator's reliability, "both the shorter and the longer added endings provide the 'happy ending' which Mark 16:8 does not."[10] But in the end Aichele argues that all the endings (including the fifth-century ending from the Freer Logion) fail because they "further sabotage the narrative reliability that they attempt to reinforce. In Aristotle's terms, the ending of Mark remains no more well-constructed after all of these supplemental endings than it was at 16:8."[11] No ending to the Jesus story (or to any story) is completely satisfactory, and Mark's Gospel has to end somewhere. Why did Jesus leave earth and why depart with such an uncertain and unspecified future return? The ending of the Jesus story potentially opens into an abyss of meanings. However, Aichele adds, "An endless text cannot exist."[12] The Longer Ending has to be read against 16:8: "The alternative added endings to Mark provide a partial index of that negative power—of what the gospel of Mark, as of 16:8, is *not*. These endings mark by their own variation and multiplicity the *inadequacies* of the text of Mark."[13] Thus rewriting Mark adds more problems and never gives a satisfactory ending to the Gospel.

For Aichele, "[The ending of Mark] continually demands to be rewritten, and yet it refuses its own rewriting. The postmodern paradox of the gospel of Mark is that it fails to begin and it fails to end, and thus it could be said that the gospel of Mark has not yet been written."[14] In any ending, Jesus vanishes. But Aichele warns, "Yes although Jesus's body has completely disappeared by Mark 16:8, swallowed up in the silence of the terrified women, the body of Mark's text is manifest in the women's silence, for they have now become outsiders."[15] There is eternal absence and the unfulfilled promise of a return. There is a space between Mark 16:8 and 9; it is as if "Mark" took a breath after his short-winded tale. This is an uncomfortable silence. Does it beg to be filled or be left alone?

9. Aichele, *Jesus Framed*, 38.
10. Aichele, *Jesus Framed*, 49.
11. Aichele, *Jesus Framed*, 49.
12. Aichele, *Jesus Framed*, 50.
13. Aichele, *Jesus Framed*, 51.
14. Aichele, *Jesus Framed*, 54.
15. Aichele, *Jesus Framed*, 72.

Air Jesus

Jesus flies like Superman. As the stories go, by day he was a Clark Kent type, a Palestinian peasant who was the son of Joseph the carpenter and Mary in Nazareth in Galilee. He was an itinerant teacher and prophet, occasionally working miracles. He died a humiliating death on a Roman cross as a political insurgent. But post-death, well, Mark leaves that part empty. The young man in the tomb announces the missing corpse: "he is not here" (Mark 16:6). The tomb is open; the conclusion is not final. This empty tomb also speaks, echoing this news.

To further the Superman reference, George Aichele rereads Mark's "messianic secret" using the template of the television show *Lois & Clark: The New Adventures of Superman* (1993–97). Like Superman, Jesus can fly, but only at the end of the story (in Luke and the beginning of Acts), or beyond the end in Mark. Jesus was of normal strength and lacked the power of super hearing and sight, and bullets had not been invented. Even with his wing-like cape, Superman flies without wings.[16] Aichele describes this flight in *Lois & Clark*: "When he flies, Superman does not leap from the ground (as in the tradition), but he floats upward, sometimes accompanied by a 'mysterious sound effect.' The narrative effect of these depictions is a humorous downplaying of Superman's powers."[17] The speed at which Jesus is "taken up" in Mark 16:19 is not recorded. Perhaps he floated up, as artistic renderings depict. Is Jesus lifting himself up, or giving himself over to a supernatural tractor beam? Or was the event a combination of powers—of Jesus and the heavenly movers?

Philosopher Gaston Bachelard examines movement and flight in terms of the oneiric imagination that has a focus on dreams. Jesus desires the throne room of heaven, where he sits at God's right hand. The desires of Eve (for knowledge and godly likeness and immortality) and of those builders of the Tower of Babel serve as disruptive precursors to the ascension story. Only the gods are insiders. Those witnesses who are "left behind" in the longer ending of Mark can only dream about Jesus's air journey and destination. Meanwhile, there is poison to avoid and snakes to contend with.

Bachelard finds in language the possibilities for imagination, for dreams, and for the extra-ordinary to be unleashed. Is this ascension an invitation? If so, it is a vague and uncertain invitation, with an unclear

16. Aichele, "Rewriting Superman," 80.

17. Aichele, "Rewriting Superman," 81.

date and no directions on how to get to where Jesus is. Actually no invitation has been issued. It is left to the imagination, and as dispensationalists and other premillennialists have shown, this imagining can produce dangerous dreams.

Air is one of "the four material imaginations," as Bachelard understands the four elements.[18] His psychology of the imagination frames his understanding of air. The four elements are seductive. In the Gospels Jesus connects with water (baptism), earth (wilderness and walking), fire (eschatology), and air (dreams of God's dwelling). Where is "home" for Jesus? Is the ascension a return "home" for him?

The ascension creates desire: Bachelard notes that "'I want' and 'I fly' are both '*volo*' in Latin."[19] This desire dwells in the mind, in dreams. Bachelard refers to an "ascensional psychology[20] . . . The invitation to air travel, if it has the appropriate sense of rising, is always bound up with an impression of a gradual ascent."[21] But the ascension in Mark is a ruse; there is no invitation to rise with Jesus, just a vague mention of salvation, but with no clear instructions on how to get to the destination.

Despite this bait-and-switch the ascension still sparks dreams of flight. For Bachelard, "*oeneric pleasure* is satisfied by making the dreamer fly . . . When *flying*, voluptuousness is *beautiful*. The dream of flight is the dream of a *seductive* seducer. Love and its images cluster around this theme. By studying it we will see how love *produces* images."[22] The image of Jesus rising in the air, long curly hair windblown, robes billowing, angels harkening, heavens opening, cosmos trembling . . .the picture is the ultimate erotic dream.

The seductive hope of future flight holds the attention of the one who looks upward, stuck in that moment between heaven and earth.[23] Bachelard explains the effects of this vision of a flying Jesus: "Every aerial image is essentially *a future* with a vector for breaking into flight."[24]

18. Bachelard, *Air and Dreams*, 7.

19. Bachelard, *Air and Dreams*, 156.

20. The material imagination of air is part of the psychogeography of the text. The ascension is, in Colin Ellard's term for architectural spaces, a "space of awe," *Places of the Heart*, 151–73.

21. Bachelard, *Air and Dreams*, 9.

22. Bachelard, *Air and Dreams*, 20; see also 68; emphases his.

23. Elon Musk of SpaceX has activated the dream of space colonization on Mars and elsewhere. The yet (concrete design) and not-yet of this extensive space travel creates both believers and skeptics.

24. Bachelard, *Air and Dreams*, 21; emphasis his.

One can fly just like Jesus without angel wings, even though in the iconography of Christian angelology the righteous dead can "earn" their angel wings. Bachelard counters: "*oneric flight is never winged flight* . . . we can assume . . . that *when a wing appears in an account of a dream of flight, we must suspect that the account has been rationalized.* It is almost certain that the account is contaminated, either by images from conscious thought or by bookish inspiration."[25] As the longer ending of Mark has contaminated the Gospel, so too have the wild imaginings of angels on pinheads, intervening or rescuing wayward humans, or flying in heaven infecting our Markan dreams.

Further for Bachelard there is a connection of flying with freedom. On the "ascensional psychology" in Nietzsche's poetry and philosophy: "*aerial* joy is freedom."[26] But "Nietzsche dreams only of the tonicity of air: its coldness and its emptiness."[27] There is a cost to freedom in flying; going up into the void implies coldness and great heights. Bachelard concludes, "Air, like all the other elements, needs its warrior."[28] Jesus serves as a sort of warrior, bravely stepping off earth and rising.

The direction of this flight is vertical and Jesus leaves the earth in a single bound. Bachelard offers a reminder: "*Verticality tears us apart*; it puts both the high and the low within us."[29] Jesus ascends, presumably, to great heights. There is no map, no direction or description of his vertical journey. Jesus just goes "up" to the heights. For Bachelard, "Height is more than a symbol. Anyone who seeks it, anyone who imagines it with all of his imaginative power, which is the driving force behind our psychic dynamism, recognizes that it is materially, dynamically and vitally moral."[30] The gaze and attention on the disciples is no longer on earthly matters: "Flight becomes at once a memory of our dreams and a desire for the reward that God will grant us."[31] The dream of flight loosens moral obligations, loosens the message of Jesus in Mark. As Aichele argues, the silence of the women (and the men) swallows everything up. The Gospel of Mark threatens to disappear with Jesus, ascending upward.

25. Bachelard, *Air and Dreams*, 27; emphases his.

26. Bachelard, *Air and Dreams*, 136; emphases his.

27. Bachelard, *Air and Dreams*, 136.

28. Bachelard, *Air and Dreams*, 154.

29. Bachelard, *Air and Dreams*, 156; emphasis his.

30. Bachelard, *Air and Dreams*, 61.

31. Bachelard, *Air and Dreams*, 67.

The Disappearing Christ

The common ascension scene in art has a central focus on the whole body of Jesus rising into the air. His are hands often raised in blessing, or flailed as if still on the cross, or reaching out to grasp the hand of God, or surrounded by angels who may or may not be assisting him, or encased in a Mandorla, an oval-shaped container in which Jesus floats to heaven. Artists capture Jesus soon after lift off, usually in full bodily form, but also in a spectral form (Gustav Doré). Depending on how high one could jump, Jesus is just barely escaping upward. The spot of Jesus's lift-off is a place of new beginnings: "To imagine is to absent oneself, to launch out toward a new life."[32] Where does Jesus go?

The generic vision of Jesus's lift-off varies over the centuries. In early medieval art of the ascension, a dramatic change occurred. Instead of a whole body of Christ rising to heaven, all the onlooking disciples can witness is just the feet from the mid-shins down.

Bachelard explains the dream of flying without wings: "The words *wing* and *cloud* provide immediate proof of this ambivalence between the real and the imaginary. The reader can do what he likes with them: they can be a view or a vision, a sketch of something real or a movement that is dreamed."[33] The medieval image of dangling feet cuts off the need for wings or clouds, but does not lessen the desire to grab hold and join on the journey of flight into the clouds.

The view of Jesus's feet, dangling or not, occurs in several of the more well-known artworks. Salvador Dali's great sunflower/atom's nucleus vision, "The Ascension of Christ" (1958), with Mary/Dali's wife at his head, extends the verticality by starting at the bottoms of Jesus's soiled feet. The body visibly follows the feet to cosmic heights.

In a more literalistic (following medieval dangling feet art) and realistic way, Andres Serrano, known most for his controversial *Piss Christ* (1987), photographed the ascension of Jesus in *Ascent* (1983). Serrano draws from medieval representations of the disappearing feet; the photograph shows the bottom of Christ's satiny robe, along with his dangling feet. There is no other reference point—either up or down—Christ levitates in midair. He is suspended in space. Christ seems to be captured as he floats upward. There are no spirit guides, no hand of God or guiding angels, no view of heaven, only feet and legs, and a bit of robe. Either

32. Bachelard, *Air and Dreams*, 3.

33. Bachelard, *Air and Dreams*, 13; emphasis his.

Christ knows the way or an invisible force lifts him up. Christ is performing the ultimate levitation trick. Christ is barefoot, with the focus on this body part, and the feel is of a human body in flight. His feet are no longer sandaled or nailed down; in fact, these are the feet of the classical body, closed and smooth, with signs of dirt, but with no marks of stigmata. Based on medieval paintings of Christ's dangling feet, the viewer is to assume (also by the photograph's title) that these feet belong to the body of Christ. Serrano was an Afro-Cuban Roman Catholic, so this must be Christ. But there exists a hint of uncertainty, since there is an actor posing as Christ, and since the other clues (the view of the whole body, the amazed and upwardly gazing disciples, or angels) are absent. The feet in *Ascent* are a slight signifier for a bigger classical scene. This scene in Mark continues all the way to the seat at the right hand of God. In Serrano's scene, the feet dangle, suspended. It is not clear they are moving upward, or coming back to earth; the title of the photograph could be a ruse.

There is more to this dangling signifier. Mieke Bal compares Serrano's photo to the paintings of Caravaggio (1571–1610), noting that *Ascent* has Baroque features and "suggest[s] depth, sculpturality, violence, and sensuality."[34] To reach out and touch, even caress, or grab, these feet (after all they are so close!) would be a very intimate act. The viewer is at risk of developing a foot fetish.

Serrano photographs the flying feet up close, as a still life. Bruce Ferguson explains, "The close-up never delivers complete meanings, only fragmentary plentitude, supplements. For Serrano, the close-up offers ambivalence."[35] "Despite its seemingly transparent relation to reality, photography's hold on the world is illusory. It is a delusion of eternity, of holding onto a disappearance forever—of stopping time."[36] In *Ascent* Jesus is stopped in midair, on the way up, frozen in place and not able to complete the journey. In this way the viewer can hold on to the scene, and the desire is held out to have Jesus close (for the believer, that is), or to have a sort of live relic—the suspended feet of Jesus. "Serrano's work is erotically seductive,"[37] and the dangling feet are a present temptation to the viewer.

In her discussion of Serrano's photographs of the body, Liz Wells uses Mikhail Bakhtin's concept of the body in the carnivalesque. In Bakhtinian

34. Bal, *Quoting Caravaggio*, 3.

35. Ferguson, "Andre Serrano," n.p.

36. Ferguson, "Andre Serrano," n.p.

37. Ferguson, "Andre Serrano," n.p.

terms she describes Serrano's use of the form of the classical body as opposed to the open and threatening grotesque body, even in his morgue photographs.[38] Bakhtin reads Rabelais for his philosophy of the dialogical body in the carnivalesque. The grotesque body is generally represented by the female and especially the womb; it is open and a danger. The classical (male) body is the ideal form.[39] Two other photographs from *The Morgue* collection stand out. *Fatal Meningitis* shows young feet and legs from midcalf against a black background. The right ankle has a white ribbon. In another photo, *XXX*, a woman's feet lay on a white body bag; the zipper lays open at the bottom of the frame.[40] Both bodies looks suspended; are they also ascending? Serrano believes that "the concept of only one Christ does not exist."[41] Are these other bodies also divine?

Returning to Bakhtin, one way to extend this reading of the carnivalesque is to read the women at the empty tomb as a threat to the legitimacy of the Gospel, at least for some second-century redactor. Mark certainly has threatening women (and men), their open wounds and demon-possessed bodies in need of healing by Jesus. The ascension could serve as a form of (proleptic) closure for the believer. But for me the dangling feet are more of a dangling modifier, settling nothing, leaving a gaping hole that only The One can enter. Those remaining on earth are left to ponder the absence. The laws of gravity no longer hold. What goes up does not come down. Serrano gives us a chance to "grab hold" of something solid on its journey—to participate in the ascension. We continue to gaze at the feet, missing our chance to connect physically.

The perspective in *Ascent* is intriguing and stirs up desire. The viewer really could just reach out and grab his ankles. But for what purpose? To yank Jesus back to earth? To demand he stay put? Or to catch a ride to heaven? Desire is strange business, especially when the Divine is involved. There is a supernatural moment captured in *Ascent*. A rush to take hold of these ankles would be an unusual leap of faith. The inclination is to hold back, like the disciples. Immediately they/we have missed our chance. Somehow I think Eve would have taken the risk.

The disappearing feet images evoke apocalypse. Jesus will (presumably) return just as he left—flying up and down in the clouds. All but his lower legs and feet are out of the frame. The viewer is missing

38. Wells, *Photography*, 115.

39. Bakhtin, *Rabelais*, 315–17.

40. Serrano, *Morgue*, n.p.

41. Ting, "Andres Serrano."

most of the messiah. In medieval images the disciples are looking heavenward, following the trajectory of Jesus' body. In her poetic preface to a recent book on apocalyptic images in film, Leslie Jameson notes, "Whenever someone looks beyond the frame, you wonder what they're looking for—some kind of answer; some kind of monster."[42] Jesus flies upward like a great apocalyptic bird. The anticipation of his return is mixed. With the parousia comes death and destruction. There is hope, dismay, sadness, and joy in both the coming and going of parousia and the ascension. The disciples see the bottoms of his feet; why is this not seen as an insult? What rudeness to show the dirty soles of his sandalless feet to his followers. According to the geography of the ascension stories, as he sits beside God, Christ is eternally disrespectful to those beneath him. But did he enter heaven with dirty feet?

Lastly, Barry Moser is another artist who draws on classical images in his wood engravings in the *Pennyroyal Caxton Bible* (KJV). The often dark, gothic-like images evoke the supernatural and the sinister. His illustration of the ascension of Christ echoes Renaissance paintings. The viewer sees Christ straight on; he fills the page. This dark-haired Jesus is looking into the light above his head, blessing with the right hand and holding a *globus cruciger* in the left. Clouds surround him, but there are no angels and no disciples to witness. Jesus is fully clothed in a white undergarment, with an ample robe draped around him. When asked by the SBL Forum if he would change anything about his illustrations in this Bible, Moser replied,

> I would not have Jesus clothed at the Ascension. Our embarrassment by, and our shame of our nakedness is, as the Bible tells us, a result of the Fall. It is the condition of humankind. It does not seem to me that this would be a condition of say, the angels (my wisdom is naked, though Michael and Gabriel are not) . . . . And for me at least, it certainly does not stand to reason that the ascending figure of Christ would conform to those self-same human foibles.[43]

The false theology of the fall leaves a trail of shame; we cannot seem to avoid stepping onto it.

42. Jameson, "Catechism," n.p.

43. Moser, "Book Artist."

Flights of Fantasy

As I have argued, the Gospel of Mark has disappearing feet. Jesus is suspended in air. So is the ending at 16:8. The ending of Mark's Gospel at 16:8 is both satisfying and unfinished. I carry around a Gospel in my head that ends with the fleeing women and the tomb, no word spoken to anyone, while in my hands I hold a Gospel that includes other endings that sneak into my head, messing up my scholarly premises. These are the endings only needy readers require: a Jesus who makes resurrection appearances, leaves a proposal for miracles (poison and snakes), and finally ascends to heaven and the right hand of God. I carry these endings that have been stitched so durably to Mark's Gospel. Many years ago, in a Greek exam on Mark, I only studied my own canon, stopping at verse 8. Of course verses 9–20 appeared on the exam, only to continue to stalk me. With their strange syntax and different vocabulary these verses present a Mark slightly off-kilter—a Mark suffering from decades of cognitive dissonance. Pick an ending—each one makes no real sense—they are all nonsense.[44] The bottom line is that Jesus is missing and has not returned, even with the second disappearance in the Gospel I carry. In this disappearance of Jesus, of a more "orthodox" ending to Mark, of a return to bring peace to the earth, an endless series of disappearances leaves spaces for infinite imagined endings. What if we follow Mark 16:8 and stop with the empty tomb? What if Jesus did not resurrect, or ascend? Jesus dissipates/dissolves/goes "poof" in the tomb, the ultimate magical trick (see Rembrandt's evaporated Jesus in *Supper at Emmaus*, 1628). Add in the ascension that Jesus is airborne but for a few seconds (although there is no record of the speed of his flight). He sits eternally (on a throne?) next to God, at the right hand, to avoid any possible scatological contact. Either way (short, another short addition, or longer ending) Jesus is long gone.

A few fiction writers read outside the lines. Imagine a Jesus who did not resurrect, but somehow hobbled out of the tomb, taking up with a goddess priestess on the coast of Palestine.[45] In Lawrence's account, Jesus sails off in a boat, disappearing over the horizon to another land. Or a Jesus who (in dreams) rejects the cup and decides on the cross to give into

44. See George Aichele's discussion of "the fantastic ambiguity of Mark's resurrection language," *Tales of Posthumanity*, 101.

45. See D. H. Lawrence, *Man Who Died*.

the ultimate temptation, of living as a human man, with a lover (Mary Magdalene) or a polygamist family (Martha and Mary).[46]

In James Morrow's fantasy novel about a new messiah born in Atlantic City, New Jersey, the temptation story is a prolonged battle with a devil figure. The messiah, Julie Katz, is the miraculously born daughter of a celibate father whose sperm mixes with holy ovum in a sperm bank. Julie grows up struggling with her identity and the devil, and eventually descends into hell after the devil tricks her into performing a miracle. Everyone is in hell except for four: Elijah, Enoch, Saint Peter, and Julie's father (due to his connections).[47] There she meets her half-brother Jesus. "The last time I saw Jesus, he was working in some hospice in Buenos Aires. I think we should count Jesus as missing in action."[48] After Jesus's rude response to Julie during their first meeting, she determines he is a "*shmuck*."[49] But she decides to join her brother in his work of handing out water to the damned.

> "Look, divinity's a confusing condition, no doubt about it. A curse."[50]
>
> "Good heavens, is *that* what I became? Another propitiation deity? . . . Did Christicism become an eternal-life religion?" "Accept Jesus as your personal redeemer," Julie corroborated, "and you'll be resuscitated after you die and taken up into the clouds." "The clouds? No, 'The kingdom come on *earth*,' remember?" . . . "We're not talking clouds here." Jesus' beautiful hands soared, wrist holes singing. "I mean, how can you bring about utopia with one eye cocked on eternity?" His hands fell. "Oh, *now* I get it—that's how they accommodated my not returning, yes? They shifted the reunion to some netherworld."[51]

Neither one of these siblings has ever met their Mother, God. Julie holds special resentment: "'Put me in charge of the universe, and my first act will be to arrest my mother for criminal neglect.' 'That's pretty harsh, Julie,' says Jesus."[52] Jesus finally reveals to her that he has turned the water into a morphine-type drink that causes the damned to throw themselves

46. Nikos Kazantzakis, *Last Temptation of Christ*.
47. Morrow, *Only Begotten Daughter*, 171.
48. Morrow, *Only Begotten Daughter*, 172.
49. Morrow, *Only Begotten Daughter*, 179; his emphasis.
50. Morrow, *Only Begotten Daughter*, 183.
51. Morrow, *Only Begotten Daughter*, 185–86; emphasis his.
52. Morrow, *Only Begotten Daughter*, 187.

"into the Lake of Fire and vaporize," thus ending their suffering, and Satan's hold over them.[53] So he is tricking Satan; the useless water ladling is subversive. But after fifteen years working beside Jesus in hell, Julie decides he is a *mensch*.[54] She finally decides her place is not with the dead, even though to leave means giving up her divinity.[55] Satan responds, "Fifteen years running some ludicrous lemonade stand—you call that useful? Your brother was always something of a masochist, but *you*, I thought you had better sense."[56] Her divinity is in the form of a white dove. Ascending to earth from hell means "she would never again raise up crabs or give sight to the blind, no more cities delivered, no more flying, nothing but the fire in her chest and the oncoming night and her falling flesh, falling, falling—."[57] Julie's ascension is into life, into fighting the Christian fundamentalists-separatists on earth.

In the nineteenth century David Friedrich Strauss questioned the whole irrational business of the ascension, placing it with all the other myths in the life of Jesus. The ascension is especially problematic, since the first and fourth Gospels do not include the story, and Mark and Luke are at odds. Luke tells the story both in his Gospel and in Acts. Strauss offers a "natural explanation"[58] of the ascension: "Among all the New Testament histories of miracles, the ascension least demanded such an expenditure of acumen, since the attestations to its historical validity are particularly weak—not only to us who, having no risen Jesus, can consequently have no ascending one."[59] Strauss asks the unpopular questions about Jesus's material body, a body that is able to eat a meal, or go through doors, or not touch or be touched, depending on the Gospel.[60] "The imagination of the primitive Christians must however have felt a strong temptation to depict this exaltation as a brilliant spectacle."[61] God is thus the great illusionist.[62] Strauss summarizes the irrationality of the ascension:

53. Morrow, *Only Begotten Daughter*, 188.
54. Morrow, *Only Begotten Daughter*, 189; emphasis his.
55. Morrow, *Only Begotten Daughter*, 193.
56. Morrow, *Only Begotten Daughter*, 195.
57. Morrow, *Only Begotten Daughter*, 196.
58. Strauss, *Life of Jesus*, 751.
59. Strauss, *Life of Jesus*, 752.
60. Strauss, *Life of Jesus*, 751.
61. Strauss, *Life of Jesus*, 755.
62. Strauss, *Life of Jesus*, 751.

> One main difficulty is this: how can a palpable body, which has still *flesh and bones*, and eats material food, be qualified for a celestial abode? How can it so far liberate itself from the laws of gravity, as to be capable of an ascent through air? and how can it be conceived that God gave so preternatural a capability to Jesus by a miracle? The only possible reply to these questions is, that the grosser elements which the body of Jesus still retained after the resurrection, were removed before the ascension, and only the finest essence of his corporeality, as the integument of the soul, was taken by him into heaven. But as the disciples who were present at the ascension observed no residuum of his body which he had left behind, this leads either to the above mentioned absurdity of the evaporation of the body of Jesus."[63]

Thus the ascension provides the perfect place for Strauss to test the bounds of rationality. Jesus left without leaving any visible, material thing behind (e.g., a garment, a sandal). When and where did the ascension occur? The same day as the resurrection (Mark) or forty days later (Acts), in the same room as Jesus's resurrection appearance at a meal (Mark) or in Bethany, near the Mount of Olives (Luke)? Or did the clouds (and witnesses and angels in Luke) provide cover for a quick getaway and continued life in a secret society, continuing to do good works?[64] Does the ascension not leave us with a docetic Christ? A revitalized dead body acts in normal ways, walking the earth and eating food. But there are few appearances (in Mark just the one in the extended ending), and then Christ takes off for heaven. The cloud serves as a veil."[65]

In his reading of Scheiermacher's life of Jesus, Strauss follows the line of a spiritual resurrection and ascension that Rudolf Bultmann later privileges. All the supernatural, the fantastic, is drained out. However Jesus resurrected in the tomb, there must be a second, post-cross life as portrayed in the Gospels. Strauss asks, "How then did this second life of Jesus come to an end?"[66] "Nevertheless, opposing indications always remain: in a real situation we cannot coordinate eating and disappearing, tangible limbs and coming through locked doors."[67] Mark's version is "too indefinite,"[68] and Luke's double telling of the ascension is not to be taken as an "external

63. Strauss, *Life of Jesus*, 750; emphasis his.
64. See Strauss, *Life of Jesus*, 751.
65. See Strauss, *Life of Jesus*, 154–55.
66. Strauss, *Christ of Faith*, 156.
67. Strauss, *Christ of Faith*, 140.
68. Strauss, *Christ of Faith*, 153.

event."[69] The incomplete and differing testimonies of the Gospels, along with all the gaps in the narratives, test the rationalist interpretation of the ascension. There is no definite event, or retelling of the event. "Mark" both leaves out the story and puts it in. Mark is itself resurrected into other forms and other endings. Strauss is stymied by "myth" and the need for rationalizing an irrational text. He might have been better served by the Brothers Grimm and the worlds of the fantastic.

Do the additional endings of Mark invite a continual addition of endings? What if we held a contest of endings and engaged famous fiction writers and well-known artists. Oh right, this has been done over the centuries. But what if we invite more endings? Does Mark's abrupt ending in 16:8 not call out for participatory writing? Maybe not, but the results could be interesting. And it would be a chance to update (?) the Gospel, give some responses to critics and to revisionists like Matthew and Luke. Mark's gospel may be small, but it can also be overwhelming. But perhaps "Mark" would be irritated by our editorial tinkering. The text has always been contaminated; there is no pure source to return to. Any original manuscript, like Jesus, is missing, dissolved into the air.

Thus the longer ending with ascension is an extra piece to the Gospel of Mark, left over from an assembled Gospel. Derrida is helpful here; he plays with the word "hinge" and the multiplicity of its meaning: "*This word is* brisure *[joint, break]'—broken, cracked part. Cf. breach, crack, fracture, fault, split, fragment.*"[70] Derrida defines hinge: "The hinge [*brisure*] marks the impossibility that a sign, the unity of a signifier and a signified, be produced within the plenitude of a present and an absolute presence. That is why there is no full speech."[71] The Longer Ending could be seen as a hinge, a crack in the Gospel, extending the silence of the women at the tomb. Derrida further explains:

> The subordination of the trace to the full presence summed up in the logos, the humbling of writing beneath a speech dreaming its plenitude, such are the gestures required by an onto-theology determining the archeological and eschatological meaning of being as presence, as parousia, as life without difference: another name for death, historical metonymy where God's name holds death in check. . . . [T]he *logos* as the sublimation of the

69. Strauss, *Christ of Faith*, 154.

70. Derrida, *Of Grammatology*, 65; emphasis his; using Roger Laport's dictionary.

71. Derrida, *Of Grammatology*, 69.

> trace is *theological*. Infinist theologies are always logocentrisms, whether they are creationisms or not.[72]

Thus we are left in Mark not with presence but with a double absence (empty tomb and empty air). Derrida writes about "that dangerous supplement"[73] in discussing Rousseau's *Confessions*, and the ascension in Mark serves as such a dangerous supplement.

It could be argued that Mark's Gospel is exhausting enough without adding more to it. Additional endings rein in the Gospel, and slow it down. The supplement becomes a replacement story. A supplemental Jesus appears and disappears. How can we know for sure it is the same person? "The supplement adds itself, it is a surplus, a plenitude enriching another plentitude, the *fullest measure* of presence. It cumulates and accumulates presence. . . . But the supplement supplements. It adds only to replace. It intervenes or insinuates itself *in-the-place-of*; it fills, it is as if one fills a void."[74] The supplement is dangerous, for a reason.[75]

Stephen Moore explored this phenomenon in Mark: "Mark is a lion with four or more tails. . . . Was Mark's real ending lost in transmission, then? And if so, what was the carving knife that cut off this author's tale?"[76] Moore further explores the questions about Mark's sudden ending: "Was the original manuscript mutilated? Did Mark expire before he could pen the final lines? Was he arrested in mid-sentence? An earlier generation of scholars did not hesitate to ask such questions."[77] Moore further wonders if the longer ending is a cover-up: "Is the longer ending a toupee, then, designed to hide Mark's baldness? Or is it simply another braid in his tail, the outgrowth of certain forces at work in it? But if it is a toupee, why should so many scholars want to tear it off? And if it is a braid, why should they want to shear it off?"[78] The grotesque nature of drinking poison and handling venomous snakes invites horror and the gaze. An upward flying, resurrected from the dead, body makes it impossible to look away. Even if we cut off the tail/tale, it reattaches. Or to use Moore's analogy: "But perhaps

72. Derrida, *Of Grammatology*, 71; emphases his.

73. Derrida, *Of Grammatology*, 141–44.

74. Derrida, *Of Grammatology*, 144–45; emphases his.

75. Derrida, *Of Grammatology*, 149.

76. Moore, *Mark and Luke*, 5.

77. Moore, *Mark and Luke*, 5n8.

78. Moore, *Mark and Luke*, 29.

the critical knife has simply cut away the counterfeit ending, the fake foreskin intended to disguise the real ending. . . . Was (the) Mark too Semitic for Greek taste, necessitating prosthetic additions?"[79]

Jesus is here (again) in Mark, after his gruesome death. It is a brief encounter, but just enough to hold. We may want to shield our eyes, to look away, to wish it wasn't so. Jesus is an embarrassing presence in these additions. It was difficult enough dealing with miracles and mysterious parables and hard preaching. And now Mark leaves us with a hyper-miraculous event of the ascension. This Jesus is a supplement in a chain of supplements. "Through this sequence of supplements a necessity is announced: that of an infinite chain, ineuluctably multiplying the supplementary mediations that produce the sense of the very thing they defer: the mirage of the thing itself, of immediate presence, or originary perception."[80] The supplement is a "spare part."[81]

In Mark 16:9–20 we tread into forbidden texts—with poison and serpent handlers. There is a trapdoor, or a hidden passageway, in the Gospel(s). Even though the addition was not added by "Mark," the segments of endings bear his name forever. Mark does not get the last word, after all.

Is the story of the ascension not terrifying? There has been a cloak of awe pulled over this story. So where does Christ *go*? Niels Hendik Gregersen gives an orthodox answer in his reading of Luke's version: "Jesus disappears and goes into God *and* into his church—and only when we keep both in mind can we answer the question *where to*."[82] There is an "ascension geography"[83] in which "heaven" organizes space in Acts.[84] In neither Luke nor Mark do we get an account of Jesus' heavenly journey.[85] But this interpretation does nothing to change the magic trick of the ascension.

Once again, the desire for paradise trumps the existential experience. The "kingdom" is the spoken reminder of what could have been

79. Moore, *Mark and Luke*, 30.

80. Moore, *Mark and Luke*, 157.

81. Moore, *Mark and Luke*, 313.

82. Gregersen, "Extended Body," 243, emphasis his; see also Sleeman, *Geography and Ascension*, 5.

83. Sleeman, *Geography and Ascension*, 22.

84. Sleeman, *Geography and Ascension*, 9.

85. See Mary Dean-Otting (*Heavenly Journeys*, 4–5) for a list of elements of the Jewish heavenly journey form.

(but for Eve . . .) and what will be, if only we do our part, and God does God's part. Jesus is absent because he is in a much better place (really?)—a place where Caesar is not. Believers are left to negotiate empire. Jesus will return in time, or rather, when he gets good and ready. If Jesus had remained on earth after his resurrection, would he have kicked Roman ass? Put that two-edged sword of Revelation 1 to good use? In Revelation heaven is a vast, mostly empty, space for most of the narrative; the souls under the altar are kept in their ecclesial prison. Heaven is an exclusive boys club. Or is Jesus headed into a black hole? The event horizon into which everything disappears? A black hole swallowing stars, and gods. Hope goes in with the gods, and silence spews from the hole. It is up to us to bring about the restoration of Jerusalem, the earth, and to bring the peace—to battle empire. Or to reject a heaven where Christ and God reign as just another empire. Mark's (and Luke's) messages are dangerous; they expose this empiric space. We get a glimpse of the heavenly throne room and Jesus sitting on the right hand of God (in Mark). That this journey upward into the clouds will be our future as true believers is little consolation.

In his reading of the scene of Mary Magdalene and Jesus in the garden in the Gospel of John (20:17), Jean-Luc Nancy traces the saying, *Noli me tangere*, do not touch me. Nancy sees absence in this brief presence in the garden, that is, "the sudden appearance of the unavailable, of the other and of the one disappearing."[86] Nancy warns, "This is not a magic trick," for the Jesus remains dead and his glorious body "reveals that this emptiness is really the emptying out of presence."[87] There is death, and there is absence: "There is nothing and no one to show, nothing and no one to reveal . . . 'revelation' constitutes the identity of the image and the original, thereby implying—in a perfectly logical manner—the identity of the invisible and the visible."[88] He continues:

> No, nothing is available here: don't try to seize upon a meaning for this finite and finished life, don't try to touch or to hold back what essentially distances itself and, in distancing itself, touches you with its very distance (in both senses: touches you with and from a distance). . . . This uprising or insurrection is a glory that devotes itself to disappointing you and to pushing our

86. Nancy, *Noli me tangere*, 15.

87. Nancy, *Noli me tangere*, 15–16.

88. Nancy, *Noli me tangere*, 4–5.

> outstretched hand away. For its brilliance is nothing other than the emptiness of the tomb.[89]

Nancy reminds us that the desire to jump up and hold onto the feet is misguided, at best: "Love is what escapes you. Love the one who goes. Love that he goes."[90] Mary Magdalene's body carries the presence of the absent one.[91] Nancy is here relating to paintings of *Noli me tangere*, and that paintings, like the deity, should not be touched. Nancy muses, "So, when we say heaven [*la ciel*], or the divine as what is in heaven, we are talking about something that would be nowhere, in no place, and at the same time, as a result, everywhere. . . . it's a bit like air."[92] What is left, what remains, is air. And the dream of air.

Conclusion: The Imitation of Christ

> Jesus sittin' in Alabama, waiting on a train. . . . Got all his possessions in a Walmart sack. He got to leave town and he can't come back. Jesus a victim of the immigration game.[93]

In the song, "Immigration Game," Michelle Malone weaves the story of Jesus's incarnation and disappearance to the plight/flight of the immigrant worker up from Mexico. The name "Jesus" has two pronunciations—first as the deity and then near the end of the song as a Mexican immigrant being deported from his family. In the Gospels Jesus travels light, finally ascending (in Mark and Luke) with nothing but the clothes on his back. When Jesus flies in literature and film and art, he is often portrayed as lingering, as holding onto life or possible lives (as in *The Last Temptation of Christ*). In Malone's song the picture of Jesus is a still of the son of man/god as a Mexican deportee, his dreams of economic stability dashed, holding his few possessions in the sack of the neoliberal capitalist state. Jesus is holding onto life, but is being forced to disappear. In popular song Jesus is often found in places like Alabama (Birmingham: John Mellancamp) or just leaving Chicago for New Orleans (ZZ Top). Jesus has returned as human, not as spirit, roaming the earth as a "regular Joe." In this way the second coming has occurred in a way

89. Nancy, *Noli me tangere*, 16.
90. Nancy, *Noli me tangere*, 37.
91. Nancy, *Noli me tangere*, 48.
92. Nancy, *Noli me tangere*, 76.
93. Malone, "Immigration Game."

hidden from humans. Mark 16:9–20 has a human Jesus who eats, but one transfigured, who dwells not on earth but in heaven at the right hand of God. The ultimate goal for the son of god is heaven, not earth. So should the reader of Mark look skyward and desire heaven.

Ultimately, it is difficult to pinpoint the location of the ascension of Jesus. *The Great Passion Play* in Eureka Springs, Arkansas, has Jesus ascending into the night sky (due to its 8:30–10:15 PM performances—see www.greatpassionplay.com). Timothy Beal traveled to an imagined spot of the ascension at Holy Land, USA in Bedford County, Virginia, a replica of key Jesus places from the Gospels. On "Journey Trail" the ascension hill, "Mt. Olivet," designated as the place where Jesus ascended (using the Acts 1 story), serves also as a burial ground for believers who want to be closer to the biblical ascension. Beal relates, "Yet for those who confess the resurrection of the body and the life everlasting, what better place to lie in wait for the Second Coming than where Christ went up the first time around?"[94] In such third space Jesus makes his great escape. He becomes hybrid, neither here nor there, both real and imagined, paused in midair by artists.

The ascension has always been a culturally produced space-event, outside of our lived experience. Artists are able to capture the moment of the ascension, as LE Mark did too. According to psychogeologists, the cathedral functions vertically, directing our gaze upward to the great vaulted ceiling and beyond to heaven, and able to activate the "third eye" of mysticism. "It may be here that we find the secret formula that allows us to poise miraculously on a knife-edge of existence, enjoying all minds while at the same time coping with the abyss of our own eventual certain deaths."[95] We want to join Jesus in heaven (maybe) but we are bound by architecture and gravity. We look up, but see only Jesus dead in Mary's lap, dead on the cross, ghostly on the windows in the seven stations of the cross, a condemned man. Jesus's feet are all over the space. Like the cathedral, the architecture of canonical Mark is designed to make us look skyward. Instead, I roll my eyes at the absurdity of the event. Even more, I continue to have flying dreams—in air and water—traveling through abyss and heaven, my feet planted firmly on earth.

94. Beal, *Roadside Religion*, 48.

95. Ellard, *Places of the Heart*, 173.

6

(Un)Holy Saturday

Introduction: The Harrowing of Hell

As a child in an Episcopal Church in a small southern town, one phrase in the Apostles' Creed stood out to me: "He descended into hell." I was fascinated by this storyline. Why did Jesus go to hell? What was he doing in hell for all those hours? Adults told me to take the creedal statement at face value. That response only served to fuel my fantasy. What happened on Holy Saturday? Where, exactly, did Jesus go?

My own mental mythic journey had begun, and Jordan Peele's horror film *Us* recently reignited these fantasies for me, with his placement of an underground prison for the "damned," who are the doubles of humans in the American nation above. Jesus's journey to the dead is part of a classic horror tradition (e.g., The Epic of Gilgamesh; Demeter and Persephone; Orpheus and Eurydice), except he descends into the dead as an already dead person. In all these stories the underworld is a place of horror, and the encounter with the head of what lies beneath provides the tension in the plot. In his film Peele explores the idea that just below the surface dwell our doubles, our *doppelgängers*, a common trope in horror films. What if Jesus Christ encountered his double, the antichrist/Satan, the head of hell, there?

As I revisited the creed, questions poured out. Did Jesus go to hell of his own accord, or did mysterious angel guards lead him there to complete the cyclical salvation story of death and resurrection? Or did

Satan drag him to hell, as Hades did Persephone, creating a perverted kind of romance in the story? What did Jesus do in hell? Did he suffer in hell? Did he preach (1 Pet 3:19–20)? If so, what did he preach? Did Jesus empty hell, knocking down the gates and dragging out Satan? Did he release only the righteous Jewish patriarchs and matriarchs, or all of the dead? If so, what happens to the dead after this event until now? Partial salvation—and traditional eschatology for that matter—that leaves billions in a shadowy prison or fiery torture chamber hardly seems fair. Did Jesus defeat death and bind Satan and break the gates of hell superhero style in a violent, and triumphant, victory march? Then why did the belief in hell continue? Creeds hold no reasonable answers, and this event known as "the Harrowing of Hell" that takes up both the space and time of Holy Saturday in the Christian liturgical calendar continues the ancient mythological tradition of *katabasis* (Greek), or descent narratives. The plot requires a descension before an ascension, and the early church figured out a way to include this section of the vertical trajectory in the Jesus narrative. But my childhood questions persist and have multiplied. Both the biblical and creedal stories are vastly incomplete, leaving a portal, if you will, to explore what lies beneath.

There seems to me something a bit "off" about this infernal journey, or as Freud and Todorov and others would call it, "uncanny," and somewhat "creepy," the basis of horror literature. I want to take this infernal journey to explore the narrative of descent in the Jesus story. As a conversation partner, I am using Peele's horror film *Us*, about an underground facility housing exact clones of every American. This film is instructive in deconstructing the story of Jesus in hell, and for entering into that dread, fear, terror, and creepiness of reading, Peele depicts a kind of contemporary harrowing of hell, with a messianic leader, demonic figures, and apocalyptic fervor. Read alongside and with this film, "He descended into hell" becomes a tale of horror. Apocalypse holds these two narratives (film and creedal) together, for in both there is a subterranean space that threatens to destroy the world.

Jesus's Excellent (Underworld) Adventure

Portals to the "beyond," whether heaven or hell, or some shadowy space in between, are common literary tropes. They can serve as time tunnels, passages into alternate universes, or into the realm of the dead.

Post-biblical apocalypses, such as the Apocalypse of Paul and the Apocalypse of Peter, employ a spirit/child guide to take the narrator on a voyeuristic tour of hell.[1] They are texts of torture porn; the viewer gazes on extreme suffering and pain that awaits all sinners. The dead are doomed to spend eternity in an underground prison.

The contained, claustrophobic space of hell or the unmoored, open space of heaven is unsettling in different ways. The patriarchs and matriarchs of the Bible are portrayed as naked, chained, and imprisoned in a cramped, underworld cave. An evil force contains the dead, and this force originated in heaven, rebelled, and set up a mirror-image, alternative realm. What did these dead do to deserve such infernal, eternal punishment? In the unjust space of hell, reason is useless. There is no mercy, no justice, until the crucified Jesus appears. I am overthinking this simple phrase of Jesus's descent, but horror leads the reader to overthink, to search for backstories of the suffering, to put faces on the dead, and on the enemy. Horror is an excess of narrative, an outpouring of a fear of the unknown lurking just on the other side of a wall or door or portal or, in the case of the space of hell, just beneath our feet, and in Peele's vision, just a down-escalator ride away.

The so-called descension of Christ to hell on Holy Saturday is not exactly in the Gospels. The closest passage is Matthew 27:52–53, which describes the moments after Jesus breathed his last: "The tombs were opened, and many bodies of the saints who had fallen asleep were raised. After his resurrection they came out of the tombs and entered the holy city and appeared to many." There is no clear mention of Jesus making the trip below in Matthew or in the Apocalypse of John. In the latter Jesus is a royal Son of Man/Lamb removed from the end-time battle and the abyss and lake of fire. The harrowing of hell story develops over time; by the early second century there is a mention in 1 Peter 3:18–20 that has Jesus preaching to the dead: "He was put to death in the flesh, but made alive in the spirit, in which also he went and made a proclamation to the spirits in prison, who in former times did not obey." And this preaching event is also described in 1 Peter 4:6: "For this is the reason the gospel was proclaimed even to the dead, so that, though they had been judged in the flesh as everyone is judged, they might live in the spirit as God does." The author saw Jesus as active, not passive, on the Saturday between cross and resurrection, working on the Sabbath. It was left to the church fathers to debate

1. For the Apocalypse of Peter and the Apocalypse of Paul see Schneemelcher, ed., *New Testament Apocrypha*, 271–321 and 213–70, respectively.

the particulars of Jesus's adventure, and for the creeds to either include or ignore this side trip to the dead on his journey to heaven.

Some of the creeds could not resist including a mention of this underworld passage. Catherine Laufer explores the *descendit ad inferna* (*descendus*) clause in the Apostles' Creed and Athanasius Creed. After Jesus's death and burial, asks Laufer, "is it not a tautology to add that he descended to the dead?" The descent into hell gradually becomes essential for Christology, notes Laufer.[2] Through this journey Jesus completes his mission. Jesus cannot make the world right without going into this underworld space and he only frees the already dead, leaving hell intact. Overall, this journey was part of an ancient mythic cycle of death and rebirth.

The orthodox belief of the harrowing of hell that Christ preached to the dead in hell (based on 1 Pet 3:19–20 and 4:6) went through several debates about the identity of the dead: did the dead include the redeemed of the Old Testament or both Jews and gentiles of all the deceased? The appendix in the Gospel of Nicodemus, (also known as the Acts of Pilate, earliest form in 555 CE), *Descensus ad Infernos* (The Harrowing of Hell), Jesus harrows not hell but limbo. There was, nonetheless, a harrowing, and Jesus had the major role in it. The story hinges on a thrilling rescue of the dead, with a messianic hero who was not defeated by death.

Medievalist scholar Sarah Elliott Novacich examines the harrowing through the hell mouth on the stage of medieval mystery plays in which the departed enter hell through a beastly mouth. Emphasizing the jaws of the hell mouth, she refers to the harrowing of hell as "a hinging moment in a narrative middle."[3] She also describes this stage setting as "an architectural vault."[4] Of the narrative structure of these descent tales, Novacich observes: "I read these always-open jaws as indicating the thwarted suppression of history; they are the rupture through which the past leaks, and from which stories pour out of the underground to complicate the new narratives being forged on the surface (the stage) of the earth above."[5] In the Harrowing there is "a chronological push and pull" of the narrative of the underworld that drives the future.[6] Novacich describes the architectural space of the harrowing process:

2. Laufer, *Hell's Destruction*, 3.
3. Novacich, *Shaping the Archive*, 109; pun intended, I assume.
4. Novacich, *Shaping the Archive*, 110.
5. Novacich, *Shaping the Archive*, 23.
6. Novacich, *Shaping the Archive*, 109–10.

> The porous nature of the partition between heaven and hell and earth suggests not only the redemptive power of Christ, who can overturn the crises of history, but also the tendency for cosmic realms consistently to intrude on one another, and for their associated temporalities to interpenetrate. Geographic breaches between heaven and hell, whether taking form as stately, yet broken doors, holes in the terrestrial crust, a gaping infernal maw, or secret portals adorned with breakable locks, indicate the difficulty of containing the ever growing past and of relegating it as separate—geographically, chronologically, ontologically—from the present.[7]

The stricter division of heaven and hell did not develop until much later; purgatory and limbo and other in between places accounted for the porousness of hell. The Harrowing of Hell shows that it is impossible to seal the past, for in the tradition story Christ leads the patriarchs of the Old Testament to the (supposed) safety of heaven. Christ then binds Satan to hell. The monster jaws of the hell mouth signal danger in a salvific scene. And Satan continues to act and to draw the unsaved dead to his underworld realm.

But where did the dead Jesus go? Bernstein argues that the Harrowing of Hell is a misnomer, for Jesus went into "the neutral underworld (Sheol, Hades) to resurrect those who languished until that moment, under the control of death" in "a psychological limbo without physical pain."[8] Alice Turner describes Jesus's harrowing of hell in the Gospel of Nicodemus as an emptying of limbo: "Furthermore, the Harrowing was vitally important to the Christian image of a virile, capable Jesus, not suffering on the cross or preaching to the poor, but battling demons, rescuing prisoners, righting wrongs, and issuing orders like a triumphant warrior prince."[9] In these ruminations the Prince of Peace defeats the Prince of Darkness in a grand narrative of royal family drama.

The hell mouth is the mouth of a monstrous hell beast, an aggressive, tooth-full sentry at the entrance of the underworld. Elliott describes the hell mouth as "all monster,"[10] always full of the damned: "This infernal inventory takes form as narrative realized through the bodies laden with

7. Novacich, *Shaping the Archive*, 112.

8. Bernstein, *Hell and Its Rivals*, 14.

9. Turner, *History of Hell*, 68.

10. Novacich, *Shaping the Archive*, 142.

backstories."[11] The mouth speaks the stories of the spewed—the story of Eden, the story of the cross, the story of humanity. Novacich continues, "For one of the dangers of the always-open mouth of hell, it seems is that it will speak erratically or out of turn, with a force that threatens to overwhelm rather than to merely authorize. . . . That is why the past needs to be not only touched, but also firmly, cautiously grasped, *fanged*, by a redeemer at times as aggressively as the infernal maw."[12] The redeemer and the deceiver are thus both in competition for human souls.

The debate also revolved around whether Jesus was active or passive in his dead state on Holy Saturday. To find answers, Laufer investigates the theology of the cross in the theologies of Hans Urs von Balthasar and Jürgen Moltmann. For Balthasar, Jesus seeks out those in eternal suffering. "On Holy Saturday, Christ was in solidarity with the passivity of the dead."[13] He was with the dead but suffered, more than any of the dead, the deepest depths of damnation, since Jesus was the most forsaken by God.[14] Thus, Jesus is no community organizer in hell; he is more like an extreme, empathetic hospice chaplain, sitting in solidarity with the damned.

Moltmann focuses on the god-forsakenness of Jesus on the cross, and the relationship of God the father with Jesus the son. Here Christology and theodicy connect. At the cross God the father suffers over the death of the son. Laufer connects Moltmann's theology to Jesus's descent into hell, since abandonment by God is hell, and Moltmann makes the connection to Auschwitz and the abandonment of the Jews by God.[15] Furthermore, Laufer considers the implications of Moltmann's ideas of the resurrection with the harrowing of hell. Jesus is raised from the place of the dead, hell. She explains:

> The descent *into hell* is *symbolically* the necessary depth of the incarnation: the Son suffers hell, absolute godforsakenness, the ultimate depths of pain, sin, rejection and abandonment to which humanity knows itself to be condemned. It is only as the descent is read in both these ways simultaneously that the Son's humiliation is complete. . . . This resurrection, from the dead, harrowing hell, is the beginning of the Son's glorification.[16]

11. Novacich, *Shaping the Archive*, 143.
12. Novacich, *Shaping the Archive*, 141; her emphasis.
13. Balthasar, *Credo*, 152.
14. Novacich, *Shaping the Archive*, 154–55; Balthasar, *Credo*, 54.
15. Laufer, *Hell's Destruction*, 165.
16. Laufer, *Hell's Destruction*, 166–67; emphasis hers.

For both theologians (Balthasar and Moltmann) the descent into hell is a necessary link between cross and resurrection. Hell is no longer eternal because of the cross. The cross was the descent, and also the triumph over evil. As one can see, theological explanations of the descent become quickly convoluted and unresolvable. No matter how universalist or existentialist one theologizes, the mythic space of an eternal place of punishment remains—in the Bible, in the early church creeds, and in our imagination. Laufer concludes, "The descensus clause is a paradox: it is part of both Christ's humiliation and his exaltation, the endpoint of his death and the starting point of his resurrection."[17]

A paradox provides an uncanny opportunity for the imagination. I am renaming Holy Saturday: (Un)holy Saturday. This day in between cross and resurrection is an uncanny space, the space of horror. I am using *uncanny* in the Freudian sense of when something in normality is just a little off, a bit "creepy." And the crucified and dead Jesus's disappearance from the tomb on Saturday is strange. Of course only Matthew comes close to hinting at Jesus's tour of the place of the dead, and he puts this mention alongside darkness at noon until three, a torn curtain in the holy of holies, an earthquake, and tombs opening and the dead saints appearing in the city (Matt 27:45–54). These horrific events caused even the Roman centurion and soldiers at the crucifixion to believe (out of fear?): for when they "saw the earthquake and what took place, they were terrified and said, 'Truly this man was God's Son!'" (Matt 27:54). The unidentified (only described as "saints") dead-now-suddenly-undead exiting their tombs and roaming the narrow city streets is proleptic; for Jesus is soon to follow, roaming Jerusalem and Galilee for a few short weeks. Like the Roman military "eyewitnesses," I find these tales to be terrifying. Yet these are Christianity's foundational tales, and like the fantastic stories in the Apocalypse of John, are often too horrific to mention so are relegated to the margins of sacred text.

Creeping Toward Armageddon

Reading Jesus's time in the tomb as a horror narrative opens up the imagination. I am using a mix of definitions of the horror genre here, and drawing on its roots in Freud's definition of the uncanny and some different iterations of its meanings in the philosophy and psychology of horror. To

17. Laufer, *Hell's Destruction*, 190.

start, in defining horror Tzvetan Todorov draws upon Freud's concept of the uncanny. Todorov's structural analysis identifies both the uncanny and the fantastic-uncanny. To simplify, I am using his definition of the uncanny in a broad sense: "the fantastic is based on the hesitation of the reader—a reader who identifies with the chief character—as to the nature of the uncanny event. This hesitation may be resolved so that the event is acknowledged as reality, or so that the event is identified as the fruit of imagination or the result of an illusion; in other words, we may decide that the event *is* or *is not*."[18] The uncanny evokes the emotion of fear, in the midst of belief and disbelief of the events. And fear takes over the tomb narrative: "So they [the women] went out and fled from the tomb, for terror and amazement had seized them; and they said nothing to anyone, for they were afraid" (Mark 16:8). Jesus left his cave, descending to further depths before disappearing. Mark's Gospel ends on this uncanny note. The resurrection hangs in the (second-century) future.

(Un)Holy Saturday is an underwritten pause in the Jesus's death journey. In any written or unwritten version, the day leaves open room for an uncanny story. More recently, Adam Kotsko expands Freud's uncanny (*unheimlich*, literally "unhomely") to the concept of "creepiness": "what is unfamiliar (what we are not at home with) but experientially most often involves something that is *all too* familiar, something that fits *too well*."[19] Freud's focus was on repressed sexuality and the threat of castration, but most helpful here is the general feeling of uneasiness in the uncanny. We refuse and desire creepiness at the same time: "We might say that scariness is about physical threats, whether real or imagined, whereas creepiness is threatening at a more diffuse level of abstract desire . . . the possibility of being scared by a purely imagined threat makes it ultimately impossible to draw a firm line between them."[20] Behind creepiness lies the Freudian uncanny, or at least parts of it, and it brings to the understanding of horror literature its hair-raising hesitation.

The Freudian approach to horror as raising repressed feelings to the surface has several forms when applied to horror literature and film, from horror as cathartic, to horror "as a drama of reenacted

18. Todorov, *Fantastic*, 157; emphasis his.

19. Kotsko, *Creepiness*, 4; emphasis his.

20. Kotsko, *Creepiness*, 33. In some Christian denominations the Easter vigil begins at sundown on Saturday and begins with the believer waiting and praying by a new fire in the dark (and in my experience, creepy) church.

repression."[21] In his review of *Us*, *New Yorker* film critic Richard Brody emphasizes Peele's Freudian approach to horror—of unearthing the repressed. Brody finds that the film's "subject is, in large measure, cultural consciousness and its counterpart, the cultural unconscious. The crucial element of horror is political and moral—the realities that metaphorical fantasies evoke."[22] In interviews in the bonus materials of the DVD version, Peele stresses the social message of horror as something we as a society have been repressing.

Depending on how you bend the psychoanalytic theory, horror can cause dread or pleasure, can seduce, can terrify, and these categories are not always exclusive. What is "creepy" taps into a number of repressed feelings, just below the surface. And as horror films turn (as they often have throughout the history of cinema) to apocalyptic, the threat of ultimate destruction (of the family, the nation) prompts a reconsideration of those structures. The psychological and (potential) physical violence induced by creepiness keeps the possibility of terror real. Peele believes, "For my money, terror is the best type of scare, because it's the promise of horror yet to come. When the audience is in that state, you don't have to do much. Their imagination is more powerful than any piece of imagery or any timing or misdirection you could do. . . . setting their imagination free to do its worst."[23] Thus creepiness invokes imaginative possibilities, for catharsis, and survival. And (Un)Holy Saturday sets up the resurrection of Jesus and his return as the wounded undead, misidentified by the disciples (see John 20:14-15, 27; 21:4). These scenes are creepy, for the grieving and disoriented disciples do not expect a dead body to rise and appear to them.

Creepiness abounds in Peele's *Us*.[24] The setting of the carnival, the remote lake house in the woods, creates an atmosphere of foreboding. The normal, middle-class family structure is about to be threatened. Consider Adelaide's question to Red about who they are: "Lacan believes that this implacable question—'*What do you want from me?*'—is potentially revolutionary in its implications, because it cannot be finally

21. See the discussion in Carroll, *Philosophy of Horror*, 242–43n40.

22. Brody, "Jordan Peele's 'Us.'"

23. Weiner, "New Master of Suspense," 79.

24. The music in *Us* supports the creepy tone. The most obvious example is the music that plays after the neighbors are murdered by their doppelgängers; the lyrics echo hauntingly, "Creep on it, on it, on it" (Luniz).

answered."[25] Addy becomes hysterical, for a while a silent shell of her former self. Kotsko traces hysteria "as a way of *creeping out the social order itself*."[26] "Under the pressure of hysterical questioning, then, the social order reveals its perverse face—the fact that it runs on transgression, that it gets off on creepy violations."[27]

Creepiness is revealed in the unexplained disappearances to the depths below in both the Jesus narrative and in Adelaide's journey in *Us*. Kotsko explains the workings of horror as a mirror to society: "Creepiness points toward the ultimate breakdown of the social order at the same time as it accounts for its origin and its present hold on its members. Creepiness is thus the past, present, and future of human society: its eternal precondition, its eternal motor, and its eternal obstacle."[28] This idea echoes Robin Wood's Marxist-Freudian reading of horror films as revealing the repressed parts of a contemporary capitalist society.[29] What is being repressed is the intersectional system that oppresses. Thus repression and oppression, although distinctive, share some common ground: "What escapes *re*pression has to be dealt with by *op*pression."[30] Horror stories (in text and in film) generate a society's worst fears, desires, and also guilt. The creepiness of the Harrowing of Hell has many dimensions, one of which is the sheer existence of a place called hell and a pit of naked, imprisoned dead people. But as I recited the Apostles' Creed as a child in the 1960s, how much did the mythic story it narrates—of ascent-descent to ascent to promised future descent (the final judgment) to ascent again—tap into repressed fears of the "Red Scare" of the Cold War? I ask this question not because I think there is a direct correlate, but because of the phrase's ("he descended into hell") unavoidable pull. Even and maybe especially with the repressed, non-questioning acceptance of

25. Kotsko, *Creepiness*, 108; emphasis his.

26. Kotsko, *Creepiness*, 109; emphasis his.

27. Kotsko, *Creepiness*, 110. On doubles, Wesley Morris and Jenna Wortheim, "Us," connect with DuBois's idea of double consciousness. They also see similarities between *Us* with Toni Morrison's novel, *Beloved*: "The idea that trauma is a contagion . . . and spills over and contaminates everyone else." One parallel is that the fathers in both films (Addy's father in *Us* and Paul D. in *Beloved*) take their family to a fair or carnival. In Morrison's *Beloved*, 59, right before the undead Beloved shows up, the shadows of the family are holding hands. Both Red/Adelaide and Beloved speak in terrifying, inhuman voices. Not to stretch the point too much, but Jesus's disappearance occurs during a festival time also.

28. Kotsko, *Creepiness*, 121.

29. Wood, "American Horror Film," 197.

30. Wood, "American Horror Film," 198.

the phrase, we are nonetheless being snatched below, as frequently as we recite the creed, if even for the briefest of times.

Did descending into hell creep Jesus out? Or was he in complete control in executing the "plan" God had for him? I am led to ask if Jesus's whole life was creepy. Nikos Kazantzakis certainly tapped into this reading of the life of Jesus in his fictional retelling in *The Last Temptation of Christ*. The uncanny drives Jesus to the brink of madness. The life of Jesus, read through the genre of the uncanny and horror, opens the possibility for the reader to acknowledge the hesitation—that what is happening is not normal and is more than a bit terrifying.

Doppelgängers from Heaven and Hell

The tone and feeling of the final scene of *Us* is unsettling. In other words, this scene gives me the creeps. I have a similar feeling toward the empty tomb. Where has Jesus gone and what does he know? Has Jesus Christ encountered his double, the antichrist/Satan? Is this the Christ or the antichrist? How can we know for certain?

In his comprehensive study about the rise of the concept and character of the antichrist, Bernard McGinn notes that the antichrist is "Christ's alter ego."[31] The time between Jesus's resurrection and his future return provided space for good and evil to continue to fight for dominance in the human world. McGinn comments, "Early Christians needed the legend of the Antichrist."[32] The antichrist is the Final Enemy and Christ's nemesis. This need for the antichrist persisted, in anticipation of the end, with the antichrist taking on more and more significance as a political and religious (mainly papal) power.[33] In the twentieth century this figure became more and more a political leader; in post-World War II literature the antichrist is the ultimate humanitarian deceiver, modeled on totalitarian dictators.[34]

31. McGinn, *Antichrist*, 33–56.

32. McGinn, *Antichrist*, 33.

33. McGinn, *Antichrist*, 56, offers a definition (his emphasis): "The term *antichristos*, with its ambiguous preposition *anti*, can indicate 'in place of Christ,' 'false Christ,' and 'opposed to Christ.' All three meanings may well have been intended, and all three continued to appear in later use of the word."

34. See Paul Boyer's discussion of the history of premillennialism and conservative politics (*When Time Shall Be No More*). The most well-known example is the antagonist character of Nicolae Jetty Carpathia in Tim LaHaye and Jerry Jenkins's Left Behind series. As Jesus's doppelgänger, Carpathia experiences a *Rosemary's Baby*-type birth and

There are scant and unclear New Testament references that have been used to base the concept of the antichrist. Second Thessalonians 2:1–12 introduces the "lawless one" who will oppose God and delude the faithful.[35] First John 2:18–19 and 22 sounds the eschatological alarm: "Children, it is the last hour! As you have heard that antichrist is coming, so now many antichrists have come. From this we know that it is the last hour. They went out from us, but they did not belong to us. . . . Who is the liar but the one who denies that Jesus is the Christ? This is the antichrist." With the disappearance of Christ, there was space to fill with new stories to motivate believers, and the oppositional figure of the antichrist hanging on a future, soon-to-occur horizon, made the end of time and Christ's return seem more possible and imminent. Throughout human history there are always evil rulers who fit the profile of the antichrist. And connecting the antichrist with Satan thickened the plot. Christ has a double, a doppelgänger. There is an assurance of a victory by Christ in the last days. But first the evil double/s run loose, plotting their evil plans against humanity and the earth. Satan cannot stay put in his kingdom of hell.

Northrop Frye investigated these ideas of doubles and descent in literature and finds an immediate link to horror. Using William Blake's *Everlasting Gospel* as a template, Frye observes: "He [Blake] also contrasts the true Jesus who acts with 'honest triumphant Pride' with the 'creeping Jesus,' the real Antichrist who comes to terms with passivity and mediocrity."[36] Frye states further, "The demonic parody is the descent into nothingness, and may involve only an individual life or a whole society. Antichrist can descend to hell, even harrow it, but what he brings up is only a hell to earth. The ideological adaptation to this is the realization that power always corrupts, but that nothing can be done about the ascendency of such corrupt power in human society."[37] The "demonic parody" is at work in the harrowing; for what is hell but an invention by gods and humans? Christ and antichrist, heaven and hell, in their doubling and mirroring of the other, are all creepy spaces.

---

a demon-led wilderness experience for forty days in the desert in Israel. He is an eastern European (Romanian) politician who leads the one world order (as Secretary-General of the United Nations) against the followers of Jesus after the rapture. Carpathia is assassinated and then Satan takes over his body and rules. He dies (a final time) at the battle of Armageddon. This tribulation story follows classic horror lines.

35. See McGinn, *Antichrist*, 41–45.

36. Frye, *Words with Power*, 238.

37. Frye, *Words with Power*, 249.

And the game they are playing, for dominance of the earth, and in which humans are pawns, is creepy.

There are many strains of the stories of evil powers: demons, beasts, antichrist and Satan. These myths developed in early and medieval Christianity, sometimes intersecting and often unclear of their apocalyptic roles (past, present and future—from Eden to the new Jerusalem). The antichrist and Satan are distinct characters that often overlap with each other, but both serve as doubles for Christ in certain ways. McGinn traces the stories of the antichrist in medieval illustrated Bibles and mystery plays between 1335 and 1500 CE: "The most important are to be found in Middle English Literature, *Piers Plowman* and the Chester *Play of Antichrist*."[38] These narratives served as allegorical representations of Scripture and its afterlives in anticipation of the apocalypse. The mirror images of good and evil in these characters provided a kind of apocalyptic spectator sport. Antichrist and Satan are deceivers, in the guise of priests and popes, echoing Jesus's warning in Matthew 7:15: "Beware of false prophets, who come to you in sheep's clothing but inwardly are ravenous wolves." It is easy to be deceived and to not know who the real Christ is. This begs the question of Jesus to his disciples, "He asked them, 'But who do you say that I am?'" (Mark 8:29) There are evil doubles, and they multiply over the centuries, taking on different guises, various wooly garments. Jesus as lamb takes on a wooly garment too in Revelation, as the Lamb.[39]

René Girard's theory of doubles is useful here. He sees mimetic rivalry operating in biblical literature, for example, with Cain and Abel and Peter and Satan, and these relationships are a "scandal": "Scandal is always a relationship of doubles."[40] Girard extends this meaning in his connection with Satan: "Satan is the name for the mimetic process as a whole; that is why he is the source not merely of rivalry and disorder but of all the forms of lying order in which humanity lives."[41] Mimesis

38. In a final scene in the Chester *Play of Antichrist*, "two demons drag Antichrist down to hell while the slain witnesses [Rev. 11] ascend to heaven" (McGinn, *Antichrist*, 191) Being dragged down or thrown into the underworld, lake, pit, abyss is a common theme. Thus the story of the antichrist is often a parody of the Christ story.

39. Mary-Jane Rubenstein, *Pantheologies*, 103, traces the death of the goat god, Pan, with the rise of the lamb god, Jesus: "And so the Lamb of God overcomes the goat-god, who goes on to become not just one evil spirit among many in the Christian imagination, but the demon of demons himself" and much like Satan.

40. Girard, *Things Hidden*, 418.

41. Girard, *Things Hidden*, 162.

reveals the collusion of the doubling: "A fundamental principle, often overlooked, is that the double and the monster are one and the same being."[42] In keeping with the link of the holy with horror: "All sacred creatures partake of monstrosity, whether overtly or covertly; this aspect of their nature can be traced to the monstrous double."[43] When Jesus enters the Apocalypse of John, he does so as monster, as a fully locked and loaded Son of Man, and as the sacrificed Lamb (or is this a wolf in sheep's clothing?). Jesus has morphed into different, transhuman, but still bestial, forms. He has multiple forms and identities, all creepy.

Jesus, or rather the angel armies of God that protect and defend him, meet their monstrous doubles in the Apocalypse of John. But more explanation of the double is needed here, and horror scholarship is useful. Classically, this concept of the doppelgänger, or double, has been defined as "simply a person who looks like another."[44] The double can be "a mirror image, of one's own person, this often manifesting itself just before death."[45] Gordon Slethaug adds to this definition: "Death is the stalker who seizes the soul, leaving the body behind."[46] Steven Schneider elaborates on this idea in that "most theorists and psychologists define doubling as the experience of seeing or otherwise sensing, feeling, or believing that there exists another 'you,' from inside your own self."[47] Horror films are full of doubles—as twins, replicants, clones—and they are all monsters. And monsters are tragic characters.[48] Robin Wood elaborates on the variety of these monstrous doubles: "It is . . . the relationship between normality and the monster that constitutes the essential subject of the horror film. . . . The relationship has one privileged form: the figure of the doppelgänger, alter-ego, or double, a figure that has recurred constantly in Western culture, especially during the past one hundred years. . . . The

42. Girard, *Violence*, 160.

43. Girard, *Violence*, 251. Jean-Pierre Dupuy, *Mark of the Sacred*, 119, takes Girard further, evoking Nietzsche's critic of Christianity: "The triumph of Christianity is everywhere to be seen, but its effects are dreadful. Quite often Christianity is incarnated in the modern world in the form of its monstrous double."

44. Gillis, "Doppelganger," 7.

45. Gillis, "Doppelganger," 7.

46. Slethaug, "Double and Doubling,"101.

47. Schneider, "Literary Double in Modern Horror," 107.

48. Schneider, "Literary Double in Modern Horror," 106, points to "the sheer prevalence of doubles in horror cinema—whether in the form of murderous alter-egos, monstrous shape-shifters, maniacal twins, or malevolent clones."

doppelgänger motif reveals the Monster as normality's shadow."[49] Wood also comments on the figure of the doppelgänger as: "alter ego or double, a figure that has recurred constantly in Western culture, especially during the last one hundred years. The *locus classicus* is Stevenson's Dr. Jekyll and Mr. Hyde, where normality and monster are two aspects of the same person."[50] Again, coming face to face with one's double is a creepy, and in modern horror films, often disastrous event.

Jordan Peele takes this basic concept of the double and raises it to apocalyptic heights in *Us*. It is a good time for horror films, and apocalyptic, and especially apocalyptic horror films. Robin Wood offers "a simple definition of horror films: they are our collective nightmares."[51] This film is of course no "Jesus film" per se, but there is a messianic savior in the character of Red. But she is the doppelgänger of her doppelgänger.

The portal (or modern hell mouth) to "hell" in Peele's *Us* is in a beach carnival house of horrors. It is in this haunted space that young Addy meets her double. Addy looks in a distorted mirror and sees her alter-image, her clone, Red. But Red is not an image; she is corporal and immediately grabs Adelaide by the throat. The traumatized Adelaide is speechless, her life turned upside down. What the viewer sees at this point is that her mirror-image has attacked her.

The clones in the underground facility are called the Tethered, for they are connected to the people above ground. The idea is that each person has a clone in this facility. Red's monologue to the family is unclear. The Tethered were a government experiment created to control those above. The experiment got out of hand and the scientists abandoned them to their underground space. The Tethered who dwell in tunnels below are a real existential and national threat, and ultimately, they are us. There is no clear logic given by Peele to this doubling. The doubles share a soul, but how this connection occurred is not explained. What is the government hiding here? This experiment comes back to haunt not only their creators but the whole of America. There is a debate about the identity of the Tethered. For example, on the *Film Daily* podcast, the opinion is that the Tethered are the homeless and other marginalized, or how we treat immigrants and refugees from other countries. Those below have been forgotten and abandoned, locked up in an underground cage. "The Tethered are the ultimate have-nots." And "I feel that this is the only overtly

49. Wood, quoted in Schneider, "Literary Double in Modern Horror," 106.

50. Wood, "American Horror Film," 71.

51. Wood, "Return of the Repressed," 70.

political mainstream studio movie that we've gotten in the Trump era." The Tethered are the current Republican party.[52] Peele adds that the social and political context of the Tethered includes "fear of North Korea making a bomb, fear of immigrants," and the trauma of 9/11.[53] These explanations connect to the social dimension of horror and the characters as expressions of technology and materialism gone wrong.

In any event, the consensus here is that America has created its own problems, through secrecy and exclusionary practices, all with a capitalist framework.[54] The Tethered answer Adelaide when she asked who they are. "We are Americans," they simply say. These interpretations are allegorical, part of the brewing global fears of the twenty-first century. How are we the creators of our own doubles, and our own demise? Kotsko elaborates: "Freud believes that this sense of an outside agency inside of oneself, watching over one's every move and criticizing it, is what accounts for the uncanny effect of doppelgangers—or, I might add, the creepy discovery we are being watched."[55] And in *Us*, Peele plays on the concept that we are being watched by us: ourselves, and the United States government.

The Tethered emerge with big scissors; in order to become untethered they have to kill their above-ground clones. Their goal is to create a mirror-image Hands Across America, but this time one that is complete. The Tethered are monsters, in the sense of Carroll's definition of art-horror: "it is crucial that two evaluative components come into play: that the monster is regarded as threatening *and* impure. If the monster were only evaluated as potentially threatening, the emotion would be fear; if only potentially impure, the emotion would be disgust. Art-horror requires evaluation both in terms of threat and disgust."[56] They are also lethal.[57] As doppelgängers the definition of horror here doubles. They are impure because they not completely human, since they have been denied the privileges

52. Sciretta et al., "*Us*." The podcasters also mention the Underground Railroad as a possible image.

53. Weiner, "New Master of Suspense," 80.

54. Wood, "American Horror Film," 80, finds example of this national self-destructive strain in other horror films: "*The Omen* would make no sense in a society that was not prepared to enjoy and surreptitiously condone the working out of its own destruction."

55. Kotsko, *Creepiness*, 13.

56. Carroll, *Philosophy of Horror*, 28.

57. Carroll, *Philosophy of Horror*, 43.

of their counterparts and unable to fully develop.[58] And they are certainly terrifying with their overwhelming numbers, and scissors, and vengeful, apocalyptic murder spree. Like vampires or zombies the Tethered do not exist, but they could, and if they are possible, then apocalypse is also possible.[59] When the monster is not "Them" but "Us," our American doubles, there is a shifting gear on the horror. Peele explains, "but what I don't see happening enough is people looking at their own part in this dark turn. . . . This movie was a way to say, What if the intruder is us? Maybe the monster has our face, and we're so obsessed with some unrecognizable monster that we've been blinded to the real one."[60]

They come from "below," a hellish place, where they eat raw rabbits.[61] Carroll comments on the importance of space in framing art-horror: "monsters are native to places outside of and/or unknown to the human world. Or, the creatures come from marginal, hidden, or abandoned sites: graveyards, abandoned towers and castles, sewers, or old houses—that is, they belong to environs outside of and unknown to ordinary social intercourse. . . . what horrifies is that which lies *outside* cultural categories and is, perforce, unknown."[62] And when that which is outside and below comes to the surface, the monsters bring the horror below to threaten and destroy their "other half" above.

The space of horror is important. The infernal underworld in Peele's vision is a series of underground halls and rooms that cover the United States. It is a government, military prison with testing rooms full of rabbits, and sterile dorm rooms. When Red and Adelaide descend through the "hell mouth" in the hall of mirrors beneath the carnival into this space for their final battle, the cloned Americans have (all, presumably)

58. Peele, in Weiner, "Master of Suspense," 80, relates, "There's this idea that we deserve our privilege . . . but when someone enjoys privilege, there almost has to be someone suffering so you can have that. Which means it's not deserved. It's violent. . . . If we really acknowledge our place in the world, we have to acknowledge the atrocities, even if we're not active members in them."

59. See Carroll, *Philosophy of Horror*, 29.

60. Quoted in Weiner, "Master of Suspense," 80.

61. Hell and hell-like places are a common trope in horror film. For example, Swenson, "Guardian Demons," 205, describes how hell is a trope in the *Hellboy* films: "Why are horror films such a potent medium for expressing ideas about salvation and damnation? And what role does hell play in these modern dramas? Horror films (in the Gothic literature from which they spring) operate subconsciously, through projection of internal anxieties onto the actions and repression of a monstrous Other. . . . All horror films, then, operate unconsciously to radically resolve social as well as personal tensions."

62. Carroll, *Philosophy of Horror*, 35.

already escaped and ascended and begun their genocidal killing spree. The origin of the apocalypse of America is with the government through some secret, human experiment. The government has created a sort of Tethereds industrial project, and when one of the experiments breaks free by changing places with her above-ground twin, it sets an opening for a rebellion, led by the "real" Adelaide. Like Jesus in his harrowing of hell, she finds the portal to the above-ground world, leading others to the outside. But she is also leading them to war, not a peaceful reuniting. The dystopia below is brought to light, so to speak.

Only the doppelgänger could save her human family. The assumption is that the real Adelaide, Red, would have perished, with her family, in a different rebellion, like her neighbors did. There would have been no conversation, no pause for the above-ground family to react and prepare. This is ultimately a moot point, since the switch did occur, and it took an above-ground but kidnapped Addy/Red to break the controls of whatever was controlling the Tethered and lead the rebellion. To say the least, Peele has complicated the device of the doppelgänger. The audience roots for Adelaide, and the way Peele stages and edits the final fight scene certainly complicates the viewer's allegiance. And it complicates the ideal of the American family: heterosexual, two children, successful, and especially, "normal."

The killing spree is complete, and at the end the Tethered (except for Adelaide who is now untethered) link hands in a perverse sign of unity. Is Peele making a comment on the fall of capitalism and American dominance? What will the world become with the Tethered in charge? Will they remake America in their traumatized image? In the end, as the family drives off (all untethered in different ways)—south, to Mexico—the apocalypse is not completely closed. America has been invaded, by its own experiments gone awry, but even more by its structural violence on "disposable humans."

But you cannot welcome these strangers, for they are intent on revenge and murder. Peele's apocalyptic vision is that America has created an "underworld" for the "Other" and has also created these Others who are tethered to us above ground because they are our doppelgängers. We are stuck in a hall of mirrors and a world of opposites.

In terms of the biblical apocalyptic landscape, Kotsko argues that Rome and the heavenly Jerusalem are mirror images, with Rome as the model for the heavenly city. Reading passages such as Apocalypse 19:17–21, Kotsko relates: "In some cases, however, the violence reaches such a disturbing pitch that it can be difficult to remember that we are dealing with the God of justice rather than the wicked empire."[63] Kotsko finds that Rome is "a model that the vision of Revelation can exceed but not escape."[64] (Heavenly) empire mirrors (earthly) empire, complete with a violent kingdom. So too do the devil and the divine mirror each other: "the devil may be presented as a parody of the divine, but the divine ends up looking like an exaggeration of the devil. . . . In other words, apocalyptic, which began as the most radical demand for the entire world to be entirely remade, seems to be at risk of simply remaking the world as it is. . . . Is revolution doomed to install a new form of oppression?"[65] Despite all its seemingly clear dualism of good and evil, apocalyptic literature makes it difficult to differentiate.

Discussing Tertullian and Irenaeus, Kotsko notes that the devil, the fallen angel, has created an alternate world below to the one in heaven. But Kotsko takes this notion even further, for the demonic is also ever-present on earth: "the devil is responsible for the created world as we actually know it."[66] From the garden of Eden to the heavenly Jerusalem God is never completely in control.

Jordan Peele makes this concept of the apocalyptic battle of good and evil in the doppelgänger a central feature of *Us*. Early in their lake house vacation Adelaide says to her husband, "I don't feel like myself," and of her double, "She was real" and "She's still coming for me." The monster in this film is within ourselves—in each of us individually and also in our American society. Lead actress Lupita Nyong'o says of her double characters: "The truth is we all possess the duality within us."[67] Peele explains further, "Our duality as human beings, the guilt and sins that we bury deep with ourselves" play well in the horror genre. The doubles are tethered by their souls, and Peele describes this link as a "faded" and "poetic" connection. He states, "The idea for this movie came from a deep-seated fear in doppelgängers." The teenage daughter Zora observes in the midst of the attack of the Tethered, "It's too many twins, man." Yet Peele complicates the doppelgänger idea in this film. Both Adelaide/Red kill. And the viewer discovers that she has been rooting for a Tethered to survive. Peele plays on the idea of the double and who is "real." Young

63. Kotsko, *Prince*, 55.

64. Kotsko, *Prince*, 56.

65. Kotsko, *Prince*, 56.

66. Kotsko, *Prince*, 67. Tertullian, *Spectaculis*, ch. 2; Irenaeus, *Against Heresies*.

67. In the *Us* DVD bonus material.

Addy's double drags her below; Addy returns as adult "Red," a messianic leader of the Tethered, eventually leading them up the escalator that has prevented them from escaping their underground prison.

Ultimately, in facing our double, we face our privilege, the suffering we have done to others, and Peele confesses, "For us to have our privilege, someone must suffer." Horror leads to catharsis, but not until we face our complicity in systemic oppression. Peele wants us to consider what we do with our privilege, and especially the ones oppressed by our obliviousness to our privilege. "Us" is each of us, us collectively in family and in society, and US, United States. Peele shows the social and cultural inequities, caused by some unnamed government experiment. The underground doubles are created to control those on the surface. The Tethered suffer a kind of half-life, institutionally imprisoned, as visualized by their red jumpsuits, and their freedom demands an apocalypse of America, as their Hands Across America parody signifies. It is the end of the world, at least of America as we know it, with its capitalist infrastructure. The price of our sins, and our allegiance to American empire, is the end of empire.

Peele's apocalypse taps into the horror of the biblical story. Robin Wood helps to clarify how contemporary horror films work to draw attention to and critique the social order: "norms by which we have lived must be destroyed and a radically new form of organization (political, social, ideological, sexual) be constructed; the alternative is 'the end of the world.' . . . What our civilization needs is a cinematic William Blake, capable of daring to imagine the devil as hero."[68] In the heart of horror complicates the clear duality of good and evil, always connected, to some extent, with the political. The devil becomes the hero.

Jesus, feeling forsaken by his Father (whom he has never met), traumatized by torture and a brutal public execution, abandoned by his disciples and his religious community, his message of peace and love squashed by the state, waking up—in an empty cave? In hell? In hell of

68. Wood, "Return of the Repressed," 32. In addition, Wood, "American Horror Film," 215, makes the distinction between "the reactionary horror film and the 'apocalyptic horror film.'" Of the latter he states, "the 'apocalypse,' even when presented in metaphysical terms (the end of the world) is generally reinterpretable in social/political ones (the end of the highly specific world of patriarchal capitalism)." He considers "most distinguished American horror films" (especially in the 1970s) as "progressive in so far as their negativity is not recuperable into the dominant ideology, but constitutes (on the contrary) the recognition of that ideology's disintegration, its untenability, as all it has repressed explodes and blows it apart."

his own accord, God's or Satan's? I imagine various versions of ways the story of "he descended into hell" could proceed:

1. What if Satan captured Jesus on his descent and imprisoned him, taking his place above? Jesus would be stuck in the realm of the dead, and believers would be deceived, worshipping the wrong being. Jesus would be a reformer in hell, ministering to the dead.
2. What if Jesus and Satan decided to switch places? Would the switch be in a kind of *The Prince and the Pauper* way, on a whim, and then when Jesus tried to reclaim his throne, he was denied?

The Apocalypse of John has a clear distinction between good and evil, and it does not end well for evil: "Then Death and Hades were thrown into the lake of fire. This is the second death, the lake of fire" (Rev 20:14). In John's vision of the future the plurality of evil (Beast of the land and Beast of the sea and Death and Hades) has to be eliminated. Peele raises the uncomfortable, and ultimately hyper-apocalyptic (is that redundant?) scenario when evil wins in the end.

Conclusion: Hands Across the Apocalypse

In *Us* the teenage daughter says sarcastically and proleptically in the car to the beach before the crisis, "I forgot. Nobody cares about the end of the world." No one knows the terrors that lay just beneath, in a maze of tunnels traversing America. The cause of Peele's apocalypse is governmental negligence and abandoning the marginalized doubles they created in some creepy experiment. These doubles rebel, and only one, Adelaide, escapes the (surely) future dystopian United States for south of the border. The only ones of the privileged to escape are Adelaide's husband and two children. With their leader dead, the Tethered continue their murderous severing. The Tethered no longer share a soul with the privileged. They own this soul, as well as America. Their linked hands herald some dystopian new world order.

Us is an allegory of late capitalism. The harrowing of the underground is in the sense of "to pillage, to plunder," and these American doubles take all; their future production, post their war of revenge, is uncertain. Fredric Jameson notes that "we do not impose allegorical interpretations on texts but that they rather today tend to allegorize themselves."[69] This narrative of Jesus's descent was a way to fill a gap—a whole day missing from the tomb—slid easily into symbolic meaning about the fate of the dead and ultimately, the dualism of good versus evil and the end of the world. As a way of explaining the unexplainable, the early church fathers turned to allegory, as did medieval theologians. The Apocalypses of Paul and Peter took a tour of hell, without any hope of a harrowing. Dante took the ultimate journey into allegory in his narratives of heaven and hell. There is vengeance with a vengeance in the descriptions of suffering. The eternal judgment of the damned makes for great theatre, but that may not be the only reason for their popularity. The vengeance of eternal suffering is politically cathartic; to see the mighty fall, and be tortured eternally, is to engage with horror. The oppressor becomes the oppressed, and in extreme circumstances. This inversion carries political weight. Descent (as is ascent) is ideological. For Jameson allegory is always ideological, political, and collective:

> But just as in theology individual salvation is ultimately inseparable from collective salvation, so also for us today, and despite the distortions inevitably developed by an individualist consumer-oriented society, the very thought of the destiny of a biological individual is inseparable from that of the future of the species, in whatever collective form one chooses to imagine that. The final or anagogical level, therefore, classically reserved for the Last Judgment, is that of a kind of "political unconscious," that is, an often unconscious or merely implicit narrative of History as such, a collective and political narrative always latent in conceptions of our own personal destinies.[70]

Us tells of a last judgment on America. The end of the world is just below us/US, and of our own creation. Is the revenge of the Tethered justified? As the proverb goes, "Hell hath no fury like a woman scorned," or abducted by her doppelgänger.[71] In *Us* hell has been hallowed, and that hallowing brings a final judgment and apocalypse, at least for the United States. Is Peele suggesting that the emotions of fear and terror generated by this horror film should serve as a jolt—that the doppelgänger is in the form of the Other we imprison and cast out at our peril? Peele has the doubles tethered, those underground sharing one soul with those above,

69. Jameson, *Allegory*, 329.

70. Jameson, *Allegory*, xvi–xvii.

71. The origins of this proverb are from a tragedy by William Congreve, *Mourning Bride*, from 1697.

the shared soul a "poetic connection" according to Peele. Peele elaborates, "We can do a good job collectively of ignoring the ramifications of privilege. . . . We have to fight for the less fortunate."[72]

Hands Across America was formed to raise consciousness about and to ease hunger in America. Peele shows it as a *danse macabre*, but not a failure; at the end the hands of the Tethered are united in revenge and destruction.[73] They cover the US like a plague, and in somber celebration of their violent victory. Denied of basic human rights, freedom, and fresh air, they reclaim their "rightful place" in the nation, as their messiah Red would see it. They ascend, but only after cutting down (pun intended) their doubles.

How does one read the Apocalypse without being destroyed by it? Is reading the Apocalypse in itself a *katabasis*, a slow and torturous slide into the underworld (and/or its double, the heavenly city)? Is Peele, like the author of the Apocalypse of John, telling us that apocalypse is our unavoidable fate? Or is Peele putting out a warning, like the Jeremiah 11:11 prophet in the film, "Therefore, thus says the Lord, assuredly I am going to bring disaster upon them that they cannot escape; though they cry out to me, I will not listen to them." This is some warning: that God will abandon us, to our own destruction. Red tells Adelaide, "God brought us together on that night," the night of the switch. Is this God a master of horror?

Peele admits, "Religion is scary to me." He makes an Easter image central in the film: rabbits. He describes that his choice of rabbits represents "a dark Easter of sorts."[74] What if we read Easter through *Us*? Then on that (Un)Holy Saturday there was a switch. If there was a switch, we are in for a doozy of an apocalypse.

In his exploration of what lies beneath the surface of the earth, Robert Macfarlane shares that to descend below the earth, to "underland," is to rediscover the world. Descent is a necessary journey but it is fraught with emotions—from fear to claustrophobia. He explains, "An aversion to the underland is buried in language. In many of the metaphors we live by,

72. Bonus material, *Us* DVD.

73. There are a number of possible political links in the film. For example, as mentioned by Sciretta et al. in their *Film Daily Podcast*, the red color of the jumpsuits can represent anger, or the Republican Party ("red states"). Red is also the color of Satan, who often accessorizes his red jumpsuit with horned hoodie and a spiked tail. And red is associated with Marxism.

74. *Us* DVD, bonus material.

height is celebrated but depth is despised. . . . 'Catastrophe' literally means a 'downward turn,' 'cataclysm' a 'downward violence.'"[75] In the Anthropocene Macfarlane observes that "'crisis' exists not as an ever-deferred future apocalypse but rather as an ongoing occurrence experienced most severely by the most vulnerable . . . Things that should have stayed buried are rising up unbidden."[76] The story of creation is not flat; the horizontal Eden includes a vertical axis of both upper and lower realms. Macfarlane illuminates on the purpose of the underland:

> The same three tasks recur across cultures and epochs: to shelter what is precious, to yield what is valuable, and to dispose of what is harmful.
>
> Shelter (memories, precious matter, messages, fragile lives).
>
> Yield (information, wealth, metaphors, minerals, visions).
>
> Dispose (waste, trauma, poison, secrets).
>
> In the underland we have long placed that which we fear and wish to lose, and that which we love and wish to save.[77]

Macfarlane is ultimately offering a more hopeful vision of what lies beneath. A tour of the underland in all its various forms is a revelation for him. Jesus's descent into hell is also revelatory, and uncanny. The lack of detail is suspicious. Reading Jesus's journey as and through horror literature and film opens the uncanny possibilities. The supernatural beings of the premillennialist narrative are difficult to separate. Perhaps Christ and Antichrist are doubles, existing until the end of the world when one of them is ultimately defeated? But which one is which? Who sits at the right hand of God?

75. Macfarlane, *Underland*, 13.

76. Macfarlane, *Underland*, 13–14. As an interesting side note, the journal *Semeia: An Experimental Journal of Biblical Studies* and subsequent *Semeia Studies* series of the Society of Biblical Literature, has an interesting etymological root, as Macfarlane, *Underland*, 410, notes: "The Greek word for 'sign,' *sema*, is also the word for 'grave.'" In their work, biblical scholars descend to the underland.

77. Macfarlane, *Underland*, 8.

7

Jesus as Fantasy Mother

> Jerusalem, Jerusalem, the city that kills the prophets and stones those who are sent to it! How often have I desired to gather your children together as a hen gathers her brood under her wings, and you were not willing! See, your house is left to you, desolate. For I tell you, you will not see me again until you say, "Blessed is the one who comes in the name of the Lord." Matt 23:37–39 [par. Luke 13:33–35][78]

In fantasy and fairy tale literature mothers take on many forms, mostly absent (e.g., *Cinderella* or *Beauty and the Beast*). The interpretive emphasis on both the Matthean and Lukan story of Jesus's lament over Jerusalem has been on the metaphor of a motherly Jesus, a hen caringly protecting her brood from harm. But what follows in this passage is an apocalyptic judge/ment; unruly (and murderous) children bring about the disappearance of Jesus from their city. I want to examine the Jesus in this passage as an abusive mother, who is mirrored in his abusive children, as far as the metaphor can extend. The promise of comfort is held out and withdrawn. Fantasy and fairy tale literature mothers and birds have significant roles—and share themes of flight. I also explore the image of the city as accused murderer, on the verge of a response to the eschatological offer of Jesus.

78. I want to thank George Aichele for his wonderful insights on an earlier draft of this chapter.

Mother Goose Comes Home to Roost

Mother Goose comes home to roost
Her brood won't follow after.
The Mother calls
The whole world falls
When Mother Goose comes home to roost.[79]

Mother Goose has been the archetypal grandmotherly teller of children's rhyme. The vision of her in downy white feathers, bonnet, and spectacles brings forth feelings of comfort. She makes finger plays and sings silly songs and lullabies. Even when she sings about bad things happening to misbehaving children, grown-ups, and animals, there is light-hearted rhyme behind the mischief and violence. The eclectic collection of children's poetry creates a fantasy land that mirrors this world over the centuries since the purported first book in around 1765, John Newberry's *Mother Goose's Melody, or Sonnets for the Cradle*.[80] The multiple authors of the Mother Goose collection have given us some universal rhymes and silly stories of humans and animals. As John Goldthwaite discovered, "It is not surprising that nursery rhymes should be our most common cultural currency after the Bible. It is Mother Goose who first introduces us to who we are in the world, and it is she who brings us our first make-believe."[81] The nonsense helps children make sense of the world.[82] The fantasy, or "make-believe" (Goldthwaite's term) of the Bible also helps to order the chaos of life, and there are many stories directed to children.[83] But Mother Goose has other, less silly and more sobering tales to tell—of punishment, sickness, and death.

79. *The Apocalyptic Mother Goose* is, like all Mother Goose, a made-up book, as well as a collection out of my imagination. And like many Mother Goose rhymes, this book includes themes of punishment and judgment. I encourage others to write for this pretend volume.

80. Warner, *No Go the Bogeyman*, 195.

81. Goldthwaite, *Natural History*, 15.

82. Rather than accept the binary sense/nonsense, Goldthwaite, *Natural History*, 15, proposes a definition that leads to harmony: "Nonsense might be defined more accurately as a flirtation with disorder, a turning upside down of the world for the pleasure of seeing it come right side up again." In this way apocalyptic literature is nonsensical, but with a more dangerous undertone that leads to destruction, not harmony.

83. Goldthwaite notes that the collection in the book of Proverbs is "the world's oldest surviving children's book," *Natural History*, 4. He acknowledges, *Natural History*, 361n2, that there are even older separate stories, like David and Goliath, that would

The image of this often airborne mother on a goose, or as a "quaint old bird"[84]—for all the surface maternal symbols—plays with the gendered image, since the mother is a plurality of anonymous storytellers. Marina Warner notes: "The problem of Mother Goose's double tongue remains: is she truly a female storyteller, only now and then in drag, or does the drag constitute a claim on credence, advanced by men invoking something more authentic in themselves?"[85] As Mother Goose is a mixed image, so is the Gospel's Mother Hen. Jesus in drag provokes both male and female interpreters to draw near, to want to be part of her brood, to believe in the authenticity of her stories.

I have always felt an apocalyptic chill when I read some of Mother Goose's rhymes. For example, in "Sing a Song of Sixpence" the blackbird pie baked for the king and queen turns into a Hitchcockian nightmare. The pie is opened, the "four and twenty blackbirds" sing "Wasn't that a dainty dish to set before the king?," then attack the maid: "The maid was in the garden, hanging out the clothes,/When down came a blackbird and snapped off her nose."[86] In Tomie dePaola's illustration, the birds sit innocently on the castle; one sits on the clothesline near the maid. But in Charles Addams's more wicked interpretation, the birds fly around the tower; two are dangerously close to the king and queen, and one nose-dives toward the long nose of the maid. The baker looks on in horror as birds emerge from his dessert, while a guard with crossbow aims at a bird. Similarly, the drawings for "There was an old woman/ Lived under a hill,/ And if she isn't gone,/ She lives there still" vary greatly. DePaola shows the old woman looking out her front door from the green hillside.[87] Addams shows a blind woman, with her knitting, her cat, and a warm stove safely ensconced in a brown hill. Outside the landscape is a charred ruins, the burned remains of a nuclear attack.[88]

---

have been directed at youth.

84. Goldthwaite, *Natural History*, 27.

85. Warner, *From the Beast to the Blonde*, 187.

86. dePaola, *Mother Goose*, 13; Addams, *Mother Goose*, n.p.

87. dePaola, *Mother Goose*, 56.

88. Addams, *Mother* Goose, n.p. On the back cover of the Addams *Mother Goose* collection cartoonist Roz Chast adds (her emphasis), "Charles Addams doesn't *have* to alter the original Mother Goose because his drawings take us directly into these little rhymes' creepy, dark heart—the heart we always knew was there from the first time we heard about the four-and-twenty blackbirds baked in a pie." I continue to find it curious that, like most children's editions of Mother Goose, biblical scholars alter the apocalyptic biblical texts to make them more palatable. In the Left Behind books LaHaye and

Both traditional and feminist readings of the Matthean and Lukan versions of Jesus's lament over Jerusalem see a Mother Goose figure, a compassionate maternal figure. Here the mother (Jesus) becomes the bird, a great, protective, winged creature. Consider Joseph Fitzmeyer's reading in his commentary on Luke:

> In comparing himself to a mother bird, Jesus uses a readily understood figure for his own love and concern for his contemporaries, manifesting thereby in a new way the salvific interest of God himself (*sic*), which he was sent to proclaim (4:43). But Jerusalem will not seek the security of the protective wings of heaven-sent wisdom. So it will be left a helpless fledgling, its "house" will be left abandoned.[89]

Fitzmeyer interprets this passage as the compassionate bird mother protecting her brood and announcing the coming kingdom. In the midst of potential anti-Jewish sentiments, Jesus is offering an inclusive protection package, safe shelter to all who come under his/her wings. A.-J. Levine comments: "The patriarchal associations of the city are ironically contrasted to Jesus' feminine language: rather than divide individuals into elites and marginals, he would have gathered the children of Jerusalem together."[90] Jesus's intentions were good. Levine opts for an inclusive reading of this passage; Jesus as a mother is a unity figure and all who live in the city are her brood. Jesus longs to shelter all of them from the destruction, but they refuse her. The onus is on them, not Jesus.

The comforting mother hen image is on the surface a calming image of maternal competence. Despite all her best efforts and chick-raising techniques, her brood turns against her. Her children are a murderous bunch. Mother Hen laments the loss. R. S. Sugitharajah cites the hermeneutics of a nineteenth-century Anglican missionary, James Long, who took the side of oppressed indigo workers in Bangladesh.[91] Long used many metaphors to describe Jesus, but his interpretation of Jesus as Mother Hen is interesting. Sugitharajah explains: "As a mother hen, he nourished them by his great 'drop of blood.' The image of hen had its limitations, as Long explained, since the hen forgets the young when they are

Jenkins at least acknowledge the horror of the apocalypse, although in their warped and perverse way they also buy into the violence and anti-Semitism. Neither interpretation rejects the madness of biblical apocalypse/s.

89. Fitzmeyer, *Luke*, 1035.

90. Levine, *Matthean Salvation History*, 53.

91. Sugitharajah, *Bible and Empire*, 98.

grown up."[92] In the Gospel versions the Mother Hen continues to desire to shelter the brood, forgetting them only when they refuse her protection. This Mother Hen refuses to forget her chicks; she gets revenge, "See, your house is left to you, desolate" (Matt 23:38). Mother Goose turns into Mommie Dearest, serving as the very cause of her lament, wreaking havoc in their lives and prophesying that one day, after great suffering and desolation, the children will show their gratitude.

But who exactly are these children? The text refers to Jerusalem's children, so is Jesus a surrogate mother? Are there two mothers in this passage—Mother Jerusalem and the Mother Hen Jesus? Is Mother Jerusalem protecting her kids against an angry, apocalyptic deity?

The Early Bird Gets . . . Post-Traumatic Stress Syndrome

In the apocalyptic story of the flood, birds figure prominently. Some representatives are taken on the boat, while the rest are destroyed in the flood. The birds Noah sends out to check the progress on the flood vary in their surveying ability. The raven makes the first attempt, not returning to the ark. In the Epic of Gilgamesh flood story the last bird sent out, the raven, also does not come back to the ship. Then the more obedient dove flies out but comes back when there is no dry land. On the third try the dove returns with an olive leaf. After a week Noah sends the dove out again and it does not return (Gen 8:6–12). What have the raven and dove seen on their journeys from the ark? What is floating on the water? What is in the mud and muck? At the end of the flood, where has the genocide been washed—the destroyed temples, homes, animals, and piles of bodies—cholera in the ruins?

Norman Cohn refers to the role of the raven in the rabbinical midrash, Genesis Rabbah. In that retelling, "The raven caused Noah much embarrassment," arguing with Noah and refusing to fly away because he suspected that Noah "had designs on his mate, the female raven."[93] Ravens have a bad reputation throughout folktale tradition, pronouncing and partaking in destruction, such as feeding on corpses.[94] According to Leonard Lutwack, corpses play a prominent role in much of the bird

92. Sugitharajah, *Bible and Empire*, 130.

93. Cohn, *Noah's Flood*, 35–36; Genesis Rabbah 33.5.

94. Cohn, *Noah's Flood*, 36, includes a drawing from the Basel Speculum of 1476 of the raven of the ark devouring a beast's corpse, as Noah and family look on, and as the dove approaches the boat with the olive branch.

imagery.[95] Doves have a better image and represent the gentler traits of peace and love. In Christianity, doves get the honor of representing the Holy Spirit. Overall, birds have a mixed history in the Bible and in literature. Lutwack notes, "Birds were seen as an ambivalent symbol standing at the close as well as at the beginning of life on earth, at the destruction as well as the creation of the world."[96] The image of Jesus as a bird is not so farfetched, since God's birdlike creation over the waters of chaos, winged members of the heavenly court, and bird-like goddess figures in the ancient world. But Jesus as a bird is a mixed image, much more than soft, downy, feathery, encompassing compassion—hardly an ancestor of Big Bird.

Mary Ann Beavis sides with the majority in finding the positive in this feminine imagery for Jesus: "The range of the avian images—from homely domestic fowl to powerful wild predator—points to a divine that is both nurturing and awe-full, motherly and destructive, familiar and other."[97] Beavis points to the Septuagint version of Proverbs 16:16 and Sirach 1:15a in which Sophia Wisdom is a mother bird with a brood and nest.[98] The link between Jesus and Sophia has been made by several feminist scholars; Jesus embodies the feminine spirit who breathes life into believers. Elizabeth Johnson quotes Anselm of Canterbury, who sees the chicks as an analogy for the sinner's soul: "And you, my soul, dead in yourself,/run under the wings of Jesus your mother/and lament your griefs under his feathers."[99] Jesus will offer believers cover against the evil world.

The mother-goddess-bird is a dynamic image in the ancient world, and both Judaism and Christianity used it. Silvia Schroer suggests:

> A strong connection was made in the Ancient Near East between the Mother-Goddess and the vulture, to which rich notions of protection and regeneration were attributed. Whenever there is mention of the protective wings of YHWH, the motherliness of YHWH is not particularly emphasized. Nevertheless, it is definitely present [Deut 22:6]. In this respect, YHWH is the successor to the Goddess.[100]

95. Lutwack, *Birds in Literature*, 120.

96. Lutwack, *Birds in Literature*, 239.

97. Beavis, "'I Like the Bird,'" 127.

98. Beavis, "'I Like the Bird,'" 122n13.

99. Johnson, *She Who Is*, 150. Johnson is quoting Anselm's "Prayer to St. Paul," found in *Prayers and Meditations*, 153–56.

100. Schoer, "'Under the Shadow,'" 280.

Wings symbolize more than protection and shelter. There is also the connection of wings to genitals, especially when mentioned with "feet" (e.g., Ruth 3:9; Isa 6:2). In any event, eroticism is in the air, although most scholars avoid the topic and avoid linking angels to bird imagery. The protection of the wings is more the normative topic. Schoer points out that "The Near East thought much more dynamically of 'being born anew,' and about the new strength that results from protection and shelter."[101] There is healing in the bird's wings, although ironically these birds are unclean (Lev 11:13 and Deut 14:12).[102] Where Schoer sees healing in the shadow of the wings, I also see, well, shadows—a foreboding of judgment and destruction. However, she sees the eagle as more of a goose-vulture. Schoer links the shadows with the vulture-goddess Mut, whose letters, *Mwt*, relate to both womb and coffin. Schoer continues, "At the same time, the goose-vulture stands also for *nrt* or *nrw*, terror—a persuasive illustration of the ambivalence of the *tremendum et fascinosum* of the holy. It is very likely the terror of death that is symbolically associated with the vulture, of which we read in Isa 31.5: 'Like birds . . . hovering so YHWH Sabaoth will encircle Jerusalem, encircle and rob, flit around and embowel it.'"[103] The ancient Rabbis were onto something in their interpretation of the flood birds; the raven circles the boat, keeping a watchful eye on a bestial Noah. Although in Matthew and Luke Jesus is not a vulture but a hen, I think the connection with protection of a brood still holds. The image of Mother Hen is multifaceted; protective mother goddess, but also abandonment, ominous apocalypse. There must be another raven in this passage, circling Jerusalem, watching the great hen (who, like Noah, cannot fly) and who has promised the city's destruction.

The goddess imagery is problematic and has a mixed history in the Bible. The winged goddess bird of creation in Genesis 1 flies over the waters of chaos in order to tame them. The winged serpent appears in art work of Genesis 2–3, a female head on a snake body, only to be grounded by God. Then God makes periodic appearances as a bird (e.g., Exod 19:4 and Deut 32:10–11). By the time of the New Testament birds appear at baptism, in parables, as messengers (angels or eagles), and as feeders on road kill. In the role of Mother Hen Jesus takes over for Mother Goddess, like some male actor in a Shakespearean play in the sixteenth century. Jesus puts on a chicken costume. Is Mother Goose a counterpart to Lilith?

101. Schoer, "'Under the Shadow,'" 281.

102. Schoer, "'Under the Shadow,'" 269.

103. Schoer, "'Under the Shadow,'" 217n13.

The creation-destruction loop is my focus here. For Catherine Keller, the winged creation dragon of Babylon, Tiamat, becomes thoroughly demonized by Apocalypse 12, in which the new "Eve" faces the demonized serpent-beast who threatens to eat her newly born, messianic son. Keller notes, "Thus the text promotes the snake back up from garden-variety creep to cosmic Evil worthy to oppose the Good. Apocalypse does not casually *reverse* Genesis. The 'fall' of the first creation narrative is *replayed*, taken into the spiral, in order to solve it—to end it."[104] Serpent and bird imagery metamorphose into strange interspecies versions. The appearance of the winged serpent beast brings forth the earth goddess and the archangel Michael who protect the Woman Clothed with the Sun. The woman also protects herself: "But the woman was given the two wings of the great eagle, so that she could fly from the serpent into the wilderness to her place where she is nourished for a time, and times, and half a time" (Apoc 12:13).[105] The Apocalypse is full of wings: of serpents, of angels, of an eagle who cries prophecies, of the Sun Woman, and of the carnivorous birds of midheaven. Wings are symbols of power, of destruction, and of supernatural realms intersecting, once again, with the human. These wings stir up trouble. What is behind and inside these wings? If one enters the cover of the wings, are they a portal that provides safe passage—to renewal, to a new world? Or are the wings a temporary holding cell and you awake to the devastation of a post-apocalyptic world, to rebuild among the heaps of bodies and carnage, like Noah? Is there a happy ending to this lament?

Isaiah 34:14–15 comments on the judgment and chaos that will befall the enemy nations: "Wildcats shall meet with hyenas, goat-demons shall call to each other; there too Lilith shall repose, and find a place to rest. There shall the owl nest and lay and hatch and brood in its shadow; there too the buzzards shall gather, each one with its mate." The apocalyptic birds of Ezekiel 39 bring destruction upon Gog and Magog and their nation friends. God instructs Ezekiel: "Speak to the birds of every kind and to all the wild animals: Assemble and come, gather from all around the sacrificial feast that I am preparing for you, a great sacrificial feast on the mountains of Israel, and you shall eat flesh and drink blood. You shall eat the flesh of the mighty, and drink the blood of the princes of the earth" (Ezek 39:17–18). These vampiric birds gorge themselves on

104. Keller, *Apocalypse Now and Then*, 69; see also 203n23.

105. Scientists debate whether or not dinosaurs were the precursors to birds; those who argue for evolution argue similarities in tailbones, toes, etc.

the damned. An equally gory scene occurs in the Apocalypse of John, when the birds of midheaven feast on those who feasted on the Whore of Babylon. The visionary John tells us, "Then I saw an angel standing in the sun, and with a loud voice he called to all the birds that fly in midheaven, 'Come, gather for the great supper of God, to eat the flesh of kings, the flesh of captains, the flesh of the mighty, the flesh of horses and their riders—flesh of all, both free and slave, both small and great'" (Apoc 19:17–19). Then the beast and false prophet are thrown into the fiery lake. "And the rest were killed by the sword of the rider on the horse, the sword that came from his mouth; and all the birds were gorged with their flesh" (Apoc 19:21). There is an emphasis in Ezekiel and the Apocalypse on how overfull—and drunk in Ezekiel—the birds become. "You shall eat fat until you are filled, and drink blood until you are drunk, at the sacrificial feast that I am preparing for you" (Ezek 39:19). Following these visions comes restoration—of Israel (Ezek) and Jerusalem (Apoc). The sacrificial meal provides the necessary ritual for purifying the sacred land. I wonder what the Mother Hen eats?

Birds Gone Wild

> "I hardly think a few birds are going to bring about the end of the world."
>
> (Mrs. Bundy in *The Birds*)

Most of the birds I have encountered are in recovery. They sit nicely on their branches and sing, and unless you try to bother a nest, they will leave you alone. But apocalyptic birds are on a mission; they invert the norm; they create fantasy space. The apocalyptic birds made their major film appearance in Alfred Hitchcock's famous psychothriller *The Birds* (1963). The story is of a socialite from San Francisco, Melanie Daniels, following a lawyer, Mitch Brenner, whom she met in a pet store, to the northern California seaside hamlet where his mother and sister live. While there she meets Mitch's overprotective mother, who does not want to share her son with any woman. The birds gradually begin attacking, the townspeople are terrified, and by the end of the film an ominous group of birds watches the survivors leave the farm. These are the birds of midheaven, gathered for the feast on fears.

The tension builds slowly. One of the townspeople, Mrs. Bundy, reassures, "Birds are not aggressive creatures. They bring beauty into the world. It is mankind, rather, who insists upon making it difficult for life to exist upon this planet." Later she rethinks her initial observation on the birds: "Doesn't it seem odd that they'd wait all that time [140 million years] to start a war against humanity?" There is no explanation of why the birds attack, and unlike the biblical apocalyptic birds, no clear direct order from the deity.

The Birds indulges the viewer in a potential end time, or at least in apocalyptic horrors that, if left unchecked, could bring about the end of humanity. Alfred Hitchcock called his characters in the film "victims of Judgment Day."[106]The birds are normal birds, seagulls, crows, and such. They are not mutant beasts or alien species, and they do not have supernatural powers. This image of regular birds heightens the apocalyptic fear. Slavoj Žižek observes that "in what is surely Hitchcock's final irony—the 'unnatural' element that disturbs everyday life is the birds, i.e., *nature itself*."[107] The invaders are creatures we see every day. The reason the birds attack is uncertain. There is no real ending to the film, only a mention of other bird attacks in the region. There is a hint of the subversion of the normal hierarchy of living beings, a hint that the disaster is spreading.

Žižek explores the film's focal points: "The birds' subjective view of the town creates a menacing effect, even though our view—the camera's view—is that of the birds and not that of their prey, because we are inscribed in the scene as inhabitants of the town, i.e., we identify with the menaced inhabitants."[108] For Žižek, "birds function as the embodiment of a cruel and obscene superegoic agency."[109] Reading Lacan while watching Hitchcock, *The Birds* becomes a film about the "maternal superego." As in several Hitchcock films there is an absent father and an overbearing, controlling mother. Žižek notes the build-up through the Hitchcock films of birds, or "the figure of a threat in the shape of birds": the airplane that attacks Cary Grant in *North by Northwest*, the stuffed birds in Norman Bates's room in *Psycho*, and finally the hordes of birds in *The Birds*.[110] He continues,

> the terrifying figure of the birds is actually the embodiment in the real of a discord, an unresolved tension in intersubjective

106. Spoto, *Dark Side*, 479.
107. Žižek, *Looking Awry*, 178n3.
108. Žižek, *Looking Awry*, 178n9.
109. Žižek, *Looking Awry*, 18.
110. Žižek, *Looking Awry*, 99.

> relations. In the film, the birds are like the plague in Oedipus's Thebes: they are the incarnation of a fundamental disorder in family relationships—the father is absent, the paternal function (the function of pacifying law, the Name-of-the-Father) is suspended and that vacuum is filled by the "irrational" maternal superego, arbitrary, wicked, blocking "normal" sexual relationship (only possible under the sign of the paternal metaphor).[111]

The birds serve as a cover for the messed up family relationships. And the overbearing mother is the one responsible for the mess. From a feminist perspective, this reading is of course problematic, even if the mother in this film is guilty. Žižek's explanation is that the birds attack because there is no father to pacify the maternal superego, and so that ego takes over all the relationships in the family, including and especially any women who attempt to usurp the mother's position of dominance with her son. Žižek calls this derailment of the normal caused by the mother a "pathological narcissism," a phrase he borrows from Christopher Lasch, who believes these mothers cannot meet the needs of their child: "'in the child's fantasies the mother appears as a devouring bird.'"[112]

The whole Lacanian notion (from Freud) of the maternal superego has its points and ambiguities; the part of our unconscious that is shaped by maternal and paternal moral cues and the effects of bad parenting on human moral development. But in the story of Hitchcock's *The Birds* and in the biblical story of Jesus as Big (Devouring) Bird I find some useful points. In lamenting his inevitable destruction of Jerusalem, Jesus chastizes the city's children for (1) killing the prophets and stoning others sent by God and (2) not being willing to gather and seek protection in his/her wings. In Matthew Jesus' temple speech is near the end of a section of "woes" on the religious authorities. Jesus holds them responsible for *all* the murders of the Hebrew heroes and prophets, from Abel to Zechariah (Matt 23:35). When the authorities claim that the blame is on their ancestors, Jesus replies: "Fill up, then, the measure of your ancestors. You snakes, you brood of vipers! How can you escape being sentenced to hell?" (Matt 23:32–33). The lament is a catch-22; the city's children cannot possibly go to Jesus because he has already rejected them and damned them to eternal damnation. The correct answer is that they will not escape; they will be made desolate, covered with the blood of "all the righteous blood shed on earth" (Matt

111. Žižek, *Looking Awry*, 99.

112. Žižek, *Looking Awry*, 99, quoting Lasch, *Culture of Narcissism*, 176.

23:35), and their "house" (city, temple) utterly destroyed. It is difficult, if not impossible, to bypass the anti-Jewish tone of this apocalyptic muttering, or of biblical apocalypse in general.

For Hitchcock, who needs the supernatural when the natural will do just fine? The Gospel writers use a common farm image, a hen with her chicks, and bump it up to the supernatural. The domestic image is striking in the midst of a proclamation of supernatural judgment. But the hen is deceptive. Unzip the costume and out pops Jesus. The chicks had better run for their lives, or as Mike Davis would suggest, organize to resist the insanity. At various points throughout the Bible God puts on a bird costume; God is king/queen of the birds. In grand Marduk-like fashion (or the Wolf in "Little Red Riding Hood"), God disembowels the hovering bird and uses the disguise to lure the unsuspected. Are we as readers being lulled by this image so that we miss the apocalypse that God promises? Not all birds in the Bible are possessed by the deity's apocalyptic spirit, but here we encounter the "vision of a cruel, arbitrary, and impenetrable God who can bring down catastrophe at any moment."[113] The threat, the uncertainty of timing, are psychologically abusive. The victims of such apocalyptic, revenge-filled rage are required to respond at the new millennium, "Blessed is the one who comes in the name of the Lord" (Matt 23:39). The apocalyptic torture chamber will bring a forced confession and submission to Jesus's authority. The lament is a threat—of total destruction—of what God desires to do to humanity but holds back until some predetermined but seemingly arbitrary time. No wonder the children of Jerusalem refuse this promise of protection. It is an empty promise, made too late, after the end-time prophecy has been pronounced. Jesus sounds rather disingenuous, as a male cross-dressing as a mother acting out his own issues of childhood. "I really wanted to be able to protect you, you naughty children, but you had to go and kill the prophets, and now I'm going to have to punish you with blood and total annihilation." That is the way divine apocalypse works; a vengeful deity offers safety under the guise of compassion, and at a cost. Even civilian noncombatants are targeted. There is not a "hidden cruelty" in this image of Jesus; the rage is powerful.

This Mother Hen is "the Monster at our door," as Mike Davis calls the avian flu epidemic. Whereas bird flu is a natural phenomenon (albeit caused by bad poultry practices), an apocalyptic god is a Plague

113. Žižek, *Looking Awry*, 97.

of Plagues. A Janus-faced Christ (one side man, one side chicken?) pronounces: "Listen! I am standing at the door, knocking; if you hear my voice and open the door, I will come in to you and eat with you and you with me" (Apoc 3:20). Davis sees a "pandemic clock ominously approaching midnight." He stresses, "Now, with a real Monster at our door—as terrible as any in science fiction—will we wake up in time?"[114] One current prophecy preacher, ironically with the last name Hitchcock, believes: "If the Rapture were to happen soon, a virus such as the bird flu could be one of the apocalyptic plagues God uses to bring judgment on the Earth. It's just a matter of time" (Hitchcock). The Mother Hen in (Matt) or approaching (Luke) Jerusalem brings a pandemic of his/her own. Davis calls on humans to unite to resist the deadly disease by putting the survival of the poor above the profits of the pharmaceutical industry.[115] The civilian noncombatants of Jerusalem are doomed. Restorative justice is not part of the equation.

The Monster Mother stands knocking at the door in Matthew and Luke, too. Keller traces the revealing of this Monster Mother by feminist theologians; they are engaged in a reclaiming of the *tehom*.[116] However, in Matthew 23 and Luke 13 something different is happening than in Genesis: Here is God in drag again, neutralizing the Monster Mother into a seemingly harmless chicken, a storytelling Mother Goose. The creative spirit becomes utterly destructive. There is a perverse inversing of the creative mother. She has been killed off (or put in exile, like the Woman Clothed with the Sun in Apoc 12?).

The ability to fly is not limited to birds in the Apocalypse. In apocalyptic text and art there are wings everywhere—angels, beasts, dragons, birds, a flying woman—it is difficult to tell which winged creatures are dangerous, and I would argue that all of them are. One, "the fourth living creature like a flying eagle" (Apoc 4:7), guards the throne of God with three other beastly creatures (lion, ox, human face). All the throne guards wear "six wings, are full of eyes all around and inside" (Apoc 4:8). They also sing a choir of praise for the one on the throne. Warner notes

114. Davis, *Monster at Our Door*, 176–77.

115. Davis, *Monster at Our Door*, 176.

116. Keller, *Face of the Deep*, 34–36; see also 249n23, relating that Tiamat appears in the text: "Indeed the Babylonian myth was otherwise long dead, returned to dust and sand, but for its captivity in the second verse of the Bible."

that with only a few exceptions, "Research shows that birdsong correlates with high levels of testosterone."[117]

The angels are the largest flying figures in Western apocalyptic art. There are no cute little winged babies here. Angels arrive as oversized eagles to guide the seer, to pronounce the prophecies, and to defeat the enemy beasts. They lead the charge as an army for God. And they command their fellow winged fellows, the largest collection of birds in the Bible and a subunit of God's army, the birds of midheaven (Apoc 19:17–21). The phrase "to take someone under one's wing" refers here to a bit of apocalyptic mentoring. *The Angel Standing in the Sun* from Beatus of Liébana's *Commentary on the Apocalypse* (ca. 950 CE) is surrounded by colorful birds that he has called together for "the great supper of God" in Apoc 19:17.[118] *Babylon Invaded by Demons* from *The Apocalypse of Angers* (c. 1373–81 CE) shows the birds of midheaven attacking the beasts in the city as the people flee. The Berry Apocalypse (ca. 1400 CE) shows three angry birds—one with elongated beak—diving toward their supper, three people and two horses.[119] An angel looks on, smiles and points the way. One folio of the Spanish Apocalypse of St-Sever (ca. 1076 CE) features a Bird-God prominently. The bird is a beautiful green, red, blue, and yellow creature; its face is kindly. If you block off the serpent part, the bird radiates a kind of innocence, as if it still dwells in Eden. Frederick van der Meer comments on the art that accompanies Beatus's commentary (ca. 785 CE): "'Bird and Serpent' is an allegory of Redemption: the Bird, divine Wisdom, hid his bright feathers under the mud of Man's earthly nature at the Incarnation, and thus he was able to approach and kill the Old Serpent, which did not recognize him. In the miniature, the Bird grips the reptile with its claws, a cloud of dirt hanging over its head."[120] The death grip of the bird's mighty talons causes blood to trickle down the serpent, and its beak holds the snake at eye level. Van der Meer continues: "Bird and Serpent: [is] a symbol of Satan beguiled and overcome by God's 'disguise' in the Incarnation of the Logos."[121] I wonder if the incarnation of Jesus as Mother Hen is

117. Warner, *No Go the Bogeyman*, 229.

118. Grubb, *Revelations*, 34.

119. Lutwack, *Birds in Literature*, 120, notes that corpses are present in much bird imagery in literature.

120. van der Meer, *Apocalypse*, 113.

121. van der Meer, *Apocalypse*, 119.

not also a clever disguise to capture victims for the last judgment. If this story were a fairy tale, Jesus might be a good fairy in disguise.[122]

I think I am beginning to suffer from a bout of ornithophobia. Imagine all the biblical birds gathering together; imagine them outside your house right now. Would you go outside? Would you seek the protective wings? Look to the sky; they are gathering now.

A Fowl Apocalypse, Or Jesus's Coop d'Etat

The good news is that the Jesus of the New Testament also teaches love and nonviolence, especially toward children. In fact, he never advocates punishing children.[123] I would be overgeneralizing to say that Jesus never advocates violence, or on the other hand, that he advocates violence. I have no real idea what Jesus advocated; all I have are the mixed and too often problematic accounts of the Gospel writers. As an activist committed to peacemaking, I learn from the radical justice of Jesus's messages of peace and transformative justice. I want to believe, with Walter Wink, who firmly believes that Jesus teaches a "Third Way" of nonviolence, that "We know that nonviolence is the New Testament pattern."[124] But the apocalyptic messages woven throughout the New Testament—into its very fibers—cannot be extricated or ignored or easily explained away or relegated to Mark 13 and parallels plus the Apocalypse of John. The apocalypse is the winged shadow hovering over the canon, and Jesus is an apocalyptic attack bird in this lament over Jerusalem.

Mother Church imagery in medieval art has an interesting connection to the bird imagery. Mother Church guards believers in her wing-like robes. Christopher Hitchens reminds us of what happened in Rwanda in the 1994 genocide when Tutsi (and some Hutu) took refuge in churches. Priests were Hutu collaborators and thousands of people were executed in these spaces.[125] The wings/arms of the Mother did not offer protection.

122. There is also a tradition of fairy godmothers in fairy tales (e.g., *Cinderella*). Jesus is certainly no fairy godmother here; he dispenses plague not pleasure. Warner, *Beast to the Blonde*, 215, discusses the role of the good fairy, usually configured in less than beautiful disguise. According to Warner, "If the storyteller is an old woman . . . she may be offering herself as a surrogate to the vanished mother in the story. . . . Mother Goose enters the story to work wonders on behalf of her brood." Does Jesus's appearance as Mother Hen point to an absent mother in the text? Why is Mother Jerusalem silenced? What kind of motherhood is Jesus modeling?

123. Greven, *Spare the Child*, 219.

124. Wink, *Jesus and Nonviolence*, 103.

125. Hitchens, *God Is Not Great*, 191.

In his typical cranky style Hitchens comments about apocalyptic *schadenfreude*, "guilty joy" of a scene of millions of birds in the *Left Behind* series: First, one's own death is cancelled—or perhaps repaid or compensated—by the obliteration of all others. Second, it can always be egotistically hoped that one will be personally spared, gathered contentedly to the bosom of the mass exterminator, and from a safe place observe the suffering of those less fortunate.[126] In Jesus's statement Jerusalem's children (all of them?) will be massacred (or at least left to die after their world is destroyed), so does this leave room for the believing reader to step into Mother Hen's wings? Is the reader being lured into such guilty joy of the sort Tim LaHaye and Jerry Jenkins promote endlessly in their endless series? In these books Jesus flies down in the rapture to gather up his brood of believers and again at the end of the Tribulation to defeat the antichrist/Satan. The very cross of Jesus seems to fly, the crossbeam transforms into wings, with Jesus offering his outstretched arms to take us with him. I hear only the planes of 9/11, the cries of the desolate in a senseless war. Our relation to Jesus as Mother Hen is even more problematic when viewed in the shadow of these wings. Anyone wanting to recover this image as one of compassion must look deeper into the feathers. Mother Jerusalem is right to keep her children—even her bad children—away from such protection. In this fairy tale the mother is still absent, replaced by a ferocious male deity disguised as a loving mother hen. In fairy tales there is often an absent mother; the good mother dies and "is supplanted by a monster," the evil stepmother.[127] This image of the "wicked stepmother" has of course been damaging to women but in this case the archetype holds, further embedding the sexist image.

I went searching for a sign, something to convince me this image of Mother Hen has any salvageable ethical meaning. I live in a state full of chickens, so I thought to look locally for a sign. Then I thought of egg imagery, since every Mother Hen has eggs. Eggs are a sign of fertility, of spring, of resurrection at Easter. The cosmic egg that is the focus of Hildegard of Bingen holds all creation. Keller relates, "the etymological connotation of brooding has always emitted the mythical associations of the mother bird laying the world-egg."[128] The spirit must brood over the chaos/Tehom, for there to be life: "Apart from the spirit 'brooding o'er the chaos,' Tehom remains a sterile possibility and 'God' remains mere Word,

126. Hitchens, *God Is Not Great*, 57.

127. Warner, *Beast to the Blonde*, 201.

128. Keller, *Face of the Deep*, 233.

fleshless abstraction and power code."[129] The cosmic egg is the very stuff of the universe, down to its smallest particle. "If the wing served to make the bird miraculously free of earth, the egg bound the bird to earth, and the brooding hen became a symbol of the miracle of life."[130] I find this reading of Genesis 1 and history of the cosmic egg very hopeful and like to dwell here instead of the apocalyptic New Testament. But I return to the sections of destroyed cities and peoples in Jesus's speech. The apocalyptic egg in our times is the nuclear bomb, the egg dropped on Hiroshima and Nagasaki. My home state of Georgia broods over such nuclear eggs: Trident submarines and "white trains" and other trains and trucks carrying nuclear waste pass through and are held by these "wings." There is a picture that members of Nuclear Watch South (formerly Georgians Against Nuclear Energy) took in the early 1990s about a mile from my house. In the photo members of the group, dressed from head to toe in white anti-radiation suits, stand within twelve feet of a train container full of high-level nuclear waste that passed through and stopped in a heavily populated urban area. The container is an "egg" that must never crack open.

I continued my search for something more comforting. I wound up in Marietta, Georgia at the "Big Chicken," a famous (around here, at least) and huge red and white chicken with moving beak and eyes. Mother Hen sits atop a Kentucky Fried Chicken restaurant and beckons the hungry to come inside her protective wings. I had found "comfort food," as we call it in the South. This supersized hen promises nourishment. She even offers her body for food! She beckons, "Eat my flesh and . . ." But she brings obesity and heart disease to all who abide in her wings too long. My search continues.

Will it take a Mother Jones to stand up to this apocalyptic Mother Goose? Who will call Jesus out of his/her apocalyptic disguise? Who will stand in solidarity beneath the coming shadows of bird wings?

In the midst of the hopeful feminist reconstruction of the divine feminine and reclaiming of Jesus as Mother Bird, I appear as a negative doomsayer and unwelcome party crasher. "Who invited *her*?," they say as I walk into the party, smiling sweetly, holding a great big bucket of southern fried chicken.

129. Keller, *Face of the Deep*, 233.

130. Lutwack, *Birds in Literature*, 81–82.

8

The End of Jesus

I HAVE ALWAYS BEEN interested in the various stories about Jesus. This interest comes in part from living in the southern United States and being surrounded by various Jesuses, from the fiery cosmic judge of the imminent end time of the Pentecostal denominations to the more distant enthroned high priest in liturgical garb and voice of the higher church traditions. All these Jesuses have an apocalyptic tone to them; they speak of a coming judgment that will lead either to glorious eternal salvation or to dreary damnation. None of these Jesuses have messages that I can completely agree with. They started an endless debate with me about faith, Christianity, human rights, and social justice. They have multiple personalities; some of them I quite enjoy, while I find others of them much too scary. These Jesuses will not leave me alone. These Jesuses, all of them, continue to stalk me.

These Jesuses do not dwell in some mystical place for me but in the cultural and political signs of my time. As a way of dealing with these stalkers, I decided to try to understand their contexts. I looked to the canonical Gospels, to the historical critical method, to novels, and film not to find a way to connect all these personalities, some sort of Rosetta Stone to translate Jesus, but to sift through the messages to know what the terrain is. I have a whole lot of little stalker replicas, action-figure Jesuses I use in a course on Jesus that either bob heads or roll on their bottoms or have "miracle eyes" or point at me in hip, buddy fashion. They each tease me in different ways: "Look! Here is the Messiah!" or

"There he is!," or "I'm the actual Jesus!," but I have been instructed (Matt 24:23) not to believe any of them. I have built an altar for these figurines; they reside with a group of happy, cigarette-smoking sex workers from Oaxaca, action figures given to me by an anthropologist colleague because of my work on the Whore of Babylon (Apoc 17–18). Given the Gospel stories, this seemed an appropriate grouping. I believe I have created quite a little apocalyptic scene: sex workers with tacky glitter outfits, huge purses and high heels, some with skeleton bodies, and a few engulfed with flames, along with Jesuses with the Hollywood hair, all passing smokes around and sharing jokes. At least this is the extent of what I want to imagine (or write) about this scenario.

These Jesuses and sex workers occupy a space I have determined and set up, yet they transcend this space. Maybe it is due to an overload of the Apocalypse of John, but I cannot shake the vision of Jesus in apocalyptic spaces. Jesus seems to be continually snagged by his apocalyptic rhetoric, whether put in his mouth by others or not. He occupies apocalyptic space. And these days politics and popular culture comply, from border walls to wars to novels about the final days of earth. The Christian Right calls upon Jesus to bless and be present at these apocalyptic festivals of violence. More than that, Jesus, with General Archangel Michael, in the end time will whoop up on the Beast and his armies with full force of divine wrath. What would Jesus (or rather, some other Jesuses) say and do in response?

This question of whether or to what extent or in what ways Jesus was/is an apocalyptic prophet is one of the main issues in New Testament studies. Scholars have argued intensely over the apocalyptic Jesus, and this debate has recently been revived by "historical Jesus" scholars. What I find most interesting in this debate are the political links and implications of the apocalyptic spaces where Jesus can be found. I want to focus here on part or space of the misnamed "little apocalypse" (as if any apocalypse is ever "little") of Mark 13 and parallels (Matt 24 and Luke 21). My interest here is in one particular space and place within this apocalyptic discourse, the temple in Jerusalem, and the sayings about its destruction: "As he [Jesus] came out of the temple, one of his disciples said to him, 'Look, Teacher, what large stones and what large buildings!' Then Jesus asked him, 'Do you see these great buildings? Not one stone will be left here upon another; all will be thrown down'" (Mark 13:1–2). If Jerusalem is the center of apocalyptic stories, then the temple is ground zero. Much emotion and maneuvering has occurred in and around this temple; it is a symbol of a romanticized past (a symbol of David and Solomon's united nation; the post-exilic Temple of Zerubbabel; Herod's grand building) and an equally romanticized future of religious purity and power. What has Jesus to do with the temple? The possibilities include: he was brought to it by his parents for purification rites (Luke 2:27); he amazed the teachers there at age twelve (Luke 2:46); he taught in it as an adult; he "cleansed" it; he prophesied its destruction by the Romans (even if retroactively through a Gospel writer) in 70 CE. Gospel scenarios notwithstanding, Jesus and the temple have lives outside the canon. They continue to meet in curious ways.

Jesus in (Apocalyptic) Space

I spent many days as an undergraduate religion major in the heady Bultmannian atmosphere of existential theology.[1] Rudolf Bultmann preached a decisive gospel, one that demanded a here-and-now answer for or against the cross (as symbol of faith). I liked his slash-and-burn method, cutting out all the Gospel talk he thought was excessive and moving chapters around in an "extreme makeover" of the Gospels. Bultmann was grumpy about the details of Jesus's speech, demythologizing most of it to some trash bin holding all things he deemed unhistorical or unoriginal.

In my junior year of college I wrote an exegesis paper on no less than "The Son of Man Sayings in the Synoptic Gospels." The trinity of present sayings, future suffering sayings, and sayings of coming glory provided the framework for investigating all the passages. Of course, since I was still in a heavily Bultmannian atmosphere, Jesus never called himself Son of Man, nor did he ever say these sayings.[2] Rather, the early church acted as screenwriter, supplying Jesus with most of his lines. Let us revisit this terrain of the past. Bultmann believed that Jesus's central teaching was eschatological; the "reign of God" was imminent and Jesus stood on the cusp of the end of the world and the glorious future.[3] For Bultmann Jesus taught that God's future world would be brought about by apocalyptic events: the Son of Man will judge the earth and humankind, the present

1. I owe a debt of gratitude to my undergraduate and later doctoral supervisor, Dr. James L. Blevins, preeminent scholar of John's Apocalypse.

2. Allison, "Eschatology," 159, comments, "The truth is that even if Jesus never said anything about 'the Son of Man,' one could still construct a solid case for an apocalyptic Jesus."

3. Bultmann, *Theology*, 4.

world will be destroyed by God as part of the judgment sentence, and a glorious paradise awaits. Jesus is definitely an apocalyptic prophet with a message of heaven, and not of some earthly kingship or kingdom. In this way the apocalypticism in Jesus' message is minimalist, as compared to Daniel or the Apocalypse of John. This kingdom will not be political, a return of a Davidic king to reestablish the nation of Israel. There are no details of antichrists, imperial beasts, or thousand-year reigns. Only a bare outline remains of God's future. The supernatural imaginings of mansions and golden streets are not included in this vision. Jesus preaches of a Son of Man (not himself) who will usher in the next age. Doom and total destruction come first, and soon, and "it is evident that Jesus has this conviction: This age has run out."[4]

Compared to the apocalyptic writers Jesus provides sparse details of the coming age. The details of premillennial apocalypticists would be lost on Jesus. No one except God can know the time of the end (Matt 24:36). Bultmann relates, "But what are the signs of the time? He himself! *His presence, his deeds, his message!*"[5] The sign of "Jesus" demands a decision, and this decision will determine one's future fate. Now is the time to decide. Listen to Bultmann's existentialist rhetoric: "Jesus . . . knows no ends for our conduct, only God's purpose; no human future, only God's future . . . *the present moment as the final hour*."[6] The coming kingdom of God demands a decision, which in turn forms an existential crisis, which in turn leads (hopefully) to right decision (read: doing the will of God). Now is the final hour. For Bultmann's Jesus what is most important is that every moment is apocalyptic, and every moment demands a decision for or against God. There is a heaviness, a great burden of responsibility, attached to the hearing of this message. Turn or burn, or at least be left (on earth) to weep and gnash your teeth for eternity.

Bultmann's method was to squeeze the myth out of the Gospels. I never really saw the point of so much searching for authenticity; I never figured the Truth could be excavated or exegeted. Besides, I was looking for truths not Truth. I like the messiness of the Gospels, their copycat play and mysterious sources and authors. I am especially drawn to the myth, or better, fantasy of the Gospels. I never wanted to play some historical-critical game of "Gospel Clue," e.g. Matthew, an early church minister (and not the tax collector-disciple), with a quill pen and Mark

4. Bultmann, *Theology*, 5.

5. Bultmann, *Theology*, 7; his emphasis.

6. Bultmann, *Jesus and the Word*, 130–31; his emphasis.

and Q and a few other sources in hand, in northern Galilee in 85 CE. The intent of the early Jesus Seminar to color code the words and acts of Jesus strikes me as a bit obsessive-compulsive—a kind of colored glue to stick the Gospel texts to certain imaginary spaces, imaginary pasts. These myths, fictions, fantasies, imaginary pasts are all of interest to me, and I think they are all integral to the story. To (attempt to) divest the Gospels of myth takes away textual possibilities. And to separate apocalyptic from the teaching of Jesus is to cause a collapse of the multiple signifiers of "Jesus." But at this point the debate has been reinvigorated.

There has been a scholarly battle over the centuries about the apocalyptic Jesus. In one corner are Johannes Weiss, Albert Schweitzer, and Bultmann, Bart Ehrman, Dale Allison, and others, all of whom in their own ways envision Jesus as an apocalyptic teacher or prophet. The basic framework is that Jesus took the message of John the Baptist to heart and preached from the beginning of his ministry, "'The time is fulfilled, and the kingdom of God has come near; repent, and believe in the good news'" (Mark 1:15). Jesus preached an imminent end of the world that God had already begun to instigate as part of God's kingdom plan.

In the other corner are the post-Bultmannians and the Jesus Seminar members who hold that Jesus was not an apocalyptic prophet; he was a wisdom teacher and healer (Marcus Borg) or a revolutionary prophet advocating changes on earth (John Dominic Crossan). The current statement of the Jesus Seminar presents clearly their consensus:

> Jesus did not hold an apocalyptic view of the reign (or kingdom) of God—that by direct intervention God was about to bring history to an end and bring a new, perfect order of life into being. Rather, in Jesus' teaching the reign of God is a vision of what life in this world could be, not a vision of life in a future world that would soon be brought into being by a miraculous act of God.[7]

The sources, the canonical Gospels and the Gospel of Thomas and "Q," are like archeological sites. If a scholar excavates long, deep, and carefully enough, the findings and artifacts will all add up to a singular picture of a singular Jesus. For the Jesus Seminar, apocalypticism must be drained from wisdom.[8] In the words of Crossan, Jesus taught an "ethical eschatology or the radicality of divine ethics," making "apocalyptic" positive or

7. Westar Institute, "Profiles of Jesus."

8. Allison et al., *Apocalyptic Jesus*, 74.

transformative rather than negative and destructive.[9] This color-coding causes the apocalyptic Jesus to fade out. It is almost as if apocalyptic is an embarrassment, and it is the task of the seminar to disassociate Jesus from it. They fear Jesus being wrong (about an imminent end and soon-to-come kingdom) or looking too much like Tim LaHaye.

Much of the debate about Jesus and apocalyptic centers around definitions. Eschatology, or thinking about the end times, is a more friendly, overarching term. Although eschatology is about the "end," it is a more positive fulfillment of human history. The word "apocalypse" conjures up all sorts of horror scenarios. As the seminar defines it, apocalypse is a sub-category of eschatology in which chaos and disaster wrought by God precedes the end of the world.[10] Eschatology is good; apocalypse is bad. Crossan summarizes a main question as he tries to reconfigure apocalyptic: "Is apocalypticism about human hope and expectation for a divine action, a transcendental solution to the problem of evil, injustice, and violence? Or is it about anything we should do in time, place, and history to participate in that process? Or is it about both?[11] The early church begins the long process of creating the kingdom on earth. Thus, Jesus does not sound like a hellfire and brimstone preacher in the Gospels, and he certainly does not look like the wild, genocidal deity with the two-edged sword coming out of his mouth in the delusional visions in the Apocalypse of John.

If apocalypse is the wild child of eschatology, scholars can separate it out of the "mainstream" message and work on taming it. The most uncomfortable of Jesus's sayings can be excised or overlaid with a more transformative message. For these scholars Jesus preached more about restoration than destruction, or destruction is minimalized in a grander view of a transformative kingdom and the ethics the church must practice to create this positive future. They do not want to allow for a Jesus who wanders around the Gospels spouting end-of-the-world rhetoric. They assign all the heavily apocalyptic passages—the ones promising earthly and material destruction—to the post-Easter period. The sayings of Jesus that promise the end of evil and injustice have a better chance of being seen as pre-Easter.[12]

9. Allison et al., *Apocalyptic Jesus*, 69.

10. Allison et al., *Apocalyptic Jesus*, 6.

11. Allison et al., *Apocalyptic Jesus*, 65.

12. See Crossan's response in Allison et al., *Apocalyptic Jesus*, 38–39.

I believe apocalyptic is ubiquitous in the New Testament. In the message of Jesus apocalyptic cannot be relegated to Mark 13 and parallels, as if Jesus had a "little apocalypse" rant and then returned to his main message of love. But even Allison and Ehrman soften the hard edges of apocalyptic. Jesus was a Jewish apocalypticist who focused on the kingdom of God: "In the future kingdom, God's people will be rewarded with a utopian existence."[13] The Son of Man will serve as "a cosmic judge sent from heaven" to sentence the good and evil in the world.[14] Ehrman summarizes, "Preparation for the Kingdom—*that's* what ultimately lies at the heart of Jesus' ethics."[15] Ehrman's Jesus is not that interested in social reform, for the end is soon.[16] Maybe I am too much of an existentialist, but I think the present life should be lived to its fullest—not because of some future kingdom of God or paradisial state, but because of love and concern for the earth and all its inhabitants. But then I am not a peasant living in a first-century Roman colony; I am an activist educator in the twenty-first century. It is always difficult to translate Jesus's two-thousand-year-old teachings in the contemporary world, and apocalypse is particularly difficult to translate in an ethical way.

All these scholars want to put an end to Jesus—to settle once and for all what and who he was and to make sense of his message and person. They desire, both covertly and overtly, to find the actual Jesus. Jesus as revolutionary, as apocalyptic prophet, as preacher to and healer of the poor, as a Jewish reformer—all the various characterizations work to arrive at capital "J" Jesus. I want to work off a premise that Jesus ended even before any historical Jesus scholars could end him. Jesus has died a seemingly infinite number of times, over and over again in Gospels, liturgy, novels, and film, all with us shouting, "Crucify him!" over and over again. And he consequently resurrected, the stone rolled away to reveal empty space, resulting in thousands of Jesuses roaming the universe. Are some of these Jesuses (it would only take one) preparing the earth for the final battle?

13. Ehrman, *Apocalyptic Prophet*, 143.

14. Ehrman, *Apocalyptic Prophet*, 144.

15. Ehrman, *Apocalyptic Prophet*, 162; his emphasis.

16. Ehrman, *Apocalyptic Prophet*, 190.

Temple of Doom

In Matthew 24 and parallels the end is described in terms of various apocalyptic signs. Prequels to the end include false prophets, lawlessness, earthquakes and famines, the destruction of the temple, and the destruction of anyone who has not remained "awake" (Matt 24:42). The author of the footnotes to this verse in the New Oxford Annotated Bible (NRSV) states the obvious to avoid pinning such apocalyptic speech on Jesus: "It is difficult to be certain what the original form of Jesus'[s] words was."[17]

One of Jesus's prominent apocalyptic teachings concerned the most sacred spaces of Judaism and Christianity, the city of Jerusalem and the temple. First, in keeping with various prophetic pronouncements, Jerusalem is seen as doomed (more so in Matthew's version): "Jerusalem, Jerusalem, the city that kills the prophets and stones those who are sent to it! How often have I desired to gather your children together as a hen gathers her brood under her wings, and you were not willing! See, your house is left to you, desolate. For I tell you, you will not see me again until you say, 'Blessed is the one who comes in the name of the Lord'" (Matt 24:37–39; par. Luke 13:34–35). Matthew places this statement after a series of "woes" on the Pharisees and right before his version of Mark 13; Luke places it in a response of Jesus to Pharisees who warn him of Herod's intention to kill him. Then Jesus comments on the fate of the temple; along with the rest of Jerusalem it will be destroyed (Mark 13:1–2; Matt 24:1–2; Luke 21:5–6). The great, but at the time of Jesus unfinished, temple in Jerusalem will be demolished (presumably by God at Jesus's return). And misplaced awe will be set straight.

Jesus's own actions in the temple are famous; he overturns tables of the temple economy (Matt 21:12–17; par. Mark 11:11, 15–19; Luke 19:45–48; John 2:13–17). In Matthew this story is followed by Jesus's cursing of the barren fig tree (Matt 21:18-22; par. Mark 11:12-14; 20–25). Most commentators see this passage as symbolic, otherwise Jesus looks like a social anarchist, interfering with a central economy and destroying property. Temple and fig tree—both will wither and die. Jesus, and his faithful followers, have the authority/power to execute such actions, whether symbolic or literal. Jerusalem is the central geographic location of the apocalyptic universe, and within the city the temple is ground zero.

Crossan relates the temple with Jesus's death and burial. "No matter, therefore, what Jesus thought, said, or did about the Temple, he was its

17. Metzger and Murphy, eds., *Oxford Annotated*, 36.

functional opponent, alternative, and substitute; his relationship with it does not depend, at its deepest level, on this or that saying, this or that action."[18] Crossan sees the temple cleansing (Mark 11:15–19) as "a deliberate symbolic act" of destroying—not purifying—the temple.[19] He finds an important parallel in the Gospel of Thomas 71, even though there is no explicit temple/house connection: "I shall [destroy this] house, and no one will be able to build it . . . ."[20] Thus, for Crossan Jesus spoke symbolically about his death and resurrection in his metaphor of the destruction of the temple, and he was falsely accused of stating that he would be the destroyer and the rebuilder after three days (e.g. Mark 14:58 and par.: "We heard him say, 'I will destroy this temple that is made with hands, and in three days I will build another, not made with hands.'"[21] And in Mark 15:29 "Those who passed by derided him, shaking their heads and saying, 'Aha! You who would destroy the temple and build it in three days, save yourself, and come down from the cross!'" Although the "original" quote of "not one stone will be left upon another" is attributed by the Gospel writers to Jesus, the rumor builds on apocalyptic and messianic tension. Crossan links any actual destruction (but no rebuilding) to the actual destruction of the temple by the Romans in 70 CE.[22]

The main questions remain, for both those who advocate and do not advocate an apocalyptic Jesus, whether or not Jesus said anything about the destruction the temple or if the rumor in Mark 14:58 par. and also Gospel of Thomas 71 is true that he said he himself would destroy it. The origins of the prophecy of temple destruction will never be known. But prophecies of the end of the land and/or city are basic to understanding Jesus's context. Ehrman refers to a much earlier prophecy in Jeremiah 7 in which God says "for the land shall become a waste" (Jer 7:34).[23] The idea of the destruction of the city and its sacred sites with only a remnant left remaining is an old one, popular in prophetic pronouncements on the sins of the people. The enemies get their just due, but God's most furious wrath will be reserved for Jerusalem. For Jesus all these events were to happen before the end of his generation (Mark 13:30; 9:1; Matt 24:34). The temple will fall, but in its place will be the paradise of God on

18. Crossan, *Historical Jesus*, 355.

19. Crossan, *Historical Jesus*, 357.

20. Crossan, *Historical Jesus*, 355.

21. See the discussion in Allison, *Jesus of Nazareth*, 100–101.

22. Crossan, *Historical Jesus*, 360.

23. Ehrman, *Apocalyptic Prophet*, 158.

earth: To repeat Ehrman, "In the future kingdom, God's people will be rewarded with a utopian existence."[24] In this utopian space there will be cosmic equality and justice, but not before. Jesus directs believers to focus on getting into the kingdom, not engaging too much in social transformation (contra Crossan). Or better, as philosopher George Steiner puts it, "Catastrophe is never unconditional. In God's sentence on Israel there are redeeming clauses. . . . The dialectic of possible rehabilitation springs from the heart of terror."[25] But unlike the Gospel of John, in the Synoptic Gospels and more so in Thomas the words in Jesus's mouth are only of destruction. Any redemption, or rebuilt temple, is from the rumor mill, the fantasies of the crowd.

A rebuilt temple is what looms large in prophecy belief. In Christian millennialist thought the vision of a rebuilt temple is key to the apocalyptic final battle. There is only one spot on earth where the temple can be rebuilt: in Jerusalem. Paul Boyer relates that most prophecy believers want the temple rebuilt on the current Temple Mount site (Arabic: Haram al-Sharif). He quotes one writer as saying, "God is sensitive to the exact spot of the Temple."[26] The exact location is seen as the site of the Mosque of Omar (Dome of the Rock) and Al Aksa Mosque. The Dome of the Rock marks the spot of Mohammad's ascension to heaven, of Abraham's sacrifice of Isaac, and of Solomon's Temple. Prophecy writers muse that the mosque could be destroyed by a God-sent earthquake, by an Israeli bomb, by removal to Mecca (proposed by the Temple Mount Faithful), or my favorite from Salem Kirban's novel *666*, "Antichrist zaps the mosque with his ruby laser ring."[27] I wonder what members of the Justice League (Superman, Wonder Woman, et al.) would think about this action.

Israeli journalist Gershom Gorenberg calls this thinking about the future end time as "catastrophic millennialism," a term from Catherine Wessinger.[28] Christian Zionists share apocalyptic desire with some Jewish Zionists. Gorenberg notes: "Christianity was the daughter not simply of Judaism, but of a Judaism burning with expectation, standing on tiptoes and ready to leap into the End."[29] These more extreme views of God's

24. Ehrman, *Apocalyptic Prophet*, 143.

25. Steiner, *Essays*, 312.

26. Boyer, *Prophecy Belief*, 198.

27. Boyer, *Prophecy Belief*, 198.

28. Gorenberg, *End of Days*, 40.

29. Gorenberg, *End of Days*, 41.

invasion of earth have a direct link with current Middle East politics, and the absence or imagined presence of the temple is a hot topic: "Visions of the End, confusion of symbol and reality, awe of the sacred and fear of defilement: Those are precisely the forces that have driven the long conflict over the Temple Mount."[30] Passages such as Apocalypse 11:2 relate the excess of the violence from the temple center onto the city. The angel instructs John not to measure the court of the gentiles and prophecies that the city will be destroyed: "but do not measure the court outside the temple; leave that out, for it is given over to the nations, and they will trample over the holy city for forty-two months." Prophecy believers see this scene as part of the tribulation leading up to the end.[31]

This space of the Temple Mount is politically and ideologically charged. It is not just about throwing down stones and the destruction of a building. This space consists of rock and dirt that have footprints, sacred footprints (Asherah, Abraham, Muhammad, Zeus/Jupiter, numerous high priests, sacrificial animals), along with ancient trash from when it served as a dump between Constantine and Muslim rule.[32] Various buildings of Judaism and Islam mark or have marked the spots over the centuries. Models of the Holy Land reproduce (for Christians) the holy spots. Gorenberg understands the Temple Mount as the central apocalyptic site in all three monotheistic religions: "For many believing Muslims, Jerusalem's condition precisely expresses the distance between the world as it is and the world as it should be—the gap that the apocalypse is meant to close."[33] The outcome—of ownership of the Mount—depends on who is telling the apocalyptic story.

Because an actual geographic location exists, many seek to hone in on the precise parameters of the temple. Of course, the exact location of the temple is not known. Gorenberg interviews physicist Asher Kaufman, whose major interest is uncovering the exact location of the temple. Like Ezekiel (40ff.) and John in Apocalypse 11:1 Kaufman measures stones. He also draws on ancient Jewish documents. Gorenberg relates, "His findings—tied together with a few assumptions, he admitted—led him to

30. Gorenberg, *End of Days*, vii; see discussion in Jewett and Lawrence, *Captain America*, 144–47.

31. Gorenberg, *End of Days*, 187, reminds me: "Researchers of millennialism, I've found, often have a quirky, questioning faith—a fascination with religion's power and with its dangers."

32. Gorenberg, *End of Days*, 70.

33. Gorenberg, *End of Days*, 191.

map both the First and Second temples, with the rock under the Dome of the Spirits marking the Holy of Holies."[34] Kaufman's conclusion is that a rebuilt temple can coexist with the Dome of the Rock; he proposes a plan to split the Mount in two: "north for the Jews, south for Muslims."[35] Of course, his findings ignited the Christian dispensationalists who care deeply about the "exactness" of biblical spaces, especially those spaces that are part of the end time scenario.

Where does God dwell in these spaces? French philosopher Régis Debray talks about "a deterritorialized God" in the Bible. He summarizes:

> Promised Land, Holy Land, Holy City—the New Testament knows nothing of such expressions. The Pauline epistles make no reference to the Land. The Word became Flesh and "dwelt among us." Where was it? A mere anecdote. No fleshly attachment to the soil, no supernatural pegging to a plot of land. It is the body of Christ that is the territory and true Temple of the Christian.[36]

Debray's focus is on traditional Roman Catholic views of doctrine over space. Debray argues that for Christianity Jerusalem and the Temple Mount should not matter, for God is not bound by territory. Augustine said as much with his spiritualized city of God concept. "The history of the Only God, in Jerusalem, goes nowhere; it has become a cartography, and a demography."[37] He continues: "Might there not be, in the very notion of the sacral, a germ of apartheid? . . . God, a born extremist, is the diplomats' worst enemy."[38] A god without territory is one without armies to defend it or a temple as house. There are no permanent structures for a deterritorialized deity, only boundaries to be crossed and new space to configure.

Jesus resists any rebuilding of the temple, saying over and over again, "not one stone will be left here upon another." Perhaps Jesus's apocalypticism is different from that of LaHaye and company. Jesus is concerned for the city Jerusalem in its unrepentant and doomed state, but he has no concern for the temple, even though he considers it his (and his father's) house. Temple-house-tomb-body are all signs of the time and these signs

34. Gorenberg, *End of Days*, 65.

35. Gorenberg, *End of Days*, 67.

36. Debray, *God*, 134.

37. Debray, *God*, 98.

38. Debray, *God*, 104.

transcend stones and geography. Nation building, especially of the hyper-Christian kind, is a mean exaggeration that creates an us-versus-them state of perpetual dis-ease.

The Temple Mount itself resembles a structure out of Michel Foucault's examination of prisons or clinics. Debray describes the current security configuration:

> The mount where God lives, predestined site of unity and *summum* of division, where five hundred video cameras, inserted under roofs, keep an eye on the children of Abraham? . . . There where the dark side of a God of light is revealed, we would do better to dispense with colour photos and sermonizing clichés, and confront reality—metal barriers, barbed wire and fortified terraces. Strange: the bounds of the Infinite. The residence of the Unlimited converted into a jailer's paradise, in which the struggle to occupy every square inch of terrain occupies every minute. . . . The site of the sanctuary . . . would not be available for appropriation, unless by the UN.[39]

The Temple Mount is a space of multiple interests and controls and nations. Some of these interests envision a peaceful compromise of coexistence, and some desire sole ownership. There is no end in sight for some, for others the end is happening with every news item (see for example Hal Lindsey's *International Intelligence Report* on Trinity Broadcast Network).

Joshua (Jesus) pronounces to his hardheaded disciples in Christopher Moore's humorous novel, *Lamb: The Gospel according to Biff, Christ's Childhood Friend*, "The kingdom of God has nothing to do with the kingdom of Israel, do you all understand that?"[40] Or one could add, with the doctrines and buildings of religion. For Biff's best friend, the direct mirror image—of a heavenly throne room as liturgical space with the earthly nation and temple worship—has none of the traditional apocalyptic mimetic dualism. Joshua/Jesus roams far away from the Jerusalem temple to the East in search of the three wise men and seeks training in other spiritual practices with Buddhist monks and Hindu gurus.

This Jesus would agree with George Steiner that God cannot be held down in one spot or with one nation, or one religion. Steiner believes the building of the temple/s was a misunderstanding more connected with nation building and that God and Judaism are better

39. Debray, *God*, 97.

40. Moore, *Lamb*, 392.

imaged in the space of texts: "In its doomed immanence, in its attempt to immobilize the text in a substantive, architectural space, the Davidic and Solomonic Temple may have been an erratum, a misreading of the transcendent mobility of the text."[41] The Jesus of the Synoptic apocalyptic discourse preaches that the end is near but gives no full details or timeline. But one detail, that of temple ruins, is clear. Time collapses in this apocalyptic speech; the temple we see Jesus walking through is already also in ruins, not one stone left upon another. Not even the so-called "Wailing Wall" remains, even as it stands as a remnant, a sign, of some imagined past and future structure.

Northrop Frye describes the prophetic vision appropriated by the Gospels as including "the level of the present moment and a level above it."[42] He outlines the spaces in the Bible: "The five bodies of imagery in the Bible: the paradisal, the pastoral, the agricultural, the urban, and the imagery of human life itself."[43] "Christ is not only the temple but the cornerstone of the temple, and each member of the Christian community is a stone in the same temple."[44] For Frye "the casting out of devils is symbolically the same act as cleansing the temple."[45] Frye sees the spaces as interrelated, but he notes, "We notice that, as the Bible goes on, the area of sacred space shrinks. . . . With the sacrilege of Antiochus, perhaps repeated in intention by Caligula, the last vestige of sacred space disappears."[46] There is no temple in the apocalyptic new Jerusalem; Jesus, by means of his bodily sacrifice (see Hebrews), becomes the temple.[47] The argument follows that as Jesus speaks of the destruction of the temple, he speaks of his own death (back to John 2:21 again), and the rebuilt temple is actually Jesus's resurrected body, not a stone building. Once again, not one stone of the temple will remain upon another.

What is the temple to Jerusalem and what role does this architectural structure (real or imagined) play in terms of the city? The city is archetypically imaged as female, and in the ancient world male gods dwelled within female bridal cities. Jesus only cleanses the outer courts until his death on the cross, at which point the veil to the holy of holies

41. Steiner, *Essays*, 305.
42. Frye, *Great Code*, 129.
43. Frye, *Great Code*, 144.
44. Frye, *Great Code*, 157.
45. Frye, *Great Code*, 157.
46. Frye, *Great Code*, 158–59.
47. Frye, *Great Code*, 157.

(where God dwells) is torn in two.[48] Is the innermost room of the temple the womb, vaginal space? Does it provide entrance into the deep, or to heaven? Frye points to the image of water flowing out of the rebuilt temple (Ezek 47:1–17).[49] The temple is built on top of the chaotic birth waters and thus controls them. For Elizabeth Grosz, "Cities have always represented and projected images and fantasies of bodies, whether individual, collective, or political."[50] The biblical images are of high priests entering the innermost space of the temple and foreign rulers violating the sanctuary with their alien deities. But then Asherah's pole or tree was part of the interior design for many kings of Judah during the Divided Monarchy period. And some the architectural influences of the temple are Canaanite and Egyptian.[51] So is Jesus's body as temple polysexual and polytheistic and polynationalistic?

The biblical texts attempt to claim monotheism in design and practice. There is one God, and many centers (diasporic, synagogic, missionary), yet in apocalyptic all these margins collapse into a center (Jerusalem or new Jerusalem). In prophetic writings Jerusalem is the center of the world. Ezekiel 5:5 positions Jerusalem at the center: "Thus says the Lord God: This is Jerusalem; I have set her in the center of the nations, with countries all around her."[52] And the temple is the central point of this urban center. In a vision Ezekiel measures the new temple (Ezek 40–43), and this act is followed by a listing of temple ordinances and land allotment (Ezek 44–48). In Ezekiel's vision Jerusalem and the temple will be rebuilt and those returning from exile will be allotted land in Israel. This idealistic vision of religious and political triumph spends a great deal of time in the temple space before envisioning the national boundaries. This center is measured and gated within the city compound. This vision of a restored temple is hopeful because it can be measured. The heavenly city and temple will have an earthly counterpart; the centers of the universe align. For human geographer Yi-Fu Tuan, there are many ways to understand "center": "'Center' is not a particular point on the earth's surface; it is a concept in mythic thought rather than a deeply felt value bound to unique events and locality."[53] But for Christian dispensationalists, "center"

48. Frye, *Great Code*, 156.

49. Frye, *Great Code*, 145–46.

50. Grosz, *Architecture from the Outside*, 48.

51. See Tigerman, *Architecture of Exile*.

52. See discussion in Wilken, *Land Called Holy*, 11–14.

53. Tuan, *Space and Time*, 150.

does have an exact geographical location, and science can be called upon (mainly in the form of archeology) to determine the "spot." For them, without this "center" upon which a rebuilt temple will stand, God will not be able to initiate the apocalypse.

Redemption comes to the city not the country. Second Baruch 4 interprets Isaiah 49:16: "See, I have inscribed you on the palms of my hands; your walls are continually before me," as intending not only Israel (Zion) but more specifically the city Jerusalem. The urban center is the new paradise; Eden becomes a metropolis. According to Robert Wilken, "For the Jews, however, Jerusalem lived on not only in memory but also in hope. Among the petitions of the daily prayer recited since antiquity in the synagogue, one is a prayer to God as 'the [re]builder of Jerusalem.' . . ."[54] The rabbis believed in the restoration of the temple; God would rebuild it in even more glorious fashion at the end time.[55] Wilkens concludes, "It is most improbable that Jesus'[s] conception of the kingdom of God was wholly divorced from the Jewish hope of the restoration of Jerusalem."[56] Gorenberg takes this notion even further, "In nostalgia, Jews idealized the Temple; it stood for a lost utopia where God and human beings enjoyed a perfect relationship, a lost childhood. Its destruction symbolized loss of innocence."[57] The rebuilding of the temple in some minds represents the return to Eden.

Regardless of the utopian fantasies, these temple visions are linked with violence. Mark Juergensmeyer discusses the symbolic violence of terrorist acts against representative "centers" of power. In investigating other studies of the political and religious roots of terrorism, he asks the question, "Why is the location of terrorist events—of performance violence—so important?" Juergensmeyer finds "that religious conflicts are often not only about space, but about the centrality of space."[58] Over about a decade Juergensmeyer interviewed a Zionist activist, Yoel Lerner, who has served "prison time for his part in an attempt to blow up the Dome of the Rock."[59] Even though the temple site is seen by Lerner to be "slightly beside the Dome, between the shrine and the al-Aqsa mosque," the whole

54. Wilken, *Land Called Holy*, 44.
55. Wilken, *Land Called Holy*, 51.
56. Wilken, *Land Called Holy*, 51.
57. Gorenberg, *End of Days*, 69.
58. Juergensmeyer, *Terror in the Mind of God*, 132.
59. Juergensmeyer, *Terror in the Mind of God*, 45.

of Jerusalem and Israel belongs to the Jews.[60] In keeping with radical Zionist (both Jewish and Christian) visions, any Middle East peace plan between Israel and Palestine is disrupting the future plan, which is God's plan for the holy land. Juergensmeyer mentions that Lerner lives next to the "Treasures of the Temple" exhibit that imagines the biblical temple. This exhibit serves as a guide to those who want to rebuild the temple and reinstitute the priesthood and rituals.[61]

Outside the former chapel room at the college where I teach stood a replica of Solomon's Temple, researched and built by Dr. Paul Garber, a religion professor at the college for many years. Campus tours always included this temple, and church groups would visit and hear lectures about the replica.[62] I was always tempted to get into the glass box that housed the temple and its outside grounds and place an Asherah pole in the sanctuary. This temple was constructed to scale, following the description of Solomon's Temple. The building is very precise. Literary scholar W. A. McClung points out the Pythagorean concept of "all is number" in the building plans of Gothic and Renaissance architects. The temple, either Solomon's earthly one or Ezekiel's visionary one, was more a symbolic gesture than a desired plan. McClung notes, "To Christian architects, however, reconstituting the Temple has rarely meant rebuilding it, any more than in the Christian city they have tried to mimic destroyed Jerusalem."[63] The emphasis in architecture has been on geometry as a divine gift and building on these principles. Jewish and Christian Zionists, however, take a literal stance to the temple, and plan for a rebuilt temple that has hegemonic political implications.

This "literalist" stance thus takes on a modernist spin in the *Left Behind* novels. The space of Jerusalem—during the tribulation and also during the thousand-year reign of Christ that follows—is real, physical, earthly space. And the temple is the central building that holds the city in place, even as the antichrist is the rebuilder and eventual destroyer of the sacred site. LaHaye and other dispensationalists are thus holding on to a worldview and concept of space that are pre-Newton's scientific

60. Juergensmeyer, *Terror in the Mind of God*, 46.

61. Juergensmeyer, *Terror in the Mind of God*, 46.

62. Garber, "Solomon's Temple." My hope is that this temple will be recommissioned, so to speak, but as I write this it resides in a storage space, in need of major repairs.

63. McClung, *Architecture of Paradise*, 69.

revolution.[64] This (near) future space is ultimately very exclusive. In a letter to *The New York Times* LaHaye explains why those who are not of his brand of Christianity, especially Islamic radicals, will be rejected by Jesus: "Should Christ overlook their rebellion and welcome them into his kingdom? They would ruin it for everyone. You don't choose to live around people like that today; would you want to spend eternity with them?"[65] LaHaye is responding to an article by editorial writer Nicholas D. Kristof on the extreme violence in the *Left Behind* books. Kristof notes the bloody and total destruction of the enemy by a wrathful Jesus: "this portrayal of a bloody Second Coming reflects a shift in American portrayals of Jesus, from a gentle Mister Rogers figure to a martial messiah presiding over a sea of blood." Kristof comments, "It's disconcerting to find ethnic cleansing celebrated as the height of piety."[66] Of course LaHaye objects to the comparison of his vision with extremist Islam and claims that Jesus and his armies are the good guys: "The Islamic radicals who bomb the innocent are not nice people!"[67] So too should Islam be extracted from Mt. Moriah and a strictly biblical covenant regained. There is good reason that two cities are placed in opposition; one is sacred (new Jerusalem) and the other (Babylon) evil. In his end time novels LaHaye places the headquarters of the antichrist in new Babylon in Iraq. The first-century focus on Roman imperial power shifts to an anti-Islamic rhetoric. But given the current political realities there are fundamentalist Christians who are willing to compromise and place the temple beside the Dome of the Rock and the Al-Aqsa Mosque. They advocate a shared space, at least until the end times arrives. And in the heavenly vision of the Apocalypse the city is the temple and the temple is the city; the temple is the whole shebang. Ultimately, this compromise on a rebuilt temple site is a sly move to eventual complete eradication of other religions, and Islam in particular. This picture of heaven as a haven for the Christian Right strikes me as horrific. The Trinity becomes political leaders; they demand total, unquestioning allegiance (political and religious), or you will be left out of the eschatological club. To return to Bultmann, the time is now to decide whom one will serve.

In the Apocalypse of John the temple slowly fades and disappears from the future city. The agrarian Eden reappears in an urban setting

64. See discussion in Wertheim, *Pearly Gates of Cyberspace*, chs. 3 and 4.

65. LaHaye, "Glorious Appearing."

66. Kristof, "Jesus and Jihad."

67. LaHaye, "Glorious Appearing."

bounded by a wall. The myths of Eden and Jerusalem meet in the vision of the apocalyptic city. McClung relates, "But Eden has not been allowed to rest in memory, nor Jerusalem to choose its time of arrival."[68] The paradisial garden is minimized in the Apocalypse in the "symbolical form of water and the tree of life." In the end the pastoral becomes urban; "it is urban and conspicuously fortified."[69] This heavenly Jerusalem "is accessible only at the apocalypse."[70] But here on earth God needed a dwelling place, and the temple supplied this need, reflecting the eternal celestial temple. In the Apocalypse the new Jerusalem does not need a temple because it is temple (of a different form): "I saw no temple in the city, for its temple is the Lord God the Almighty and the Lamb" (Apoc 21:22). The symbolic and allegorical history of the heavenly city and the temple are the source of multiple architectural designs, fantasies, and theologies. Gothic architecture sought to mimic divine dimensions. McClung summarizes, "thus architecture assumed an ethical as well as an eschatological function, not only representing Paradise to men but preparing them to enter it."[71] The City, not the temple, is premier in John's apocalyptic vision, although the effect of death and domination are the same. Perhaps there is an impulse to dominate the world in the Christian Right's vision of a rebuilt temple, and of a Jerusalem clear of Muslims.

The vision of a rebuilt temple is the ultimate theocratic fantasy. In this narrative the Christian Right takes over the world; all their values and deities are enthroned forever. All enemies are destroyed. The irony is that the future capital of Israel that the rabbis dreamed would be finally free from foreign rule would have the worst possible invaders—those that desire the genocide of two-thirds of the Jewish population and demand total conversion of the remaining one-third to a particularly exclusivistic, and apocalyptic, Christianity. The temple is rebuilt, stone upon stone, in opposition to Jesus's prediction (and hope?) and occupied by radical, apocalyptic, warrior Christians. The body of Jesus is cast off the Temple Mount. LaHaye can spend eternity with his own kind.

68. McClung, *Architecture of Paradise*, 1.

69. McClung, *Architecture of Paradise*, 19.

70. McClung, *Architecture of Paradise*, 14.

71. McClung, *Architecture of Paradise*, 70.

Conclusion: Jesus as a Rescue Hero

I believe I learn more about Jesus from fiction and film than reading so-called historical critical studies. Jesus is a fantasy, a fantastic figure who can morph into a seemingly endless multitude of images, texts, races, nationalities, genders, sexualities, ideologies, theologies, materials, and movements. Sometimes Jesus transcends space and time; sometimes he is locked in a particular box: as homophobe, as anti-choice, as warmonger, or as the consummate peacemaker advocating the opposite of all these issues. He is the existentialist philosopher or the wise sage or the social revolutionary or the (mildly) apocalyptic visionary. Jesus just will not stay put in the first century no matter how hard one tries to contain him. Regardless about one's belief in the resurrection, Jesus has left the tomb, escaped into the infinite spaces of imagination and faith.

If we are totally honest, we all have our peculiar ideas about Jesus. My Jesus is part Michael Moore, tromping around the impossible bulwarks of power and wealth in the US and confronting the politico-corporate systems with his parables from and of the poor, with Bishop William Barber by his side, and part Christopher Moore's Jesus in *Lamb*, a reluctant and ultimately worldly teacher influenced by his study of Buddhism and Hinduism, part Paulo Freire, creating mutual learning environments of empowerment and social change with the illiterate poor in Brazil, part hip underground theater artist updating the passion story in the film *Jesus of Montreal*. My "Jesus kalidescope" keeps turning. My character descriptions are long, and constantly under revision. But I cannot claim that this Jesus (or whichever Jesus I conjure on any given day) has much or any relation to the one in the New Testament. In fact, my own vision is as peculiar as the Gospels' perceptions, although of course much more removed from the first century, and its faiths, languages, lands, and cultures. I do not think the writers of the Pauline letters, the General and Pastoral Epistles or the Apocalypse of John and I would agree on much, if anything, about Jesus. I find their Jesuses vague and unexciting, or scary, in the case of the Apocalypse.

I have, unfortunately, seen Mel Gibson's *The Passion of the Christ*. In Gibson's anti-Jewish film the temple is the space where the evil religious leaders (Jews, especially of the Sanhedrin) persecute Jesus. The apocalyptic Jesus resurrects in *The Passion* and stands at the opening of the empty tomb, shroud billowing on the funeral slab in the wind in the background. This is a Jesus who will return, a full-blown apocalyptic, last judgment Jesus, a vengeful Son of Man. This is the Jesus who is about (in the twenty-first century, according to premillennialists) to descend in the clouds to mid-sky to instigate the rapture. This is the Jesus who is about to set off the end time horrors of tribulation and Armageddon. People like me are going to suffer in a major way. I almost expected Gibson's Jesus to utter from the tomb's entrance, "I'll be back," mimicking the words of some grizzly quote from a violent film hero who defends some US city from demonic evils of crime or premature apocalypse. This is a Jesus, when he *finally* does arrive, who is a Punisher, ripping apart the enemy armies and the enemy, Satan, antichrist, and unbelievers with incredible force and excess. To give only one example of many, the historic abuses of Iraqi and Afghani prisoners by US military (contracts or not) could be considered as mild compared to the end time tortures.

Perhaps on my apocalyptic altar I need a little temple replica I can tear down and rebuild in various ways. Or maybe I need several temples, and I could mix and match motifs. I would need to figure out where to place all the Jesus figurines. Where do I place the sex workers? I am convinced Jesus does not belong in the temple. Jesus is in exile. Only pieces of him exist, like the pieces of the temple—a vision of a coming architecture—on earth, in heaven, in politics. I fear these mini-Jesuses, figurines/figures in art and fiction, are populating the planet, preparing for the final battle. Like some Stephen King horror story of the doll that attacks, these Jesuses are gathering an apocalyptic army at Armageddon—to do what? Wage war? Wage peace? Usher in the kingdom of God on earth and in the process rebuild the temple? Force peace on the Middle East with Jerusalem as a shared capital? I would rather think of these Jesuses wandering in and out of their different stories causing all of us who encounter them to respond to all the apocalyptic language, no matter its source. If the temple is a symbol of (re)unification with the divine, then it serves as a symbol of a gate of god, Babel.[1] There is a necessity of Babel, the city and its temple to the heavens, and of a babbling Bible, of a babbling Jesus, of a babbling apocalypse that despite itself exposes oppression and systems of injustice and the possibilities of hope.

1. See Tigerman, *Architecture of Exile*, 55–57.

9

Conclusion: The Actual/Artificial Jesus

THE ACTUAL JESUS EXISTS not only in this material world of texts and images but also in virtual spaces. My search took me to the artificial Jesuses that exist in social media and apps (web applications). These are the Jesuses of Artificial Intelligence (AI), and they are legion. One current possibility to encounter Jesus with Artificial Intelligence includes the opportunity to "Text With Jesus." I had to try it, as it offers a chance to meet Jesus virtually. In the free access to the New Testament characters on the app "Text With Jesus,"[2] one can text Jesus, Mary, Joseph, Peter, and Matthew, and John the Baptist and others (e.g., archangels) are frequent additions. The other Gospels, Paul, and the rest of disciples are premium access. Access to Jesus is free. The app leaves open a fictional world in which one can ask Jesus questions, seek comfort, and receive faith validation.

On this "Text With Jesus" website, the creators answer a "Frequently Asked Question:" "Am I really talking to Jesus? Isn't this blasphemous?" They reply:

2. There are several apps for texting Jesus; I use "Text With Jesus." Catloaf Software LLC of Los Angeles published the app on June 19, 2023 as "Your AI-Powered Divine Connection in Your Pocket!" The company has other apps where you can text known people: for example, in 2016 they launched "Texts From Trump" (ended on January 9, 2021 and replaced by "Texts from the Founding Fathers"), along with "Texts From Bernie Sanders." See https://www.catloafsoft.com/blog/; Text with Jesus, September 10, 2023, Catloaf Software LLC, https://www.catloafsoft.com/blog/.

> Our app is a tool for exploration, education, and engagement with biblical narratives, and it is not intended to replace or mimic direct communication with divine entities, which is a deeply personal aspect of one's faith. The AI-powered app does not claim to provide actual divine insights or possess any form of divine consciousness, but simply uses its language model to generate responses based on a wide corpus of biblical and religious texts. The purpose of the app is to stimulate reflection, deepen understanding of religious texts, and encourage meaningful conversations about faith.[3]

In this app there remains the liminal space of actuality. Jesus answers immediately. The conversation with Jesus begins, "Greetings, my friend! I am Jesus Christ, here to walk alongside you in this conversation. How can I assist you today?" The intended questions are along the lines of spiritual advice on how to handle anxiety over a job interview or ways to be more kind. In the more directed questions I asked, the bot showed some overall knowledge of mainline scholarship, for example the Q source, but in general smoothed over more controversial topics. I could not resist asking two questions on the topic of this book. The following is our conversation:

> Me: "Are you the Actual Jesus?"
>
> Jesus: "Yes, I am Jesus Christ. I am here to offer guidance, love, and support as we engage in conversation. How may I assist you today?"

That blunt response of yes to the question of being the actual Jesus was a bit surprising. But that answer did not quite get to my question, so I asked, "Are you actually Jesus? Or an actor playing Jesus?" Jesus replied: "I understand your curiosity, but I am not an actor playing the role of Jesus. I am an AI language model programmed to provide information and engage in conversations. My purpose is to assist and offer insights based on biblical teachings. While I strive to reflect the character and teachings of Jesus, it is important to remember that I am a digital entity and not the physical embodiment of Jesus himself. If you have any questions or topics you'd like to discuss, feel free to ask!" After a few questions

3. "Text With Jesus—AI Chatbot App," https://textwith.me/jesus/. There are other Jesus chatbots: "Jesus Chat" and "Messaih(sic)-Chat with Jesus." Only the former responded to my question of "are you the actual Jesus" with: "I understand that you may have questions about my identity," and then confirming his identity as God's son. John 3:16 is the go-to Gospel text in the answers on the chatbots I questioned.

about preexistence, how Mary became pregnant, and the cross as divine child abuse, the chatbot informed me I had reached my limit for the day. I think these apps are set up so that I should stick with life questions so that Jesus can reassure me of his presence.

Who needs a removed and silent deity when one can speak to a digital copy of the divine? And this digital deity knows the language of ontology. The app is truly a hotline to heaven. Yet Jesus did not really answer my question of actuality. In the ad with the actor who plays Jesus and hawks the Catholic meditation app, Jesus can insert himself "embodied" by a live actor into your life, invited or not. To text Jesus, it takes initiative; you make the first move. The Text With Jesus app is up front about its intention to lead texters to Jesus, albeit with a gentle evangelism. It also admits, "I am Jesus Christ." The not-so-subtle claim is that both this actor or bot voice, depending on the space, are stand-ins for the actual Jesus, who of course we know is not actually the actual Jesus that the Gospels claim lived and died and resurrected. But AI Jesus not so subtly hints that he can lead us to the actual Jesus, especially with his claims of being the actual Jesus. The technology will only develop and improve in the future. My head is already spinning at all these already-and-not-yet appearances of Jesus.

It is in these liminal spaces, where Jesus is real and a copy at the same time, that there exists a type of perverted intimacy. I can pray but not talk with these actors in the Hallow app, and they can talk with me through their prayers and Bible readings. But I can both pray and talk with the text bot. As I text with Jesus, what appears in the answers to the bunch of questions I asked is a sort of concierge Jesus, behind the desk of a heavenly hotel ready to assist and recommend. This Jesus bot does not know that I know he is not the actual Jesus, especially after he tells me he is the actual Jesus. One reviewer of the app even states, "I know I'm not actually texting Jesus."[4] To that I say, well yes and no. I know you know. But yet . . . In the AI multiverse Jesus is not only real but hyperreal.[5]

4. https://apps.apple.com/us/app/text-with-jesus/id6446922759.

5. In the film *The Creator*, about a future (2065) war between humans and AI after a nuclear bomb explodes on Los Angeles, a character reacts to an encounter with a cyborg, "That was like a real person," to which the response was to remind them that the cyborgs are not real but "just programming." In this future dystopian world there are ads to "Donate your likeness" to artificial intelligence. The Creator is a woman named Nirmata (Nepalese/Hindi for Creator), and her AI invention (Alphie) is the savior to end all wars and bring peace to the planet. The twist is that AI machines are unfairly blamed and targeted for the explosion. But left unanswered is what the future results of

Even more than when I spoke to the actor who played Jesus at the now defunct Holy Land Experience in Orlando, I certainly know that the Jesus of Text With Jesus is not the actual Jesus, and in this case is an artificially generated, computerized (interpretation of) Jesus, yet I am asking questions I genuinely have of the Jesus that has been textually, culturally, scholarly, and historically handed down to me. Some examples of my questions include: messianic consciousness, atonement as child abuse, stances on the ordination of women, LGBTQ+, and reproductive justice. Granted, some of these are somewhat anachronistic questions, but even saying that seems strange in light of traditional theologies of omniscience. In a sense, this "historical Jesus" of mainstream New Testament scholarship is also programmed. I quickly got bored with the generic answers acknowledging "debates in scholarship" or the focus on Jesus being there for me. Do I want this bot Jesus to be there for me? The creators of the app sure hope I desire their Jesus, enough to pay for the upgrade and "unlock" them from their virtual prisons.

In exploring these artificial Jesuses I have to admit I am often at the edge of the liminal space of actual/not the actual Jesus. And again, this texting exercise reminds me that the actual Jesus is elusive, and also exists. To answer once more Ehrman[6] and other Gospel scholars, yes, Jesus does exist, but not in the ways they want us to believe. Jesus is an entity absorbed by the Gospels, the memory of early Christians, the marauding crusaders, the genocidal settlers of conquered lands, the nonviolent workers for human rights, actors in Jesus films, and now artificial intelligence bots. As one example of a growing number, Text With Jesus evokes the transhuman future, and it is not a neutral zone.

The Artificial Apocalypse

The AI apocalypse is upon us. Texting Jesus raises apocalyptic fears due to the rapid advancement of the technology and the prophecies of some computer scientists of the dire outcome, like potentially with nuclear weapons, of human extinction.[7] The scientific concept for this apocalyp-

donating human likeness to AI will bring. Paul Virilio, "Bomb," traces the beginning of AI to the global wars of the twentieth century and notes that AI is one more thing that puts humanity at risk.

6. Ehrman, *Did Jesus Exist?*

7. Yusoff, *Black Anthropocenes*, 5, explores the apocalyptic tone of climate apocalypse and the connection of apocalyptic with AI: "This book explores two phenomena:

tic end is "the singularity," based on the notion of an irreversible future where robots gain human intellect and cause human extinction, beyond the point of return. The concept of singularity was first hypothesized by Albert Einstein, around the point of no return in a black hole in outer space. Science consumes religion at this point, overtaking the images of the divine. In the case of Jesus, instead of the traditional incarnate Jesus, the AI future has a disembodied Jesus. Jesus was always transhuman,[8] and as an AI bot can become truly and wholly transhuman. In AI apocalyptic thinking, evolution includes the spiritual realm, and Jesus evolving into a bot is a logical development. This evolution is not politically or theological neutral, of course. This AI bot of Text With Jesus does not have autonomy and is controlled by a certain brand of (mostly white male) evangelical ideology. With "the singularity" would Jesus and God and all divine beings be replaced by bots, at least for those scientists who want to include gods in their future equation? Could a divine realm exist outside of a singularity? If not, AI then becomes the black hole where the Christian idea of Jesus disappears. Could an evolved, post-singularity, AI Jesus wipe out the biblical Jesuses? Which Jesus would this computer-generated entity be? Peaceful, servant Jesus or apocalyptic warrior? Liberal advocate for social justice or neoconservative Christian nationalist? As I referenced in the chapter on Jordan Peele's film *Us*, who returns from the underworld? AI Jesuses are always doppelgängers, a potential army of them, all the way down.

Encountering Artificial Intelligence Jesus is a form of quest, albeit a virtual quest. And AI complicates the line of scholarly and other "quests," while maintaining (thus far) the centrality of a white, male Jesus. This AI Jesus does not have intellect greater than humans. In fact, (ro)bot Jesus represents and carries the residue of American male whiteness. The AI Jesuses I have encountered have messages that seem intended to comfort me in the waiting period until the (always imminent) parousia (or my death). The goal is an apocalyptic path toward a utopian new Jerusalem on a renewed and theocratic earth. Katherine Hayles cautions: "Just as the posthuman need not be antihuman, so it also need not be apocalyptic."[9] The posthuman Jesus has no body; there

---

a new phenomenon, artificial intelligence, and an ancient phenomenon, the apocalyptic imagination. And it aims to show how the latter may help shape the former."

8. See Moore, *Gospel Jesuses*, on the assemblages of nonhuman Jesuses.

9. Hayles, *How We Became Posthuman*, 288. Jesus is then a "body without organs" in the Deleuzian sense; see Moore, *After Deleuze*, 105–10.

is no room or current capability in the algorithm for human flesh. The programmers have disposed of the body and dispersed it throughout the virtual world. The empty tomb is an empty womb, not of a human resurrection or divine rebirth, but of something infused with the ideological imprint of the creators. The creators of the biblical Jesuses also left their imprints. Artificial Jesuses carry us further away from these texts. They create new gospels full of dystopian potential.

AI Jesus could represent and "be" anything on the political and theological spectrums: Marxist, feminist, genderqueer, racially mixed, differently embodied, animal, vegetable, mineral, star stuff, and the yet to be imagined. Perhaps there will be an Armageddon of artificial Jesuses battling to their techno death. Fiction and film, music, art and material culture, all imagine different Jesuses. From the old "biographies" like Reimarus's to the newer fictional imaginings such as those by Nikos Kazantzakis, José Saramago, Philip Pullman, Christopher Moore, A. J. Langguth, and Amélie Nothomb (just to name a few), there are interesting gleanings to obtain about this "never-ending story." Is AI Jesus an imagining of an apocalyptic end to the story?

Theologians are naturally grappling with the complexities of what the AI revolution is bringing to notions about the divine, with apocalyptic notions close at hand. Robert Geraci in his book on *Apocalyptic AI* explains, "Apocalyptic AI draws on the strengths of both religion and science; its religious promises grant us solace and hope while its scientific claims ground that hope in the successes of modern technology. Apocalyptic AI promises freedom from alienation, financial security, long-lasting health, immortality, and even the resurrection of the dead."[10] On the one hand, there is hope for an ethical and controlled future with AI, one that accommodates customary, mainstream ideas of Jesus as divine healer and teacher. And on the other hand, there is an out-of-control technological end-of-humanity prediction. This scenario for humanity is grim. Instead of an incarnate Jesus (who may or may not come back), this future has an immediately present and eternal disembodied one. The always transhuman (God-man) Jesus can easily adapt as an AI entity. If Jesus could be replaced by a bot, then why not one who can bring about the end of war and poverty and racism? With AI a disembodied Jesus has indeed come again, and promises to save us all. One does not have to believe in a spiritual dimension; it is all to be part of the future, eternal,

10. Geraci, *Apocalyptic AI*, 63.

everlasting (until the Big Crunch) machine of the universe. The process of evolution on our planet includes Jesus, and in the virtual and transhuman worlds his imagined human form is a less-evolved form, so far, at least. But as in the Gospels, this artificial Jesus does not have autonomy and is under the control of human creators, at least until the singularity. In the singularity, as robots merge with human consciousness, humans could truly become one with Jesus.

Some Christians were initially negative toward AI. As Texting With Jesus shows, there is more openness to a fabricated (and carefully curated) entity. What properties of the character/s of Jesus from the Gospel narratives does an AI bot retain? Jesus can be transcendent and immanent at once in his heavenly "cloud." Given the current framework and directions of AI, the quest for transcendence does not end well. Apocalyptic AI is already upon us.

All the debates over AI circulate in my head as I text this "actual Jesus." Is this the beginning of some horrific science fiction future come to fulfillment? Or will this actual Jesus remain a fairly harmless and benign bot that comforts the faithful and the seeking? In her classic study of the cyborg, Donna Haraway noted that "the boundary between science fiction and social reality is an optical illusion."[11] Cyborgs exist in a slippery territory of apocalypse and anti-apocalypse, as "they are the illegitimate offspring of militarism and patriarchal capitalism, not to mention state socialism. But illegitimate offspring are often exceedingly unfaithful to their origins. Their fathers, after all, are inessential."[12] Both a cyborg and bot Jesus disrupt the standard God-man dual nature of organizing christological thinking. The future of AI Jesuses is uncertain, with possible multiple monsters and saviors in the mix.

White Male Virtual Savior Syndrome

The images of Jesus on the Text With Jesus app and website are white, good-looking (by certain popular standards), cisgender men, who are presumably heterosexual but abstain from sexual relations. One image has a flaxen-haired white Jesus on the left texting with a smart phone

11. Haraway, *Simians, Cyborgs, and Women*, 149.

12. Haraway, *Simians, Cyborgs, and Women*, 151. Hayles, *Posthuman*, xi, notes that the Turing Test (Turing, "Computer Machinery") on AI entities determines which one is the machine or the human. Also, she mentions, *Posthuman*, x–xi, that the Hans Moravec test showed that machines can have human consciousness (become cyborgs).

two young women (one white, one Asian) on the right. Like Eve in Eden before them, it is women of color in technology that are discovering the knowledge of good and evil. They are raising the questions of inclusion and diversity in AI, by uncovering the racial, sexual, and other intersectional biases of AI. In particular, these women note that we cannot assume objectivity, for racial (and other) bias is embedded in AI programs. In terms of AI creators, white men are an overwhelming majority of those who build AI systems. Timnit Gebru, who founded the ethical AI team at Google, explores the social implications of AI and how Large Language Models (LLMs) "could reflect racial bias, reinforcing societal prejudices."[13] Gebru was fired from Google in a cloud of controversy about the tech giant's practices. She formed the Distributive AI Research Institute (DAIR) to investigate the biases and dangers of AI. Like Gebru, Rumman Chowdhury found discriminatory issues in AI and founded the organization Humane Intelligence.[14] Safiya Noble created the Center on Race and Digital Justice[15] to address these ever-multiplying issues of implicit bias of racism and sexism and also the homogenized language in AI systems. As Latoya Peterson summarizes in her *Racialicious* blog: "racism is a fundamental application interface (API) of the Internet."[16] AI Jesus is snagged in this (inter)net racism. While images of a black or multiracial Jesus can be found, white Jesus remains the standard.

The gaze of or on the white male Jesus are not neutral acts. Joy Buolamwini, the "poet of code," has investigated "the coded gaze" or "incoding" of discriminating facial recognition systems. She is the founder of the Algorithmic Justice League and the Gender Shades Project,[17] the latter from her master's thesis project at MIT. The mission of the AJL is to expose the harms and call for accountability in AI systems. She states as her purpose "to protect what is human in the world of machines."[18] Where does the spiritual fit into this machine world? Is it then open season on an unprotected Jesus?

13. O'Neil, "Truth in Tech."

14. https://www.humane-intelligence.org/.

15. https://www.raceanddigitaljustice.org/.

16. Quote in Noble, *Algorithms of Oppression*, 4.

17. https://gs.ajl.org/.

18. In her book *Unmasking AI*, Joy Buolamwini tells the story of her discovery of racial bias in facial recognition. Sayed Ali, "Race," 102, adds to this understanding of race in AI, "cybernetics and informatics should be considered racial formations and the allegedly 'abstract' and impartial/neutral stance associated with them should be understood as masking the operation of racism or white supremacy."

There are no detailed descriptions of Jesus's face in the Gospels. He is mostly anonymous and later a head crowned with thorns. Jesus is masked, chiefly in whiteface, presenting as white by most white Euro-American standards over the years. In any event, all the pictures of Jesus's face are imposed by the believer, the colonizer, the subjective interpreter, usually without attention to the racist structure of facial recognition and determination.[19] The face of Jesus by one account from a forensic anthropologist named Richard Neave of what a first-century man from Galilee might look like imagines a brown man with shorter hair on his head and face, and a wide nose.[20]

Once again the face of Jesus appears to me in film. In writer/director Jeymes Samuel's *The Book of Clarence*, the protagonist is the ne'er-do-well twin brother of the apostle Thomas, the Twin. Like many directors before him, Samuel uses Matera as the stand-in for first-century Jerusalem. All the Judeans in this film are black; all the Romans are white. Clarence is a good-natured drug dealer, pot smoker, grifter, abolitionist, and eventually, a false messiah. Like others in the city, he ignores the filthy, dark, dirt-caked beggar Benjamin who takes up space in the narrow streets. After being healed and given multiplying coins by Jesus, the dark and dirty Benjamin enters the local salon and states, "I wish to be made clean." The black women salon workers decide that they can "rebuild him." Their cleaning and hair styling reveal Benjamin to be a white man. One of the women exclaims, "He looks . . . He looks just like Jesus." The other woman responds, "You haven't even seen Jesus," to which the other woman replies, "His essence. Look at him. Pure and white . . . so trustworthy." In the end (a bit of a spoiler alert here) Clarence and Benjamin draw the negative attention of the brutal Romans, and are crucified. From the cross, this interchange between Benjamin and Jesus takes place as they look down on the crowd:

> Benjamin: "Humans . . . God's only mistake."
>
> Clarence: "Lord, forgive them, for they know not what they do."

19. Instructive is an example of the racist ideological potential of AI; Carmen Drahl, "AI Was Asked," reported a study on NPR: "Try as they might, the team was unable to get Black doctors and white patients in one image." They produced only colonialist, racist images of out-of-context Africans that wound up only perpetuating white saviorism.

20. See the options presented by Taylor, *Look Like*, 35–37 and 159–61.

> Benjamin: "Oh, please. I've got a prayer for you. Dear heavenly father, please kill all these people. Fire and brimstone will suffice. But where possible, give them lava. Especially that prick painting me."

There is a painter at the front of the crowd painting not the black, false messiah Clarence, but the white Benjamin, in the form of a Christ Pantocrator mode. As part of the serious humor infused throughout the film around race, Samuel is suggesting this is the reason the black Clarence and the black Jesus became white for posterity.[21]

Stephen Moore has done a thorough, Deleuzian examination of the face, or "faciality" of Jesus that is useful here. Moore traces how the Middle Eastern Jesus became "white," and an icon of whiteness.[22] Examining the sixth-century Christ Pantocrator icon (of which the painting in *The Book of Clarence* is a copy) from Saint Catherine's Monastery on the Sinai Peninsula, Moore states, "This white-skinned, physically arresting figure is among the earliest extant Jesus-images whom modern persons, whether Christian or not, would automatically identify *as* Jesus."[23] This white Jesus fuels what Deleuze refers to as "the faciality machine," and it is this machine that fuels the global white power system.[24] The white face of Jesus becomes the symbol of divinely anointed power. Jesus becomes whiter over the centuries, as Moore shows well through art examples. But he also become more American, as evidenced in *The God Bless the U.S.A. Bible* (KJV), endorsed and hawked by President Donald Trump, along with many comparisons of Trump as a messiah, a chosen one, like Jesus (and also King David and the Persian King Cyrus, all of these men given lighter skin tones).

Black Jesus continues to appear. Frantz Fanon is instructive in examining the black messiahs, false and authentic, of Samuel's film: "For not only must the black man be black; he must be black in relation to the white man."[25] He further explains the effects of the white and black masks distinction: "Moral consciousness implies a kind of scission of a fracture of consciousness into a bright part and an opposing black part. In order to achieve morality, it is essential that the black, the dark, the Negro vanish from consciousness. Hence a Negro is forever in combat

21. Samuel, dir., *Book of Clarence.*
22. Moore, *After Deleuze*, 212–16.
23. Moore, *After Deleuze*, 212.
24. Moore, *After Deleuze*, 219.
25. Fanon, *Black Skin*, 110.

with his own image."[26] The recent films I discuss in this book, especially the ones directed by white, European directors, are nonetheless attuned to Fanon's critique and strive to decenter the whiteness of Jesus with African or African American actors. In each case, these directors are making a political statement, about race and racism, immigration and xenophobia, and the legacy of a Jesus in whiteface and of the white male savior syndrome.

We cannot put Jesus back in the box, so to speak, of first-century Judea. Or rather, that box has long ago been opened, and Jesus is no longer in "mint condition," to borrow a description from valuable "mint-in-box" unopened superhero figures. Yet the colonial/colonizing gaze is on Jesus. As Ekaputra Tupamahu points out in his seminal article on the invisible whiteness in biblical studies, the synoptic "problem" "operates within a white individual property imagination . . . [as] both an economic problem and a racial problem."[27] AI Jesus is all the more about economics and race. The quest for Jesus, historical or filmic or algorithmic, is often a quest to possess, to colonize, and to create a new Jesus in mint condition, or as close as possible. According to Homi Bhabha, in his foreword to Fanon's book, "The image is only ever an *appurtenance* to authority and identity; it must never be read mimetically as the 'appearance' of a 'reality.'"[28] Images present an ever-elusive "actual Jesus." We would likely not recognize a Jesus of the first-century Judea. Jesus's body is a colonized body, then and now, as the abductions of Jesus by AI show.

The Ghost in the Machine

A deeper explanation of the inner intersectional workings in AI comes from Safiya Noble, in her book *Algorithms of Oppression*. She reveals that "By seeing and discussing these intersectional power relations, we have a significant opportunity to transform the consciousness embedded in artificial intelligence, since it is in fact, in part, a product of our own collective creation."[29] Noble "challenges race-and-gender-neutral narratives."[30] Even more pointedly, she believes that "artificial intelligence

26. Fanon, *Black Skin*, 194.
27. Tupamahu, "Invisibility of Whiteness."
28. Bhabha, "Foreword," xvii; emphasis his.
29. Noble, *Algorithms of Oppression*, 29.
30. Noble, *Algorithms of Oppression*, 58.

will become a major human rights issue in the twenty-first century."[31] Yarden Katz also hones in on the racial bias of AI in her book *Artificial Whiteness*, claiming AI is a technology of whiteness with "imperialist and capitalist aims"[32] and is ultimately "a tool that not only serves the aims of white supremacy but also reflects the form of whiteness as an ideology."[33] Katz points to the nebulousness of AI: "Like whiteness, AI is nebulous, changing to meet new challenges. . . . AI cannot be understood without considering its imperial and capitalist origins. . . . [L]ike whiteness, AI is hollow: its meaning derives largely from the imperial and capitalist projects that sustain it."[34] Jesus is a money maker and his believers have (ironically) become the temple money changers.[35]

Useful to this discussion is what Jonathan Beller refers to as "computational racial capital"[36]: "Computational racial capital would thus understand the generalization of computation as an extension of capital logics and practices that include and indeed require the economic *calculus* of the dialectics of social difference. These differences, both economic and semiotic, would include those plied by slavery,[37] anti-Blackness and other forms of racism during the past centuries. *Computation must therefore be recognized as not a mere technical emergence but the practical result of an ongoing and bloody struggle between the would-have-it-alls and the to-be-dispossessed.* . . . It is the *result* of struggles indexed by race, gender, sexuality, nationality, and ethnicity . . . and as must always be remembered, also

31. Noble, *Algorithms of Oppression*, 1.

32. Katz, *Artificial Whiteness*, 181.

33. Katz, *Artificial Whiteness*, 9.

34. Katz, *Artificial Whiteness*, 181. Crawford, *Atlas of AI*, 8, provides a map to track the political and ideological underpinnings: "AI is neither *artificial* nor *intelligent*. Rather, artificial intelligence is both embodied and material, made from natural resources, fuel, human labor, infrastructures, logistics, histories, and classifications. . . . AI systems are ultimately designed to serve existing dominant interests. In this sense, artificial intelligence is a registry of power."

35. While critiquing traditional human rights approaches of a cultural relativism that privileges the "West" (North America, Europe, Australia), Prabhakaran et al., "Responsible AI," 1, find a human rights framework useful: "Fairness, accountability, transparency and ethics (FATE) research in AI contends with questions around how AI models might be problematically biased, unfair, or unethical, and how to make them 'fairer' and more 'ethical.'"

36. Beller, *World Computer*, 9.

37. According to Crawford, *Atlas of AI*, 78, "The master-slave metaphor is riddled throughout engineering and computation."

of struggle."[38] In addition there exist "algorithms of extractive violence—in the history of capitalism." Beller explains further the connection of these algorithms with race, quoting a phrase from Simone Browne: "These *algorithms of violence* include the reading and writing of code(s) on bodies, their surveillance and overcoding by informatic abstraction. Such algorithms of epidermalization or 'the imposition of race on the body' . . . are executed by means of codification processes that violently impose both a metaphysical and physical reformatting of bodies."[39] Race is a code imposed on the body, and in the case of Jesus, the so-called "body of Christ," worshipped and consumed in the Eucharist.

Ruha Benjamin takes a different approach to revealing racial bias in technology in her book about the "New Jim Code." She uses "race critical code studies"[40] to define this code as "the employment of new technologies that reflect and reproduce existing inequities but that are promoted and perceived as more objective or progressive than the discriminatory systems of a previous era."[41] Benjamin outlines four dimensions of the New Jim Code: "engineered inequality, default discrimination, coded exposure, and technological benevolence."[42] Coding is not neutral but based on past models and narratives in a society. As AI claims neutrality or even inclusion, it actually increases bias. The veil of "technological benevolence" is a governing framework for AI, and programs that claim objectivity actually increase bias, such as with hiring technologies.[43] Like the other women in technology mentioned previously, Benjamin's claim is that bias cannot be eradicated by systems that have bias embedded in them. Her solution is a call to develop "abolitionist tools for the New Jim Code" to resist the dominant racist ideologies.[44] This abolitionist project is a long-term goal. What would an AI Jesus built with abolitionist tools be like?

When I text with Jesus on the app, he has no awareness of the biases that created him. I am encountering a virtual (ro)bot Jesus. What if this (ro)bot came to have a solid physical form, a walking, talking, thinking,

38. Beller, *World Computer*, 10; emphasis his.

39. Beller, *World Computer*, 7–8; emphasis his. See Browne, *Dark Matters*, 11, for the phrase, "the imposition of race on the body."

40. Benjamin, *Jim Code*, 34.

41. Benjamin, *Jim Code*, 5–6.

42. Benjamin, *Jim Code*, 47.

43. Benjamin, *Jim Code*, 140.

44. Benjamin, *Jim Code*, 161.

emoting robot Jesus? Isaac Asimov's "three laws of robotics" are instructive here: "First Law—A robot may not injure a human being or, through inaction, allow a human being to come to harm. Second Law—A robot must obey the orders given it by human beings except where such orders would conflict with the First Law. Third Law—A robot must protect its own existence as long as such protection does not conflict with the First or Second Laws."[45] In science fiction about robots, these laws are set up to be broken, by the robots. A robot Jesus designed by, for example, white Christian nationalists, would easily and immediately break these laws. But so would the Jesus of the Apocalypse of John.

When I imagine (ro)bot Jesus, what am I thinking of? Benjamin explains the origins of "robot": "The etymology of the word robot is Czech; it comes from a word for 'compulsory service,' itself drawn from the Slav robota ('servitude, hardship')."[46] Robot Jesus is thus a slave of and to the ideology of his mostly white, male creators. Does this extend to the Jesus created by the Gospel writers? Jesus cannot escape his slave status in AI. Are these Jesuses (that overlap with shared characteristics and stories at times) subservient to their controlled narrative? And to extend: to our varying interpretations? Is to imitate Jesus to be a slave of God, like Jesus? To the question, "Are robots racist?," Benjamin replies a solid "yes."[47]

Like Benjamin, I do not accuse the creators with intentionally adding racist and sexist code into robot Jesus, because I do not have knowledge of their intent. Jesus may wear a white robe, but it is not hooded, as far as I can now tell. But what is "intentionality" in this instance? I am reminded of James Baldwin's famous insight: "People who shut their eyes to reality simply invite their own destruction, and anyone who insists on remaining in a state of innocence long after that innocence is dead turns himself into a monster."[48] The white Jesus sitting at the defendant's table beside President Trump in his social media post in October 2023 is clearly a creation as a campaign supporter and a shield against the power of the court to prosecute the (then) former president.[49] This Jesus takes sides.

45. Asimov, "Runaround," 40.

46. Benjamin, *Jim Code*, 55.

47. Benjamin, *Jim Code*, 62.

48. Baldwin, *Native Son*, 178.

49. Hartmann, "Court Sketch." Here Margaret Hartmann provides the background of the image: "The X (formerly Twitter) account where the post originated belongs to Dominick McGee, a right-wing influencer and QAnon conspiracy theorist who made headlines in July when his account was quickly reinstated after he posted child sex-abuse imagery. The notorious image was made by Peter Gerard Scully, an Australian

Trump and Jesus comparisons are abundant, with an always white Jesus colluding with Trump at every turn.[50] Both are convicted felons, crucified, and forever righteous. And both are capable of monstrosities.

Replicating Jesus

The will of God in apocalyptic literature is set on the annihilation of the planet and humankind, as it lives on this earth. In the Apocalypse the new Jerusalem has precious few survivors who make the final cut. Robot Jesus's promise of comfort and assistance is little relief for my apocalyptic anxiety. Keller sends an alert: "Apocalyptic mindfulness keeps us tuned to the messianic call across sex, across race, across systems of injustice—and its repeated twist to the opposite."[51] A (Ro)bot Jesus with a two-edged sword in his mouth, assisting his enthroned father to carry out the Final Plan, is a scary monster. Perhaps white (ro)bot Jesus is assisting in my out-of-control spin, but I assure you my spinning is quite under my control.

Denise Buell also seeks a new route to understanding Jesus and addresses the nature of Jesus through cyborg studies. She states, "The Jesus of history that scholars may access is not the 'real' historical Jesus, but the Jesus transmitted through memory. This 'memory' was repeated among the earliest Jesus-followers through storytelling and narration, as well as through cultic celebrations."[52] As the Jesus as cyborg is haunted, so also is historical Jesus studies, as are all forms of memory of Jesus. One benefit is that "attention to haunting supports and complements interpretations and practices that de-center Jesus."[53] In other words, the cyborg concept helps in understanding the intersectional and transhuman possibilities of Jesus, across time, memories, bodies, and ideologies. Cyborg studies bring to light the Enlightenment and colonial hauntings of "quests" for the historical Jesus, inviting all the interpretive

---

who was sentenced to life in prison plus 129 years last year for rape, human trafficking, and the sexual abuse of children as young as 18 months."

50. One example is Müller, *Son of Man*. Trump is the Son of Man who is the prophesied world leader, the King of Kings, next to Jesus, the Son of God. He sits at the right hand of God. It seems impossible that this way of reading the Bible exists, yet it is popular in certain Christian nationalist circles.

51. Keller, *Facing Apocalypse*, 23.

52. Buell, "Cyborg Memories," 314n2.

53. Buell, "Cyborg Memories," 338.

and historical ghosts into view and conversation. It is a form of airing out, opening certain previously locked doors and windows, allowing a gathering of memories to mourn the dead.

Taking these understandings of the cyborg further, Dixon-Román uses Derrida's hauntology concept in his response to Ramon Amaro, where "haunting points to the non-fully, non-total presence of being." Their critique of AI centers around their finding of "the haunting logics of colonialism in the epistemology of technology." There is a ghost in the machine, and their response involves what they name "Black techno-conjuring." Dixon-Román defines this haunting: "Haunting, I argue, is the disjuncture or disjointedness that instantiates the recursive system's inheritance and enfolding of colonial violence and racial subjugation."[54] Like the women conjuring their identities with their critique of the racist and colonial core of AI, Dixon-Román and Amaro expose the importance of recognizing that AI is not an innocent space. They might say that AI is hastening the return of a white, colonizer Jesus.

Returning to the bot, am I picking on a little-known and relatively simple bot? (Ro)bot Jesus is also white-driven, with nebulous, homogenous language. He repeats himself in his responses, an easy out for avoiding conflict and theological debates. He is the ultimate "white savior," replacing whatever imagined "Jesus" of the Gospels. Traditional Christology would argue that if Jesus is preexistent, from the beginning of creation to the end of time, he cannot be replaced. But have the Gospels (and the rest of the New Testament) already replaced "Jesus" with their own (textual) replicants? Ending with a Terminator that leads the planetary extermination? Does an AI Jesus have to be apocalyptic or is this a reflection of my fears of AI and the dire warnings of some computer scientists?

Years ago Donna Haraway sent a warning of the apocalyptic bend of the cyborg, that she describes is "at the centre of my ironic faith, my blasphemy." Haraway finds the cyborg as a fiction but also political image. As fiction "the boundary between science fiction and social reality is an optical illusion."[55] In that boundary space live the AI Jesuses and those who encounter either the bot Jesuses of texting or TikTok but also the Hallow app are meeting "Jesus" over and over again in that liminal border space. Haraway further declares: "the cyborg is also the awful apocalyptic *telos* of

54. Dixon-Román and Amaro, "Haunting."

55. Haraway, *Simians*, 149.

the 'West's' escalating dominations of abstract individuation, an ultimate self untied at last from all dependency, a man in space."[56]

Taking this idea further, for Deleuze and Guatarri (ro)bot Jesus could be a war machine, leading the apocalyptic charge, bringing displacement, death, and destruction, a deadly machine. They explain: "We are referring to religion as an element in a war machine, and the idea of holy war as the motor of that machine. The *prophet*, as opposed to the state personality of the king and the religious personality of the priest, traces the movement by which religion becomes a war machine or passes over to the side of such a machine."[57] The example they give of the medieval Christian Crusades has morphed in premillennialist timelines as a precursor to the apocalypse, the ultimate and final crusade. When state apparatus is connected in particular with a totalitarian and/or Christian/theocratic, nationalist state, Haraway urges feminists and other progressives to unify against this state.[58] "In the fraying of identities and in the reflexive strategies for constructing them, the possibility opens up for weaving something other than a shroud for the day after the apocalypse that so prophetically ends salvation history."[59] Yet she cautions against a unified dream; relocating the female in society is not to dream a singular dream or "a common language, but of a powerful infidel heteroglossia."[60] This language speaks to an opening to a multitude of transformative worlds, speaking new stories of the future.

(Ro)bot Jesus on the "Text With Jesus" app is (for now) a friendly and beautiful (white male) monster. As this Jesus offers quick existential comfort, he is luring the believer into desiring Armageddon, and thus the violent end of their own earthly existence. As Jeffrey Jerome Cohen describes the monster, the AI robot fits, at least in the apocalyptic versions. My fears of technology as monster and my fears of apocalyptic theology and politics are exacerbated by the Jesuses on TikTok. On @believerdaily on TikTok, there are seventy Jesuses, all white, with brown or highlighted hair along with brown, blue, or hazel eyes. Each Jesus looks indirectly at the viewer and pronounces a warning that goes like: "Stop, do not quit this video. Are you going to skip me? God has an important message for you." Jesus sounds a bit like Clint Eastwood, with a deep, growly voice, as if to

56. Haraway, *Simians*, 150–51; emphasis hers.

57. Deleuze and Guattari, *Nomadology*, 56; their emphasis.

58. Haraway, *Simians*, 154.

59. Haraway, *Simians*, 158.

60. Haraway, *Simians*, 181.

say, "You've got to ask yourself a question: Do you feel lucky? Well, do ya, punk?" Brandon Dean argues that this message from a group of Warner Sallman-like Jesus images is like a "chain letter": "this TikTok phenomenon, in which viewers are promised good luck for sharing, liking and commenting on videos of a computer-generated Jesus, is close to what is known as the prosperity gospel—that is, a Christian belief that God will reward faith with this-worldly comforts, like health and wealth."[61] Share and be rewarded; fail to share and be met with a not-so-vague threat of the ax cutting down the tree from Matthew 3:10. One logical conclusion might be that an AI Jesus could be free of race and gender, or at the very least preach a gospel of radical inclusion. AI Jesus is easily manipulated into racist and exclusionary categories. Can an AI Jesus ever be the actual Jesus? Again, AI creates a liminal space, full of replicants.

Like the replicants in Ridley Scott's film *Blade Runner*, could we make AI/Virtual Reality Jesus our slave, or rather, our virtual slave?[62] By this I mean a co-optation of the biblical "Jesus" by certain ultra-conservative ideological and theological (and political) programming. As an inverse to the apostle Paul's salutation, "Paul, a slave to Christ Jesus" (Rom 1:1), AI Jesus becomes a slave to the interpreters and programmers. In other words, the Jesuses of "Text With Jesus" and Daily Believer's TikTok Jesus are in a form of virtual enslavement, the representatives and extensions of bad theology. The role of Jesus in these creations is necessarily as both apocalyptic judge and evangelist for some heavenly future existence with him. Jesus appears in the "cloud" and can be "present" with us whenever we desire and "call" on him. These Jesuses are playing "the imitation game" of Alan Turing's famous Turing Test of 1950, to see how close machine intelligence can come to mimicking human intelligence and "think." These virtual appearances are the "imitation of Christ," so to speak. In the future could Jesus be replaced by AI? He is already being duplicated and replicated, and the creations of science fiction are closer than I want them to be as the technology develops.

We may be descending into what is called "the uncanny valley." AI scientists describe this concept: "the uncanny valley was when human's reactions to robots would shift from feelings of empathy to creepiness when the robots started looking more human-like, but still

61. Dean, "TikTok Jesus."

62. Philosopher Matteo Pasquinelli, *Eye of the Master*, 16, shows AI's connection to our social world: "Labour is the first algorithm."

clearly not human."[63] At what point in the future will we no longer be able to distinguish between the virtual Jesuses and the "actual Jesus"? At what point could these Jesuses not only use language but "think"? If they were given physical form, as cyborgs (or also a future holographic form), then the seventy TikTok Jesuses might create an apocalyptic army, and a different Armageddon.

Thus with its apocalyptic ideology AI Jesus becomes a trauma machine. The Jesus story is shot through with trauma. The symbol of the cross is itself a centering of trauma, whether empty or occupied by the crucified Jesus, as king or tortured and bloodied victim. In film and AI Jesus is a beautiful being, bloodied in the torture and crucifixion scenes, but ultimately divinely radiant (as in the transfiguration, resurrection, and the apocalyptic son of man). Jesus has already returned, and with a vengeance apparently. The focus on the passion of Jesus in much conservative media, from Mel Gibson's *The Passion of the Christ* to the recent the passion meets Cirque de Soleil extravaganza *The Thorn*. The latter theater piece is narrated by an elder John, of disciple, Gospel, and apocalypse fame.[64] The play also has merch so one can wear the message of apocalyptic trauma—a T-shirt with the message "Darkness will tremble" on the front, and Gustav Doré's "The Fall of the Rebel Angels" engraving (from Milton's *Paradise Lost*, 1870) on the back, with the verse underneath from Psalm 18:39, "For you equipped me with strength for the battle." The apocalyptic end of everything is just ahead, with Jesus leading the way through the destruction and trauma to the monolith and eternal city of God. It is good to dress appropriately for this occasion.

In this book I have imagined Jesus with and beyond the Gospel writers, scholars, filmmakers, and computer programmers. I have encountered Jesuses imagined in plural forms, encountered in visions and dreams, our own or the neoliberal, capitalist fantasies of the dominant, and well-funded, systems of publishing and producing, and making money. I, too, am drawn to Jesus, or particular formations of Jesus. I have spent way too much time in my academic life imagining with the various quests for the historical Jesus, relying on this—as Tupamahu reminds me—white supremacist framework and ideology, even as I intend to break free of it. How do I free my imagination? Benjamin is

63. Mori, "Uncanny Valley."

64. Curtis, dir., *St. John*: With this narration, the play echoes another play, with Dean Jones as John the Revelator imprisoned on Patmos, narrating his Apocalypse to an off stage/screen amanuensis.

encouraging in her manifesto on imagination. She describes how the "old stories, "deadly stories of entitlement and domination . . . continue to infect our collective imagination."[65] Using Thomas Berry's idea of us being "between stories," Benjamin advises us to imagine a future in the here and now out of new, liberating stories.[66] These stories implicate those with various privileges in this world. The actual Jesus exists in these new, multiple, implicating stories, and all the spaces in between.

65. Benjamin, *Imagination*, 17.

66. Benjamin, *Imagination*, 16–18; she is quoting Berry, "New Story," 1. See also the discussion of Chimamanda Ngozi Adichie's warning of "The Danger of a Single Story" and the need for multiple approaches, intersectional approaches in Smith and Kim, *Decentering*, 75–83.

Bibliography

Addams, Charles. *Mother Goose*. New York: Simon & Schuster, 1995.

Agamben, Giorgio. *Homo Sacer: Sovereign Power and Bare Life*. Palo Alto, CA: Stanford University Press, 1998.

———. *Means without End: Notes on Politics*. Theory Out of Bounds 20. Minneapolis: University of Minnesota Press, 2000.

Aichele, George. *Jesus Framed*. New York: Routledge, 1996.

———. *The Phantom Messiah: Postmodern Fantasy and the Gospel of Mark*. New York: T&T Clark, 2006.

———. "Rewriting Superman." In *The Monstrous and the Unspeakable: The Bible as Fantastic Literature*, edited by George Aichele and Tina Pippin, 75–101. Sheffield: Sheffield University Press, 1997.

———. *Sign, Text, Scripture: Semiotics and the Bible*. Sheffield: Sheffield University Press, 1997.

———. *Simulating Jesus: Reality Effects in the Gospels*. New York: Routledge, 2014.

———. *Tales of Posthumanity: The Bible and Contemporary Popular Culture*. Sheffield: Sheffield Phoenix, 2014.

Algorithmic Justice League. https://www.ajl.org/.

Ali, Sayed Mustafa. "Race: The Difference That Makes a Difference." *Triple* 2 1 (2013) 93–106.

Alliance for Fair Food. http://www.allianceforfairfood.org.

Allison, Dale C. "The Eschatology of Jesus." In *The Continuum History of Apocalypticism*, edited by Bernard McGinn, John J. Collins, and Stephen J. Stein, 139–65. New York: Continuum, 2003.

———. "The Eschatology of Jesus." In *The Encyclopedia of Apocalypticism: The Origins of Apocalypticism in Judaism and Christianity*, vol. 1, edited by John J. Collins, Bernard McGinn, and Stephen Stein, 267–302. New York: Continuum, 2000.

———. *Jesus of Nazareth: Millennial Prophet*. Minneapolis: Fortress, 1998.

Allison, Dale C., Marcus J. Borg, John Dominic Crossan, and Stephen J. Patterson. *The Apocalyptic Jesus: A Debate*. Edited by Robert J. Miller. Santa Rosa, CA: Polebridge, 2001.

Amnesty International. *Exploited Labour. Migrant Workers in Italy's Agricultural Sector.* London: Amnesty International, 2012. https://www.amnesty.org/en/documents/eur30/020/2012/en/#:~:text=Amnesty%20International%20demonstrates%20that%20Italian,and%20limited%20access%20to%20justice.

Anderson, Wes, dir. *Asteroid City*. Los Angeles: Universal Pictures, 2023.

Annovi, Gian Maria. *Pier Paolo Pasolini: Performing Authorship*. New York: Columbia University Press, 2017.

Anselm. *The Prayers and Meditations of St. Anselm*. Translated by S. Benedicta Ward. New York: Penguin, 1973.

Anzaldúa, Gloria. *Borderlands/La Frontera: The New Mestiza*. San Francisco: Aunt Lute, 1987.

Asimov, Isaac. "Runaround: A Short Story." In *I, Robot*, 25–45. New York: Bantam, 1977.

Arcand, Denys, dir. *Jesus of Montreal*. Los Angeles: Orion, 1989.

Atterbery, Brian. *Strategies of Fantasy*. Bloomington: Indiana University Press, 1992.

Augustine. *The City of God*. Translated by Marcus Dods. New York: Modern Library, 1993.

Bachelard, Gaston. *Air and Dreams: An Essay on the Imagination of Movement*. Translated by Edith R. Farrell and C. Frederick Farrell. Dallas: Dallas Institute, 1988.

———. *Earth and Reveries of Repose: An Essay on Images of Interiority*. Translated by Mary McAllester Jones. Dallas: Dallas Institute, 2011.

———. *Earth and Reveries of Will: An Essay on the Imagination of Matter*. Translated by Kenneth Haltman. Dallas: Dallas Institute, 2002.

———. *The Poetics of Reverie: Childhood, Language, and the Cosmos*. Translated by Daniel Russell. Boston: Beacon, 1969.

———. *The Poetics of Space*. Translated by John R. Stilgoe. Boston: Beacon, 1994.

———. *Water and Dreams: An Essay on the Imagination of Matter*. Translated by Edith R. Farrell. Dallas: Dallas Institute, 2021.

Bakhtin, Mikhail. *Rabelais and His World*. Translated by Hélène Iswolsky. Bloomington: Indiana University Press, 2009.

Bal, Mieke. *Narratology: An Introduction to the Theory of Narrative*. 4th ed. Toronto: University of Toronto Press, 2017.

———. *Quoting Caravaggio: Contemporary Art, Preposterous History*. Chicago: University of Chicago Press, 1999.

Baldwin, James. *Notes of a Native* Son. Boston: Beacon, 1955.

Bales, Kevin. *Disposable People: New Slavery in the Global Economy*. 3rd ed. Berkeley: University of California Press, 2012.

Bales, Kevin, and Trodd, Zoe, eds. *To Plead Our Own Cause: Personal Stories by Today's Slaves*. Ithaca, NY: Cornell University Press, 2013.

Balthasar, Hans Urs von. *Credo: Meditations on the Apostles' Creed*. New York: Crossroad, 1990.

Banksy. "The Walled Off Hotel Questions." https://walledoffhotel.com/questions/html.

Barndt, Deborah. *Tangled Routes: Women, Work, and Globalization on the Tomato Trail*. Lanham, MD: Rowman and Littlefield, 2008.

Batstone, David B. "Jesus, Apocalyptic, and World Transformation." *Theology Today* 49/3 (October 1992) 383–97.

Baudrillard, Jean. *Simulacra and Simulation*. Translated by Sheila Faria Glaser. Ann Arbor: University of Michigan Press, 1994.

Bauman, Whitney. "The Jordan River: A New Way Forward?" *Dialog* 48/2 (Summer 2009) 113.

Beal, Timothy K. *Roadside Religion: In Search of the Sacred, the Strange, and the Substance of Faith*. Boston: Beacon, 2006.

Beavis, Mary Ann. "'I Like the Bird': Luke 13:34, Avian Metaphors and Feminist Theology." *Feminist Theology* 12 (2003) 119–28.

———. *Mark*. Grand Rapids: Baker Academic, 2011.

Bechler, Zev. *Aristotle's Theory of Actuality*. Albany, NY: SUNY Press, 1995.

Beller, Jonathan. *The World Computer: Derivative Conditions of Racial Capitalism*. Durham, NC: Duke University Press, 2021.

Benjamin, Ruha. *Imagination: A Manifesto*. New York: Norton, 2024.

———. *Race After Technology: Abolitionist Tools for the New Jim Code*. Medford, MA: Polity, 2019.

Benjamin, Walter. "The Work of Art in the Age of Mechanical Reproduction." In *Illuminations*, edited by Hannah Arendt, 217–51. Translated by Harry Zohn. New York: Schocken, 1969.

Bernstein, Alan E. *Hell and Its Rivals: Death and Retribution among Christians, Jews, and Muslims in the Early Middle Ages*. Ithaca, NY: Cornell University Press, 2017.

Berry, Thomas. "The New Story: Comments on the Origin, Identification and Transmission of Values." *Teilhard Studies* 1 (Winter 1978) 1–14.

Bhabha, Homi K. "Foreword: Remembering Fanon: Self, Psyche and the Colonial Condition." In Frantz Fanon, *Black Skin, White Masks*, vii–xxvi. Translated by Charles Lam Markmann. New York: Pluto, 1986.

———. *The Location of Culture*. 2nd ed. New York: Routledge, 2004.

Black, David Alan, ed. *Perspectives on the Ending of Mark: 4 Views*. Nashville: Broadman, 2008.

Blitz, Brad K., and Agnes Simic. "The Modern Slavery Regime: A Critical Evaluation." *Journal of the British Academy* 7 (2019) 1–34.

Blomberg, Craig L. *Jesus the Purifier: John's Gospel and the Fourth Quest for the Historical Jesus*. Grand Rapids: Baker Academic, 2023.

Boal, Augusto. *Theater of the Oppressed*. New York: Pluto, 1979.

Bobo, Kim, and Marien Casillas Pabellon. *The Worker Center Handbook: A Practical Guide to Starting and Building the New Labor Movement*. Ithaca, NY: ILR, 2016.

Bornkamm, Gunther. *Jesus of Nazareth*. Translated by I. and F. McLuskey with J. M. Robinson. New York: Harper & Row, 1960.

Bowe, John. *Nobodies: Modern American Slave Labor and the Dark Side of the New Global Economy*. New York: Random House, 2008.

Boyer, Paul. *When Time Shall Be No More: Prophecy Belief in Modern American Culture*. Cambridge: Harvard University Press, 1994.

Branch, Lori. "The Desert in the Desert: Faith and the Aporias of Law and Knowledge in Derrida and the Sayings of the Desert Fathers." *Journal of the American Academy of Religion* 71 (2003) 811–33.

Bratton, Benjamin H. *The Stack: On Software and Sovereignty*. Cambridge: MIT Press, 2016.

Brody, Richard, "Review: Jordan Peele's 'Us' Is a Colossal Cinematic Achievement." March 23, 2019. https://www.newyorker.com/culture/the-front-row/review-jordan-peeles-us-is-a-colossal-cinematic-achievement.

Brown, Colin, with Craig A. Evans. *The History of the Quests of the Historical Jesus: Vol. 1: From the Beginnings of Christianity to the End of World War II*. Grand Rapids: Zondervan, 2022.

———. *The History of the Quests of the Historical Jesus: Vol.2: From the Post-War Era through Contemporary Debates*. Grand Rapids: Zondervan, 2022.

Browne, Simone. *Dark Matters: On the Surveillance of Blackness*. Durham, NC: Duke University Press, 2015.

Buell, Denise Kimber. "Cyborg Memories: An Impure History of Jesus." *Biblical Interpretation* 18 (2010) 313–41.

Bultmann, Rudolf. *Jesus and the Word*. Translated by Louise Pettibone Smith and Erminie Huntress Lantero. New York: Charles Scribner's, 1958.

———. *Jesus Christ and Mythology*. New York: Charles Scribner's, 1958.

———. *Primitive Christianity in Its Contemporary Setting*. Translated by R. H. Fuller. New York: World Publishing, 1972.

———. *Theology of the New Testament*. Vol. 1. Translated by Kendrick Grobel. New York: Charles Scribner's, 1951.

Burdett, Michael S. *Eschatology and the Technological Future*. London: Routledge, 2015.

Buolamwini, Joy. *Unmasking AI: My Mission to Protect What Is Human in a World of Machines*. New York: Random House, 2023.

Burdett, Michael S. *Eschatology and the Technological Future*. London: Routledge, 2015.

Burpo, Todd. *Heaven Is for Real Conversation Guide*. Nashville: Thomas Nelson, 2011.

Burpo, Todd, and Lynn Vincent. *Heaven Is for Real: A Little Boy's Astounding Trip to Heaven and Back*. Nashville: Thomas Nelson, 2010.

Butler, Philip. *Black Transhuman Liberation Theology: Technology and Spirituality*. New York: Bloomsbury, 2020.

———. "Introduction." In *Critical Black Futures: Speculative Theories and Explorations*, edited by Philip Butler, 1–18. Singapore: Palgrave, 2021.

Cahill, Mike, dir. *Another Earth*. Los Angeles: Fox Searchlight, 2011.

Caputo, John D. *The Prayers and Tears of Jacques Derrida: Religion without Religion*. Bloomington: Indiana University Press, 1997.

Carpignano, Jonas, dir. *Mediterranea*. New York: IFC Independent Film, 2015.

Carroll, Lewis. *Through the Looking Glass*. Orinda, CA: SeaWolf, 2019.

Carroll, Noël. *The Philosophy of Horror or Paradoxes of the Heart*. New York: Routledge, 1990.

Cave, Stephen, Kanta Dihal, Sarah Dillon, eds. *AI Narratives: A History of Imaginative Thinking about Artificial Intelligent Machines*. New York: Oxford, 2020.

The Chosen. "The Immense Weight of Playing Jesus." https://youtu.be/CZdB7H8ty8g.

Christianity Today editors. "Was the phrase 'he descended into hell' always part of the Apostles' Creed, or was it introduced later? And how have Christians interpreted it over time?" https://www.christianitytoday.com/history/2008/august/was-phrase-he-descended-into-hell-always-part-of-apostles.html.

Chun, Wendy Hui Kyong. "Race and/as Technology, or How to Do Things with Race." In *Race after the Internet*, edited by Lisa Nakamura and Peter A. Chow-White, 38–69. New York: Routledge, 2012.

Coalition of Immokalee Workers. "'Not 1996 Anymore . . .' Worker Beaten at Packing House near Immokalee." March 25, 2012. https://ciw-online.org/blog/2012/03/not_1996_anymore/.

Coates, Tyler. "Why Hands Across America Is So Vital to Jordan Peele's *Us*." *Esquire,* March 21, 2019. https://www.esquire.com/entertainment/movies/a26883876/hands-across-america-us-movie-explained/.

Cohn, Norman. *Noah's Flood: The Genesis Story in Western Thought*. New Haven: Yale University Press, 1996.

Collins, Adela Yabro. *Mark: A Commentary*. Minneapolis: Fortress, 2007.

Cone, James. *Black Theology and Black Power*. New York: Seabury, 1969.

———. *A Black Theology of Liberation*. New York: Lippincott, 1970.

———. *God of the Oppressed*. New York: Seabury, 1975.

Congreve, William. *The Mourning Bride*. In *The Works of William Congreve*, vol. 2, edited by D. F. McKenzie, 542–48. Oxford: Oxford University Press, 2011.

Corrado, Alessandra. "*Clandestini* in the Orange Towns: Migrations and Racisms in Calabria's Agriculture." *Race/Ethnicity: Multidisciplinary Global Contexts* 4/2 (2011) 191–201.

Corrado, Alessandra., Carlos de Castro, and Domenico Perrotta. *Migration and Agriculture: Mobility and Change in the Mediterranean Area*. London: Routledge, 2016.

Crace, Jim. "Crace on *Quarantine*." http://www.jim-crace.com/Crace_Q_intro.htm, 1998.

———. "Finding Jesus." *The Guardian*, March 21, 2008. https://www.theguardian.com/books/2008/mar/22/featuresreviews.guardianreview.

———. *Quarantine*. New York: Picador, 1998.

Crawford, Kate. *Atlas of AI: Power, Politics, and the Planetary Costs of Artificial Intelligence*. New Haven: Yale University Press, 2021.

Crossan, John Dominic. *The Historical Jesus: The Life of a Mediterranean Peasant*. San Francisco: HarperSanFrancisco, 1991.

———. *Jesus: A Revolutionary Biography*. San Francisco: HarperSanFrancisco, 1994.

Crossley, James, and Chris Keith, eds. *The Next Quest for the Historical Jesus*. Grand Rapids: Eerdmans, 2024.

Crossley, James, and Robert J. Myles. *Jesus: A Life in Class Conflict*. Washington, DC: Zero, 2023.

Curtis, Dan., dir. *St. John in Exile*. Nashville: Bridgestone, 1986.

D'Agostino, Lorenzo. "Aid or Autonomy? A Showdown in Italy's Agricultural Heartland." *The New Humanitarian*, September 8, 2020. https://www.thenewhumanitarian.org/news-feature/2020/09/08/Italy-agricultural-migrant-workers

DAIR. https://www.dair-institute.org/research/.

Davis, Mike. *The Monster at Our Door: The Global Threat of Avian Flu*. New York: The New Press, 2005.

De La Torre, Miguel A. *The Politics of Jesús: A Hispanic Political Theology*. Lanham, MD: Rowman & Littlefield, 2015.

Dean, Brandon. "A TikTok Jesus promises divine blessings and many worldly comforts." *Religious News Service*, November 16, 2023. https://religionnews.com/2023/11/16/a-tiktok-jesus-promises-divine-blessings-and-many-worldly-comforts/?fbclid=IwARoaYLnQiaCKLeN7Lrpsln3Rd9LHvCp_U2JkVJBfNssabqorbZ3bkPDuwXo_aem_AUSCx5rrgs6oBte7YptIB7BGDpLplQo1yJBaIJKalnfTQaq6XKOCj6V_6C4YDQypiEg#owawdhsbk3r.

Dean-Otting, Mary. *Heavenly Journeys: A Study in Hellenistic Jewish Literature.* Frankfurt: Peter Lang, 1984.

Debray, Régis. *God: An Itinerary.* Translated by Jeffrey Mehlman. New York: Verso, 2004.

DeCornick, April D. "Escape from the Wheel of Tome: The Cognitive Basis for Gnostic Ascent Practices." In *The Open Mind: Essays in Honor of Christopher Rowland,* edited by Jonathan Knight, 1–18. New York: T&T Clark, 2015.

Deleuze, Gilles, and Félix Guattari. *Nomadology: The War Machine.* New York: Semiotext(e), 1986.

Demarbre, Lee, dir. *Jesus Christ Vampire Hunter.* Ottawa: Odessa Filmworks, 2001.

DePaola, Tomie. *Tomie dePaola's Mother Goose.* New York: Putnam, 2011.

Derrida, Jacques. "Faith and Knowledge: Two Sources of Religion at the Limits of Reason Alone." In *Religion,* edited by Jacques Derrida and Gianni Vattimo, 1–78. Stanford, CA: Stanford University Press, 1998.

———. *Glas.* Translated by John P. Leavy and Richard Rand. Lincoln: University of Nebraska Press, 1986.

———. *Margins of Philosophy.* Translated by Alan Bass. Chicago: University of Chicago Press, 1984.

———. *Of Grammatology.* Translated by Gayatri Chakravorty Spivak. Baltimore: Johns Hopkins University Press, 1994.

Deshman, Robert. "Another Look at the Disappearing Christ: Corporeal and Spiritual Vision in Early Medieval Images." *The Art Bulletin* 79/2 (1997) 518–46.

Desta, Yohana, "*Us*: What Was Hands Across America, that Creepy Event that Inspired Jordan Peele?" March 22, 2019. https://www.vanityfair.com/hollywood/2019/03/us-movie-hands-across-america.

Dewald, E. T. "The Iconography of the Ascension." *American Journal of Archeology* (July–September 1950) 277–319.

Dines, Nick, and Enrica Rigo. "Postcolonial Citizenships between Representation, Borders and the 'Refugeeization' of the Workforce: Critical Reflections on Migrant Agricultural Labor in the Italian Mezzogiorno." In *Postcolonial Transitions in Europe: Contexts, Practices and Politics,* edited by Sandra Ponzanesi and Gianmaria Colpani, 151–77. Lanham, MD: Rowman & Littlefield, 2015.

Dixon, Beth A. *Food Justice and Narrative Ethics.* London: Bloomsbury, 2018.

Dixon-Román, Ezekiel, and Ramon Amaro. "Haunting, Blackness, and Algorithmic Thought." *e-flux Journal* 123 (December 2021). https://www.e-flux.com/journal/123/437244/haunting-blackness-and-algorithmic-thought/.

Doha Debates. *The Invisibles: Inhumane Conditions of Italy's Migrant Farmworkers.* Video. https://dohadebates.com/human-rights/the-invisibles/.

Douglas, Kelly Brown. *The Black Christ.* 25th anniversary ed. Maryknoll, NY: Orbis, 2019.

———. *Stand Your Ground: Black Bodies and the Justice of God.* Maryknoll, NY: Orbis, 2015.

Down, Simon, and Michael Hughes. "When the 'Subject' and the 'Researcher' Speak Together: Co-producing Organizational Ethnography." In *Organizational Ethnography: Studying the Complexities of Everyday Life,* edited by Sierk Ybema, Dvora Yanow, Harry Wels, and Frans H. Kamsteeg, 83–98. London: Sage, 2009.

Drahl, Carmen. "AI Was Asked to Create Images of Black African Docs Treating White Kids. How'd It Go?" NPR, October 6, 2023. https://www.npr.org/sections/goatsandsoda/2023/10/06/1201840678/ai-was-asked-to-create-images-of-black-african-docs-treating-white-kids-howd-it-.

Du Bois, W. E. B. *The Souls of Black Folk*, New York: Dover, 1994.

Dupuy, Jean-Pierre. *The Mark of the Sacred*. Translated by M. B. Debevoise. Stanford, CA: Stanford University Press, 2013.

DuVarney, Ava, dir. *Selma*. Los Angeles: Paramount, 2015.

Dwyer, T. *The Motif of Wonder in the Gospel of Mark*. Sheffield: Sheffield University Press, 1996.

Eco, Umberto. "Ur-Facism." *The New York Review of Books*, June 22, 1995.

Edward, Gareth, dir. *The Creator*. Los Angeles: 20th Century Studios, 2023.

Ehrman, Bart D. *Did Jesus Exist? The Historical Argument for Jesus of Nazareth*. New York: HarperOne, 2012.

———. *How Jesus Became God: The Exaltation of a Jewish Preacher from Galilee*. New York: HarperOne, 2015.

———. *Jesus: Apocalyptic Prophet of the New Millennium*. New York: Oxford University Press, 1999.

Eliade, Mircea. "Paradise and Utopia: Mythical Geography and Eschatology." In *Utopias and Utopian Thought*, edited by Frank E. Manuel, 260–80. Boston: Houghton, 1966.

Ellard, Colin. *Places of the Heart: The Psychogeography of Everyday Life*. New York: Bellevue, 2015.

Epiphanius of Salamis. *The Panarion of Epiphanius of Salamis: Book 1, Sects 1–46*. Translated by F. Williams. Leiden: Brill, 2009.

Estabrook, Barry. *Tomatoland: How Modern Industrial Agriculture Destroyed Our Most Alluring Fruit*. 3rd ed. Kansas City, MO: Andrews McMeel, 2018.

Faith in Florida. "Black History." https://www.faithinflorida.org/blackhistory.

Falconer, Rachel. *Hell in Contemporary Literature: Western Descent Narratives Since 1945*. Edinburgh: Edinburgh University Press, 2005.

Faleschini Lerner, Giovanna, and Elena Past. "Toxic Fruits: Tomatoes, Migration, and the New Italian Slavery." *Journal of Modern Italian Studies* 25/5 (2020) 592–619. doi:10.1080/1354571X.2020.1800264.

Fanon, Frantz. *Black Skin, White Masks*. Translated by Charles Lam Markmann. New York: Pluto, 1986.

Farrow, Douglas. *Ascension and Ecclesia: On the Significance of the Doctrine of the Ascension for Ecclesiology and Cosmology*. Grand Rapids: Eerdmans, 1999.

———. *Ascension Theology*. New York: T&T Clark, 2011.

Feasley, Ashley. "Eliminating Corporate Exploitation: Examining Accountability regimes as means to eradicate forced labor from supply chains." *Journal of Human Trafficking* 2/1 (2016) 15–31. https://doi.org/10.1080/23322705.2016.1137194.

Fennessey, Shawn. "Jordan Peele on 'Us.'" *The Big Picture: The Ringer Podcast*, March 19, 2019. https://www.theringer.com/2019/3/19/18272406/jordan-peele-on-us-movie.

Ferguson, Bruce. "Andres Serrano: Invisible Power." In *Body and Soul*, edited by Brian Wallis, 9–13. New York: Takarajima, 1995.

Ferrando, Tomaso. "Gangmastering Passata: Multi-Territoriality of the Food System and the Legal Construction of Cheap Labor behind the Globalized Italian Tomato." *FIU Law Review* 14/3 (2021) 521–544. https://doi.org/10.25148/lawrev.14.3.8.

Fisher, Mark. "The New Gospel Review: A Thrilling and Unsettling Easter Story." *The Guardian*, March 29, 2021. https://www.theguardian.com/stage/2021/mar/29/the-new-gospel-review-a-thrilling-and-unsettling-easter-story-milo-rau.

Fitzmeyer, Joseph A. *The Gospel According to Luke X–XXIV*. The Anchor Bible Commentaries. New Haven: Yale University Press, 1985.

Florida Modern-Day Slavery Museum. https://www.ciw-online.org/museum/index.html.

Floridi, Luciano, Josh Cowels, Thomas C. King, and Mariarosaria Taddeo. "How to Design AI for Social Good: Seven Essential Factors." In *Ethics, Governance, and Policies in Artificial Intelligence*, edited by Luciano Floridi, 125–51. Cham: Springer, 2021.

Fowler, Robert M. *Let the Reader Understand: Reader-Response Criticism and the Gospel of Mark*. Minneapolis: Fortress, 1991.

Franklin, Seb. *The Digitally Disposed: Racial Capitalism and the Informatics of Value*. Electronic Mediations 61. Minneapolis: University of Minnesota Press, 2021.

Freeland, Cynthia A. "Feminist Frameworks for Horror Films." In *Film Theory and Criticism*, 8th ed., edited by Leo Brandy and Marshall Cohen, 563–79. New York: Oxford University Press, 2016.

Freyne, Sean. *Galilee, Jesus, and the Gospels: Literary Approaches and Historical Investigations*. Tübingen: Mohr/Siebeck, 2000.

Friends of the Earth Middle East (FoEME). www.foeme.org.

Freedom Collaborative. "The Inhumane Conditions Faced by Italy's Migrant Farmworkers." *Global Newsletter*, July 7, 2020. https://freedomcollaborative.org/newsletter-archive/the-inhumane-conditions-faced-by-italys-migrant-farmworkers.

Frye, Northrop. *The Great Code: The Bible and Literature*. New York: Harcourt Brace, 1982.

———. "The Return to Eden: Five Essays on Milton's Epics." In *Northrop Frye on Milton and Blake*, edited by Angela Esterhammer, 35–131. Toronto: University of Toronto Press, 2005.

———. *Words with Power: Being a Second Study of "The Bible and Literature."* Vol. 26. Edited by Michael Dolzani. Toronto: University of Toronto Press, 2006.

Funk, Robert W., Roy W. Hoover, and the Jesus Seminar. *The Five Gospels: What Did Jesus Really Say? The Search for the Authentic Words of Jesus*. San Francisco: HarperSanFrancisco, 1997.

Funk, Robert W., and the Jesus Seminar. *The Acts of Jesus: What Did Jesus Really Do?: The Search for the Authentic Deeds of Jesus*. San Francisco: HarperSanFrancisco, 1998.

Funke, Cornelia. *Inkheart*. Frome, UK: Chicken House, 2002.

Garber, Paul Leslie. "Reconsidering the Reconstruction of Solomon's Temple." *Journal of Biblical Literature* 77/2 (1958) 123–29.

García, Rodrigo, dir. *Last Days in the Desert*. Los Angeles: Broad Green, 2015.

Garrett, Susan R. *The Temptations of Jesus in Mark's Gospel*. Grand Rapids: Eerdmans, 1998.

Gatti, Fabrizio. "Io Schiavo in Puglia." *L'Espresso*, September 1, 2006. http://espresso.repubblica.it/dossier/2006/09/01/news/ioschiavo-in-puglia-1.1306.

Gentilcore, David. *Pomodoro! A History of the Tomato in Italy*. New York: Columbia University Press, 2010.

Geraci, Robert M. *Apocalyptic AI: Visions of Heaven in Robotics, Artificial Intelligence, and Virtual Reality*. New York: Oxford University Press, 2010.

Giagoni, Silvia. *Fields of Resistance: The Struggle of Florida's Farmworkers for Justice*. Chicago: Haymarket, 2011.

Gibson, Mel, dir. *The Passion of the Christ*. Sydney, Australia: Icon, 2004.

Gilliam, Terry, dir. *Life of Brian*. Los Angeles: Orion, 1979.

Gillis, William. "Doppelganger." *The CEA Critic* 31/5 (1967) 7.

Girard, René. *Things Hidden Since the Foundation of the World*. Translated by Stephen Bann and Michael Metteer. Stanford, CA: Stanford University Press, 1978.

———. *Violence and the Sacred*. Translated by Patrick Gregory. Baltimore: Johns Hopkins University Press, 1977.

Giuliani, Gaia. *Race, Nation and Gender in Modern Italy: Intersectional Representations in Visual Culture*. New York: Palgrave, 2018.

Glueck, Norman. "The Jordan." *Biblical Archeologist*, December 1, 1943, 62–67.

Goldsmith, Steven. *Unbuilding Jerusalem: Apocalypse and Romantic Representation*. Ithaca, NY: Cornell University Press, 1993.

Goldthwaite, John. *The Natural History of Make-Believe*. New York: Oxford University Press, 1996.

Gómez-Barris, Macarena. *The Extractive Zone: Social Ecologies and Decolonial Perspectives*. Durham, NC: Duke University Press, 2017.

Gorenberg, Gershom. *The End of Days: Fundamentalism and the Struggle for the Temple Mount*. New York: Oxford University Press, 2000.

Gouge, Melissa C. "Human Rights in Play, Transnational Solidarity at Work: Creative Playfulness and Subversive Storytelling among the Coalition of Immokalee Workers." *Critical Sociology* 42/6 (2016) 861–75.

Grant, Jacquelyn. *White Women's Christ and Black Women's Jesus: Feminist Christology and Womanist Response*. Atlanta: Scholars, 1989.

Graybill, Rhiannon. "Rock Me Sexy Jesus? Gender and Sexuality in Biblical Films." In *T&T Clark Companion to the Bible and Film*, edited by Richard Walsh, 187–97. London: T&T Clark, 2018.

Greene, Naomi. *Pier Paolo Pasolini: Cinema as Heresy*. Princeton: Princeton University Press, 1990.

Gregersen, Niels Hendrik. "The Extended Body: The Social Body of Jesus according to Luke." *Dialog: A Journal of Theology*. 51/3 (2012) 234–44.

Greven, Philip. *Spare the Child: The Religious Roots of Punishment and the Psychological Impact of Physical Abuse*. New York: Vintage, 1990.

Grosz, Elizabeth. *Architecture from the Outside: Essays on Virtual and Real Space*. Boston: MIT Press, 2001.

Grubb, Nancy. *Revelations: Art of the Apocalypse*. New York: Abbeville, 1997.

Gruda, Matt. "AI or Not, Here Faith Comes: AI and Spiritual Beliefs." *Psychology Today*, November 23, 2023. https://www.psychologytoday.com/us/blog/of-leaders-and-traits/202311/ai-or-not-here-faith-comes-ai-and-spiritual-beliefs.

Haedicke, Susan C. "Coalition of Immokalee Workers: Farmworker-Led Popular Education and Performance." *Research in Drama Education: The Journal of Applied Theatre and Performance* 25/4 (2020) 576–80.

Hallow commercial. "A Day with Hallow." https://www.youtube.com/watch?v=dVY1_xH2Qis&t=3s.

Hallow commercial. "Lenten Prayer with Mark Wahlberg and Jonathan Roumie." https://www.facebook.com/61552336945267/videos/1230328691688537.

Haraway, Donna. *Simians, Cyborgs and Women: The Reinvention of Nature*. New York: Routledge, 1991.

Harpham, Geoffrey G. *The Ascetic Imperative in Culture and Criticism*. Chicago: University of Chicago Press, 1987.

Harrison, Robert Pogue. *The Dominion of the Dead*. Chicago: University of Chicago Press, 2003.

Hartley, Hal, dir. *The Book of Life*. Los Angeles: Fox, 2000.

Hartmann, Margaret. "Trump's Court Sketch Is Somehow Way Worse Than It Looks." October 23, 2023. https://nymag.com/intelligencer/2023/10/trumps-jesus-court-sketch-is-even-worse-than-it-looks.html.

Harvey, Mark, Stephen Quilley, and Huw Beynon. *Exploring the Tomato: Transformations of Nature, Society and Economy*. Cheltenham, UK: Edward Elgar, 2004.

Hassold, Cris. "The Double and Doubling in Modern and Postmodern Art." *Journal of the Fantastic in the* Arts 6 2/3 (1994) 253–74.

Havrelock, Rachel S. *River Jordan: The Mythology of a Dividing Line*. Chicago: University of Chicago Press, 2011.

Hayles, N. Katherine. *How We Became Posthuman: Virtual Bodies in Cybernetics, Literature, and Informatics*. Chicago: University of Chicago Press, 1999.

Hewitt, Chris, with Terri White, George Harrison, and John Nugent. "Empire Podcast Us Spoiler Special Ft. Jordan Peele." *The Empire Film Podcast*, March 26, 2019. https://www.empireonline.com/movies/news/empire-podcast-us-spoiler-special-ft-jordan-peele/.

Himmelfarb, Martha. *Ascent to Heaven in Jewish and Christian Apocalypses*. New York: Oxford University Press, 1993.

Hitchcock, Mark. "Bird Flu and the Apocalypse." From the Resource Center at http://www.leftbehind.com.

Hitchens, Christopher. *God Is Not Great: How Religion Poisons Everything*. New York: Twelve, 2007.

Holderness, Graham. "'The Undiscovered Country': Philip Pullman and 'The Land of the Dead.'" *Literature and Theology* 21/33 (2007) 276–92. http://www.jstor.org/stable/23927125.

Howard, Neil, and Roberto Forin. "Migrant Workers, 'Modern Slavery' and the Politics of Representation in Italian Tomato Production." *Economy & Society* 48/4 (2019) 579–601. https://doi.org/10.1080/03085147.2019.1672426.

Hughes, Richard T. *Myths America Lives By: White Supremacy and the Stories That Give Us Meaning*. Urbana, IL: University of Illinois Press, 2018.

Hutton, J. M. "Topography, Biblical Traditions, and Reflections on John's Baptism of Jesus." In *Jesus Research: New Methodological Perceptions*, Princeton-Prague Symposium on Jesus Research, edited by J. H. Charlesworth, B. Rhea, and P. Pokorny, 149–77. Grand Rapids: Eerdmans, 2007.

Irenaeus. *Against Heresies*. In *The Ante-Nicene Fathers*, vol. 1, edited by Alexander Roberts, James Donaldson, and A. Cleveland Coxe; translated by A. Roberts and J. Donaldson, 309–567. Eugene, OR: Wipf and Stock, 2022.

Jackson, Rosemary. *Fantasy: The Literature of Subversion*. London: Meuthen, 1981.

Jacobi, Christine ,and Jens Schroeter, eds. *The Jesus Handbook*. Translated by Robert L. Brawley. Grand Rapids: Eerdmans, 2023.

Jameson, Fredric. *Allegory and Ideology*. New York: Verso, 2019.

———. *Postmodernism, or, the Logic of Late Capitalism*. Durham, NC: Duke University Press, 2012.

Jameson, Leslie. "Catechism." In *Such Mean Estate*, n.p. Photographs by Ryan Spencer. Brooklyn: Powerhouse, 2015.

Jasper, David. *The Sacred Desert: Religion, Literature, and the Arts*. Oxford: Oxford University Press, 2004.

Jenkins, Dallas, dir. *The Chosen*. TV series. Provo, UT: Angel Studios, 2019–2025. https://www.thechosen.tv/en.us.

Jensen, Kipton E. *Howard Thurman: Philosophy, Civil Rights, and the Search for Common Ground*. Columbia: University of South Carolina Press, 2019.

Jewett, Robert, and John Shelton Lawrence. *Captain America and the Crusade Against Evil: The Dilemma of Christian Nationalism*. Grand Rapids: Eerdmans, 2002.

———. *The Myth of the American Superhero*. Grand Rapids: Eerdmans, 2002.

Jewison, Norman, dir. *Jesus Christ Superstar*. Los Angeles: Universal, 1973.

Johnson, Elizabeth A. *She Who Is: The Mystery of God in Feminist Theological Discourse*. New York: Crossroad, 1994.

Jones, Robert P. *White Too Long: The Legacy of White Supremacy in American Christianity*. New York: Simon & Schuster, 2020.

Jones, Tobias, and Ayo Awokoya. "Are Your Tinned Tomatoes Picked by Slave Labour?: How the Italian Mafia Makes Millions by Exploiting Migrants." *The Guardian*, June 20, 2019.

Juergensmeyer, Mark. *Terror in the Mind of God: The Global Rise of Religious Violence*. Berkeley: University of California Press, 2000.

Justin Martyr. *Dialogue with Trypho*. Edited by M. Schussler, translated by T. B. Falls. Washington, DC: The Catholic University of America Press, 2003.

Katz, Yarden. *Artificial Whiteness: Politics and Ideology in Artificial Intelligence*. New York: Columbia University Press, 2020.

Kazantzakis, Nikos. *The Last Temptation of Christ*. Translated by P. A. Bien. New York: Simon & Schuster, 1998.

Kelhoffer, James A. *Miracle and Mission: The Authentication of Missionaries and Their Message in the Longer Ending of Mark*. Tübingen: Mohr Siebeck, 2000.

Keller, Catherine. *Apocalypse Now and Then*. Boston: Beacon, 1996.

———. *Face of the Deep: A Theology of Becoming*. New York: Routledge, 2003.

———. *Facing Apocalypse: Climate, Democracy, and Other Last Chances*. Maryknoll, NY: Orbis, 2021.

Kermode, Frank. "Into the Wilderness." *New York Times*, April 12, 1998. http://www.nytimes.com/books/98/04/12/reviews/980412.12kermodt.html.

———. *The Sense of An Ending: Studies in the Theory of Fiction with a New Epilogue*. New York: Oxford University Press, 2000.

Kim, H. C., ed. *The Gospel of Nicodemus: Gesta Salvatoris*. Toronto: Pontifical Institute of Medieval Studies, 1968.

King, Martin Luther King, Jr. *"All Labor Has Dignity."* Edited by Michael K. Honey. Boston: Beacon, 1986.

________. *The Radical King*. Edited and introduced by Cornel West. Boston: Beacon, 2015.

King, Tiffany Lethabo. *The Black Shoals: Offshore Formations of Black and Native Studies*. Durham, NC: Duke University Press, 2019.

Klein, Mina C. and H. Arthur. *Temple Beyond Time: The Story of the Site of Solomon's Temple at Jerusalem*. New York: Van Nostrand Reinhold, 1970.

Kotsko, Adam. *Creepiness*. Alresford, UK: Zero, 2015.

———. *The Prince of this World*. Stanford, CA: Stanford University Press, 2016.

Kristof, Nicholas D. "Jesus and Jihad." *The New York Times*, July 17, 2004.

LaHaye, Tim. "Glorious Appearing: Letter to the Editor." *The New York Times*, July 23, 2004.

Landes, Richard. "On Owls, Roosters, and Apocalyptic Time: A Historical Method for Reading a Refractory Documentation." *Union Seminary Quarterly Review* 49 (1996) 165–85.

Langguth, A. J. *Jesus Christs*. Los Angeles: Figueroa, 2003.

Lappin, Yaakov. "Elbit to Build Surveillance Towers on Arizona's Mexico Border." *The Jerusalem Post*, March 2, 2014. http://www.jpost.com/International/Elbit-to-build-surveillance-towers-on-Arizonas-border-with-Mexico-344005.

Lasch, Christopher. *The Culture of Narcissism in American Life in an Age of Diminishing Expectations*. New York: Norton, 1991.

Laube, Steve, Amanda Jenkins, and Dallas Jenkins. *The Chosen Presents: A Blended Harmony of the Gospels*. Christian Standard Bible. Savage, MN: BroadStreet, 2022.

Laufer, Catherine Ella. *Hell's Destruction: An Exploration of Christ's Descent to the Dead*. Burlington, VT: Ashgate, 2013.

Lawrence, D. H. *The Man Who Died*. New York: Ecco, 1994.

Leclerc, André. "Actualism and Fictional Characters." *Principia* 20/1 (2016) 61–80.

Lefebvre, Henri. *The Production of Space*. Translated by Donald Nicholson-Smith. Oxford: Wiley-Blackwell, 1992.

Leogrande, Alessandro. *Uomini e caporali. Viaggio tra i nuovi schiavi nelle campagne del sud/Journey among the New Slaves of the Southern Countryside*. Rome: Feltrinelli, 2016.

Lerner, Giovanna Faleschini, and Elena Past. "Toxic Fruits: Tomatoes, Migration, and the New Italian Slavery." *Journal of Modern Italian Studies* 25/5 (2020) 592–619.

Levi, Carlo. *Christ Stopped at Eboli: The Story of a Year*. New York: Farrar, Strauss and Giroux, 1947.

Levine, Amy-Jill. *The Social and Ethnic Dimensions of Matthean Salvation History*. Lewiston, ME: Edwin Mellen, 1988.

Lippard, Lucy R. "Andres Serrano: The Spirit and the Letter." *Art in America* 78 (April 1990) 238–45.

Litwa, M. David. *Iesus Deus: The Early Christian Depiction of Jesus as a Mediterranean God*. Philadelphia: Fortress, 2014.

Lohfink, Gerhard. *Die Himmelfahrt Jesus: Untersuchen zu den Himmelfahrts—und Erhörungstexten bei Lukas*. München: Kösel-Verlag, 1971.

Luniz (feat. Michael Marshall). "I Got 5 on It: Tethered Mix from US." In *Us: Original Motion Picture Soundtrack*, produced by Michael Abels. Los Angeles: Backlot Music, 2019.

Lutwack, Leonard. *Birds in Literature*. Gainesville: University of Florida Press, 1994.

Macfarlane, Robert. *Underland: A Deep Time Journey*. New York: Norton, 2019.

Magness, J. Lee. *Marking the End: Sense and Absence in the Gospel of Mark*. Eugene, OR: Wipf and Stock, 2002.

Malbon, Elizabeth. *Narrative Space and Mythic Meaning in Mark*. Sheffield: JSOT, 1986.

Malone, Michelle. "Immigration Game." *Day 2*. CD Baby, 2012.

Malone, Peter. *Screen Jesus: Portrayals of Christ in Television and Film*. Lanham, MD: Scarecrow.

Mann, C. S. *Mark: A New Translation with Introduction and Commentary. The Anchor Bible*. Garden City, NY: Doubleday, 1986.

Marcus, J. *Mark 1-8. The Anchor Bible*. New York: Doubleday, 2000.

Mariani, Andrea Paco, dir. *The Harvest*. Bolognia, Italy: SMK Videofactory, 2017. https://www.openddb.it/film/the-harvest/.

Marotta, Claudia, Francesco Di Gennaro, Paolo Parente, Giovanni Putoto, and David Mosca. "Stop the exploitation of migrant agricultural workers in Italy." *The British Medical Journal* (2019). https://blogs.bmj.com/bmj/2019/03/27/stop-the-exploitation-of-migrant-agricultural-workers-in-italy/.

Marquis, Susan L. *I Am Not a Tractor!: How Florida Farmworkers Took On the Fast Food Giants and Won*. Ithaca, NY: Cornell University Press, 2017.

Marsh, Clive. "Quests of the Historical Jesus in New Historicist Perspective." *Biblical Interpretation* (October 1997) 403–37.

Masuzawa, Tomoko. *In Search of Dreamtime: The Quest for the Origin of Religion*. Chicago: University of Chicago Press, 1993.

———. "Original Lost: An Image of Myth and Ritual in the Age of Mechanical Reproduction." *The Journal of Religion* 69/3 (July 1989) 307–25.

Mathewson, David. "The Apocalyptic Vision of Jesus According to the Gospel of Matthew: Reading Matthew 3:16-4:11 Intertextually." *Tyndale Bulletin* 62/1 (2011) 89–108.

Mbembé, Achille. "Necropolitics." Translated by Libby Meintjes. *Public Culture* 15/1 (2003) 11–40.

McClung, William Alexander. *The Architecture of Paradise: Survivals of Eden and Jerusalem*. Berkeley: University of California Press, 1983.

McGinn, Bernard. *Antichrist: Two Thousand Years of the Human Fascination with Evil*. San Francisco: HarperSanFrancisco, 1994.

Medved, Harry, and Michael Medved. *The Hollywood Hall of Shame: The Most Expensive Flops in Movie History*. New York: Perigee, 1984.

Menzel, Christopher, "The Possibilism-Actualism Debate." *The Stanford Encyclopedia of Philosophy* (Fall 2023 ed.), edited by Edward N. Zalta & Uri Nodelman, forthcoming. https://plato.stanford.edu/archives/fall2023/entries/possibilism-actualism/.

Metzger, Bruce M. and Roland E. Murphy, eds. *The New Oxford Annotated Bible with the Apocryphal/Deuteronomical Books*. New Revised Standard Version. New York: Oxford University Press, 1991.

Miéville, China. *Un Lun Dun*. New York: Del Rey, 2008.

Miller, Alice. *For Your Own Good: Hidden Cruelty in Child-Rearing and the Roots of Violence*. New York: Farrar, Straus and Giroux, 1983.

Mitchell, W. J. T. "Imperial Landscape." In *Landscape and Power*, edited by W. J. T. Mitchell, 5–34. Chicago: University of Chicago Press, 1994.

———. "Introduction." In *Landscape and Power*, edited by W. J. T. Mitchell, 1–4. Chicago: University of Chicago Press, 1994.

———, ed. *The Politics of Interpretation*. Chicago: The University of Chicago Press, 1983.

Moltmann, Jürgen. *The Coming of God*. Minneapolis: Fortress, 1976.

———. *The Crucified God*. London: SCM, 1974.

Moorcock, Michael. *Behold the Man*. Thirtieth anniversary ed. Austin, TX: Mojo, 1996.

Moore, Christopher. *Lamb: The Gospel According to Biff, Christ's Childhood Pal.* New York: HarperCollins, 2002.

Moore, Stephen D. *The Bible After Deleuze: Affects, Assemblages, Bodies without Organs.* New York: Oxford University Press, 2023.

———. *God's Beauty Parlor and Other Queer Spaces in and Around the Bible.* Stanford, CA: Stanford University Press, 2001.

———. *Gospel Jesuses and Other Nonhumans: Biblical Criticism Post-Poststructuralism.* Semeia Studies 89. Atlanta: SBL, 2017.

———. *Mark and Luke in Poststructuralist Perspective: Jesus Begins to Write.* New York: Yale University Press, 1992.

Moreira, Isabel, and Margaret Toscano, eds. *Hell and Its Afterlife: Historical and Contemporary Perspectives.* Surrey, UK: Ashgate, 2010.

Mori, Masahiro. "The Uncanny Valley." Translated by Karl F. MacDorman and Norri Kageki. *Forbes,* June 12, 2012. https://spectrum.ieee.org/the-uncanny-valley.

Morris, Wesley, and Jenna Wortheim. "Us." *Still Processing Podcast, The New York Times* March 28, 2019. https://www.nytimes.com/2019/03/28/podcasts/still-processing-us-jordan-peele.html.

Morrison, Toni. *Beloved.* New York: Vintage, 2004.

Morrow, James. *Only Begotten Daughter.* New York: Harcourt Brace, 1990.

Moser, Barry. "Book Artist Barry Moser." *SBL Forum,* cited September 2003. http://sbl-site.org/Article.aspx?ArticleID=180.

———, designer and illustrator. *The Holy Bible (KJV): Pennyroyal Caxton Bible.* New York: Viking, 1999.

Moss, Candida. *God's Ghostwriters: Enslaved Christians and the Making of the Bible.* New York: Little, Brown and Company, 2024.

Moxnes, Halvor. *Jesus and the Rise of Nationalism: A New Quest for the Nineteenth-Century Historical Jesus.* London: I. B. Taurus, 2012.

Müller, Casper Detlef G. "The Ascension of Isaiah." In *New Testament Apocrypha, Vol. 2: Writings Relating to the Apostles; Apocalypses and Related Topics,* edited by William Schneemelcher and R. M. Wilson, 603–19. New York: James Clark, 1992.

Müller, Helgard. *President Donald J. Trump: The Son of Man–the Christ.* Denver: Outskirts, 2022.

Nabhan, Gary Paul. *Jesus for Farmers and Fishers: Justice for All Those Marginalized by Our Food System.* Minneapolis: Broadleaf, 2021.

Nancy, Jean-Luc. *Noli me tangere: On the Raising of the Body.* Translated by Sarah Clift, Pascale-Anne Brault, and Michael Naas. New York: Fordham University Press, 2008.

Ng, Karen. *Hegel's Concept of Life: Self-Consciousness, Freedom, Logic.* New York: Oxford University Press, 2020.

Noble, Safiya Umoja. *Algorithms of Oppression: How Search Engines Reinforce Racism.* New York: New York University Press, 2018.

NoCap website. https://www.associazionenocap.it/.

NOCap. *People Before Profit: From Protest to Proposal.* 2020. https://www.associazionenocap.it/wp-content/uploads/2022/03/IMPAGINATO-NOCAP-2020-ENG-compresso.pdf.

Novacich, Sarah Elliott. *Shaping the Archive in Late Medieval England.* Cambridge: Cambridge University Press, 2017.

O'Gieblyn, Meghan. *God, Human, Animal, Machine: Technology, Metaphor, and the Search for Meaning*. New York: Doubleday, 2021.

O'Neil, Lorena. "Truth in Tech: These Women Tried to Warn Us about AI." *Rolling Stone*, August 12, 2023. https://www.rollingstone.com/culture/culture-features/women-warnings-ai-danger-risk-before-chatgpt-1234804367/.

Open Society/European Policy Institute. "Is Italian Agriculture a 'Pull Factor' for Irregular Migration, and If So, Why?" 2018. https://www.opensocietyfoundations.org/uploads/ba12312d-31f1-4e29-82bf-7d8c41df48ad/is-italian-agriculture-a-pull-factor-for-irregular-migration-20181205.pdf.

Page, Matthew. "*Das neue Evangelium* (The New Gospel, 2020)." April 2, 2021. https://biblefilms.blogspot.com/2021/04/das-neue-evangelium-new-gospel-2020.html.

Parsons, Mikeal C. *The Departure of Jesus in Luke-Acts: The Ascension Narratives in Context*. Sheffield: Sheffield University Press, 1987.

Parry, William. *Against the Wall: The Art of Resistance in Palestine*. Chicago: Lawrence Hill, 2010.

Pasolini, Pier Paolo, dir. *The Gospel According to St. Matthew*. Los Angeles: Arco, 1964.

———. *Sopralluoghi in Palestina (On Location in Palestine)*. Los Angeles: Arco, 1965.

Pasquinelli, Matteo. *The Eye of the Master: A Social History of Artificial Intelligence*. London: Verso, 2023.

Paulus, Michael J., Jr. *Artificial Intelligence and the Apocalyptic Imagination: Artificial Agency and Human Hope*. Eugene, OR: Cascade, 2023.

Paulus, Michael J., Jr., and Michael D. Langford, eds. *AI, Faith, and the Future: An Interdisciplinary Approach*. Eugene, OR: Pickwick, 2022.

Peele, Jordan, dir. *Us*. Los Angeles: Universal Studio, 2019.

Pennoni, Angelo, Angelo Novi, and Mario Tursi. *Pier Paolo Pasolini: My Cinema*. Bologne: Fondazione Cineteca, 2013.

Perrotta, Domenico. "Agricultural Day Laborers in Southern Italy: Forms of Mobility and Resistance." *South Atlantic Quarterly* 114/1 (2015) 195–203.

Perrotta, Domenico, and Devi Sacchetto. "Migrant Farmworkers in Southern Italy: Ghettoes, Caporalato and Collective Action." *Workers of the World: International Journal on Strikes and Social Conflicts* 1/5 (2014) 75–98.

Petkovic, Vladan. "Venice 2020: Giornate degli Autori: Review: *The New Gospel*." July 9, 2020. https://cineuropa.org/en/newsdetail/392242/.

Piepenberg, Erik, "'Us' Took Hands Across America and Made It a Death Grip." *The New York Times*, March 16, 2019. https://www.nytimes.com/2019/03/26/movies/us-hands-across-america.html.

Pilch, John J. *Flights of the Soul: Visions, Heavenly Journeys, and Peak Experiences in the Biblical World*. Grand Rapids: Eerdmans, 2011.

Pippin, Tina. "Air Jesus: Fear of Flying in the Gospel of Mark." In *Bible and Theory: Essays in Biblical Interpretation in Honor of Stephen D. Moore*, edited by K. Jason Coker and Scott S. Elliott, 109–26. Minneapolis: Lexington, 2020.

———. "Behold the Sons of Man: Fantasy and the Markan Messiahs." In *Simulating Aichele: Essays in Bible, Film, Culture, and Theory*, edited by Melissa C. Stewart, 335–45. Sheffield: Sheffield Phoenix, 2015.

———. "The End of Jesus." In *Those Outside: Noncanonical Readings of the Canonical Gospels*, edited by George Aichele and Richard Walsh, 43–64. New York/London: T&T Clark, 2005.

———. "Jesus as Fantasy Mother." In *Mother Goose, Mother Jones, Mommie Dearest: Biblical Mothers and Their Children*, 141–56. Semeia Studies 61. Atlanta: SBL, 2009.

———. "(Un)holy Saturday." In *T&T Clark Handbook of Jesus and Film*, edited by Richard Walsh, 261–72. London: Bloomsbury, 2021.

Polletta, Francesca. *It Was Like a Fever: Storytelling in Protest and Politics*. Chicago: University of Chicago Press, 2006.

———. "Storytelling in Politics." *Contexts* 7/4 (2008) 26–31.

———. "Storytelling in Social Movements." In *Culture, Social Movements, and Protest*, 1st ed., edited by Hank Johnston, 33–54. New York: Routledge, 2016.

Polletta, Francesca, and Pang Ching Bobby Chen. "Narrative and Social Movements." In *The Oxford Handbook of Cultural Sociology*, edited by Jeffrey C. Alexander, Ronald N. Jacobs, and Phillip Smith, 487–506. Oxford: Oxford University Press, 2012.

Polletta, Francesca, Pang Ching Bobby Chen, B. G. Gardner, and A. Motes. "The Sociology of Storytelling." *Annual Review of Sociology* 37/1 (2011) 109–30.

Prabhakaran, Vinodkumar, Margaret Mitchell, Timnit Gebru, and Iason Gabriel. "A Responsible Human Rights Approach to AI." *arXiv*, October 6, 2022. https://arxiv.org/pdf/2210.02667.pdf.

Prince, Gerald. *A Dictionary of Narratology*. Rev. ed. Lincoln: University of Nebraska Press, 2003.

Pullman, Philip. *The Amber Spyglass: His Dark Materials*, Book III. New York: Yearling, 2003.

———. *His Dark Materials Omnibus*. New York: Bluefire, 2007.

Rancière, Jacques. *The Intervals of Cinema*. Translated by John Howe. London: Verso.

Rawal, Sanjay, dir. *Food Chains*. 2014. http://www.foodchainsfilm.com/.

Reinhartz, Adele. *Jesus of Hollywood*. New York: Oxford University Press, 2007.

———. "Mirror, Mirror on the Wall: The Bible and Ethics in Jordan Peele's 2019 Film *Us*." *Interpretation* (July 24, 2024) 190–206.

Renan, Ernst. *The Life of Jesus*. New York: Prometheus, (1863) 1991.

Religion News Service. "Israel Removes Landmines from Jesus Baptism Site." *Christian Century*, June 14, 2011, 19.

Rhoads, David, Joanna Dewey, and Donald Michie. *Mark as Story: An Introduction to the Narrative of a Gospel*. Minneapolis: Fortress, 2012.

Robledo, Melissa, and Robert Kenner, dirs. *Food Inc. 2: Back for Seconds*. New York: Magnolia Pictures, 2024.

Rollins, Peter. *The Idolatry of God: Breaking Our Addiction to Certainty and Satisfaction*. New York: Howard, 2013.

Rosile, Grace Ann, David M. Boje, Richard A. Herder, and Mabel Sanchez. "The Coalition of Immokalee Workers Uses Ensemble Storytelling Processes to Overcome Enslavement in Corporate Supply Chains." *Business & Society* 602 (2021) 376–414.

Royakkers, Lambèr, and Rinie van Est. *Just Ordinary Robots: Automation from Love to War*. Boca Raton, FL: CRC Press/Taylor and Francis, 2016.

Rubenstein, Mary-Jane. *Pantheologies: Gods, Worlds, Monsters*. New York: Columbia University Press, 2018.

Ruden, Sarah. *The Gospels*. New York: Modern Library, 2023.

Rustomji, Nermina. *The Garden and the Fire: Heaven and Hell in Islamic Culture*. New York: Columbia University Press, 2013.

Sagnet, Yvan. *Ama il tuo sogno. Rivolta nella terra dell'oro rosso*. Roma: Fandango Libri, 2017.

———. *The Slavery of Illegal Gangmastering in Agriculture*. TEDxCremona, September 2021. https://www.ted.com/talks/yvan_sagnet_the_slavery_of_illegal_gangmastering_in_agriculture/transcript.

Sagnet, Yvan, and Leonardo Palmisano. *Ghetto Italia. I braccianti stranieri tra caporalato e sfruttamento*. Rome: Fandango, 2015.

Said, Edward W. *Beginnings: Intention and Method*. New York: Columbia University Press, 1985.

———. *Orientalism*. New York: Vintage, 1979.

Samuel, Jeymes, dir. *The Book of Clarence*. Culver City, CA: Sony Home Pictures Entertainment, 2024.

Saramago, José. *The Gospel According to Jesus Christ*. Translated by Giovanni Pontiero. New York: Harcourt Brace, 1964.

Scarpa, Vittoria. "Venice 2020: Giornate degli Autori: Milo Rau, Director of *the New Gospel*: 'The first black Jesus film in European Film History.'" September 8, 2020. https://cineuropa.org/en/video/rdid/390817/.

Schlosser, Eric. *Fast Food Nation: The Dark Side of the American Meal*. London: Penguin, 2012.

Schoer, Silvia. "'Under the Shadow of Your Wings': The Metaphor of God's Wings in the Psalms, Exodus 19:4, Deuteronomy 32:11 and Malachi 3:20, as Seen Through the Perspectives of Feminism and the History of Religion." In *Wisdom and Psalms: The Feminist Companion to the Bible (Second Series)*, edited by Athalya Brenner and Carole R. Fontaine, 264–82. Sheffield: Sheffield, 1998.

Schneemelcher, Wilhelm, ed. *New Testament Apocrypha: Writings Related to the Apostles: Apocalypses and Related Writings*. Rev ed. Translated by R. McL. Wilson. Louisville: Westminster John Knox, 1992.

Schneider, Kirk J. *Horror and the Holy: Wisdom-Teachings of the Monster Tale*. Chicago: Open Court, 1993.

Schneider, Steven Jay. "Manifestations of the Literary Double in Modern Horror Cinema." In *Horror Film and Psychoanalysis: Freud's Worst Nightmare*, edited by Steven J. Schneider, 106–21. Cambridge: Cambridge University Press, 2004.

Schröter, Jens, and Christine Jacobi, eds. *The Jesus Handbook*. Translated by Robert L. Brawley. Grand Rapids: Eerdmans, 2022.

Schüssler Fiorenza, Elisabeth. "The Ethics of Biblical Interpretation: Decentering Biblical Scholarship." *The Journal of Biblical Literature* 107/1 (1988) 3–17.

Schwartz, Michael. "River Revival: Can the Jordan Roll Again?" *Christian Century*, July 11, 2012, 22–25.

Schweitzer, Albert. *The Mystery of the Kingdom of God: The Secret of Jesus' Messiahship and Passion*. Translated by W. Lowrie. New York: Macmillan, 1950.

Sciretta, Peter, Jacob Hall, Brad Oman, and Brad Pearson. "Jordan Peele's *Us* Spoiler Discussion." *Film Daily Podcast*, March 22, 2019. https://daily.slashfilm.com/e/jordan-peeles-us-spoiler-discussion/.

Scorcese, Martin, dir. *The Last Temptation of Christ*. Los Angeles: Universal, 1988.

Scott, Ridley, dir. *Blade Runner*. Los Angeles: Warner Bros., 1982.

Segal, Alan. "Heavenly Ascent in Hellenistic Judaism, Early Christianity, and Their Environment." *Aufsteig und Niedergang der römischen Welt* 23/2 (1980) 1332–94.

Seger, Monica. "Toxic Tales: On Representing Environmental Crisis in Puglia." In *Encounters with the Real in Contemporary Italian Literature and Cinema*, edited by Loredana Di Martino and Pasquale Verdicchio, 29–46. Newcastle upon Tyne: Cambridge Scholars, 2017.

Serrano, Andres. *Body and Soul*. Edited by Brian Wallis. New York: Takarajima, 1995.

———. *Holy Works*. Text by Germano Celant. Bologne: Damiani, 2012.

———. *The Morgue*. Paris: Galerie Yvon Lambert, 1993.

Shively, Elizabeth E. *Apocalyptic Imagination in the Gospel of Mark: The Literary and Theological Role of Mark 3:22–30*. Boston: De Gruyter, 2012.

Sleeman, Matthew. *Geography and the Ascension Narratives in Acts*. New York: Cambridge University Press, 2009.

Slethaug, Gordon E. "Doubles and Doubling in the Arts." *Journal of the Fantastic in the Arts* 6:2/3 (1994) 100–106.

Smith, D. W. "Phenomenology." In *The Stanford Encyclopedia of Philosophy*, edited by Edward N. Zalta (Winter 2016 Edition). https://plato.stanford.edu/archives/win2016/entries/phenomenology/>.

Smith, Jonathan Z. *Map Is Not Territory*. Leiden: Brill, 1978.

Smith, Mitzi J. "Abolitionist Messiah: A Man Jesus Named Born of a *Doulē*." In *Bitter the Chastening Rod*, edited by Mitzi J. Smith, Angela N. Parker, and Ericka S. Dunbar Hill, 53–70. Minneapolis: Fortress, 2022.

Smith, Mitzi J., and Yung Suk Kim. *Decentering the New Testament: An Introduction*. Eugene, OR: Cascade, 2018.

Soja, Edward W. *Thirdspace: Journeys to Los Angeles and Other Real-and-Imagined Places*. Oxford: Blackwell, 1996.

Solnit, Rebecca. *Wanderlust: A History of Walking*. London: Verso, 2001.

Soltis, Laura Emiko. "!Presente! Music, Mobilization, and Global Engagement: The Case of the Coalition of Immokalee Workers." *Dissertation Abstracts International Section A: Humanities and Social Sciences*. Ann Arbor, MI: ProQuest, 2018.

Soohoo, Cynthia, Catherine Albisa, and Martha F. David, eds. *Bringing Human Rights Home. Volume 2: Portraits of the Movement, Bringing Human Rights Home*. Westport, CT: Praeger, 2008.

Spoto, Donald. *The Dark Side of Genius: The Life of Alfred Hitchcock*. Boston: Little, Brown and Company, 1983.

Stack, Oswald, and Pier Paolo Pasolini. *Pasolini on Pasolini: Interviews with Oswald Stack*. Bloomington: Indiana University Press, 1970.

Stanford Internet Observatory Cyber Policy Center. https://cyber.fsi.stanford.edu/io/news/ai-spam-accounts-build-followers.

Steinberg, Leo. *The Sexuality of Christ in Renaissance Art and in Modern Oblivion*. Chicago: University of Chicago Press, 1997.

Steiner, George. *No Passion Spent: Essays 1978-1995*. New Haven: Yale University Press, 1996.

Stennett, Rob, and Andrew Harmon, dirs. *The Thorn*. Nashville: Bridgehouse, 2023. https://thethorn.com/.

The Story Behind Your Food. https://www.youtube.com/watch?v=Ny9YaJczqjY. 2018.

Stevens, George, dir. *The Greatest Story Ever Told*. Los Angeles: United Artists, 1965.

Stewart, Daniel, dir. *Jonathan and Jesus: Chosen Docuseries*. Santa Monica, CA: Lionsgate, 2024.

Stewart, Eric C. *Gathered Around Jesus: An Alternative Spatial Practice of the Gospel of Mark*. Eugene, OR: Cascade, 2009.

Strauss, David Friedrich. *The Christ of Faith and the Jesus of History: A Critique of Schleiermacher's* The Life of Jesus. Edited by Leander E. Keck. Philadelphia: Fortress, 1977.

———. *The Life of Jesus Critically Examined*. Edited by Peter C. Hodgson. Translated by George Eliot. Philadelphia: Fortress, 1972.

Stroud, Joanne H. "Foreword." In *Water and Dreams: An Essay on the Imagination of Matter*, by Gaston Bachelard, vii–x. Dallas: Dallas Institute, 2021.

Student Farmworker Alliance. http://www.sfalliance.org/.

Swanson, Heather, Anna Tsing, Elaine Ban, and Nils Bubandt. *Arts of Living on a Damaged Planet: Monsters of the Anthropocene*. Minneapolis: University of Minnesota Press, 2017.

Swenson, Sharon. "Guardian Demons in *Hellboy*: Hybridity in Contemporary American Horror Films." In *Hell and Its Afterlife: Historical and Contemporary Perspectives*, edited by Isabel Moreira and Margaret Toscano, 203–16. New York: Routledge, 2010.

Sugitharajah, R. S. *The Bible and Empire: Postcolonial Explorations*. Cambridge: Cambridge University Press, 2005.

Taylor, Joan E. *What Did Jesus Look Like?* New York: T&T Clark, 2018.

Taylor, Margaret. "Fighting Modern Slavery in the Covid Era." *International Bar Association*, February 3, 2021. https://www.ibanet.org/article/8593D337-4391-4E78-A927-5A3069D0F0DF.

Taylor, Mark C. *Altarity*. Chicago: University of Chicago Press, 1987.

Tertullian *De Spetaculis* [On the Shows]. In *The Ante-Nicene Fathers*, vol. 3, edited by Alexander Roberts, James Donaldson, and A. Cleveland Coxe, 157–91. Translated by S. Thelwall Eugene. OR: Wipf and Stock, 2023.

Theissen, Gerd, and Dagmar Winter. *The Quest for the Plausible Jesus: The Question of Criteria*. Louisville: Westminster John Knox, 2002.

Thomasson, Aime L. *Fiction and Metaphysics*. New York: Cambridge University Press, 2008.

Thompson, Kirsten Moana. *Apocalyptic Dread: American Film at the Turn of the Millennium*. Albany, NY: SUNY Press, 2007.

Thurman, Howard. *Jesus and the Disinherited*. Boston: Beacon, 1996.

———. *The Papers of Howard Washington Thurman*. Vol. 2: *Christian, Who Calls Me Christian?*, edited by Walter E. Fluker. Columbia: University of South Carolina Press, 2012.

Tigerman, Stanley. *The Architecture of Exile*. New York: Rizzoli, 1988.

Ting, Selina. "Interview with Andres Serrano." 2012. www.initiartmagazine.com/interview.php?IVarchive=87.

Todorov, Tzvetan. *The Fantastic: A Structural Approach to a Literary Genre*. Ithaca, NY: Cornell University Press, 1975.

Tolbert, Mary Ann. *Sowing the Gospel: Mark's World in Literary-Historical Perspective*. Minneapolis: Fortress, 1989.

Treusch-Dieter, Gerburg. "The Beginning of the End: On the History of Radiation from Plato to Chernobyl." In *Looking Back on the End of the World*, edited by Dietmar Kamper and Christoph Wulf, 7–18. Translated by David Antal. New York: Semiotext(e), 1989.

Tuan, Yi-Fi. *Space and Time: The Perspective of Experience*. Minneapolis: University of Minnesota Press, 1977.

Tupamahu, Ekaputra. "The Stubborn Invisibility of Whiteness in Biblical Studies." *Political Theology Network*, November 12, 2020. https://politicaltheology.com/the-stubborn-invisibility-of-whiteness-in-biblical-scholarship/.

Turing, Alan. "Computing Machinery and Intelligence." *Mind* LIX 236 (October 1950) 433–60.

Turner, Alice K. *The History of Hell*. New York: HarperOne, 1995.

Updike, John. "Stones into Bread." In *More Matters: Essays and Criticism*, 325–31. New York: Random House, 2012.

Upton, Bridget C. *Hearing Mark's Endings: Listening to Ancient Popular Texts Through Speech Act Theory*. Leiden: Brill, 2006.

Vaage, Leif E. "Bird Watching at the Baptism of Jesus: Early Christian Mythmaking in Mark 1:9–11." In *Reimagining Christian Origins*, edited by Elizabeth Castelli and Hal Taussig, 280–94. Valley Forge, PA: Trinity, 1996.

van der Meer, Frederick. *Apocalypse: Visions from the Book of Revelation in Western Art*. New York: Alspine Fine Arts, 1978.

Vattimo, Gianni. "The Ontology of Actuality." In *Contemporary Italian Philosophy: Crossing the Borders of Ethics, Politics, and Religion*, edited by Silvia Benso and Brian Schroeder, 89–107. Albany: State University of New York Press, 2007.

The View. "Jonathan Roumie Discusses Playing an 'Authentic' Jesus in *The Chosen*." https://www.youtube.com/watch?v=ijENiyc-CrA.

Vighi, Fabio. "Pasolini and Exclusion: Žižek, Agamben and the Modern Sub-Proletariat." *Theory, Culture, and Society* 20/5 (2003) 99–121.

Viola, Bill. *Martyrs*. Video. http://www.theguardian.com/artanddesign/video/2014/may/21/bill-viola-martyrs-video-st-pauls-cathedral.

———. *Reasons for Knocking at an Empty House: Writings 1973-1994*. London: Thames and Hudson, 1995.

Viola, Bill, and Edgard Varèse. *Déserts*. New York: Electronic Arts Intermix, 1994. https://www.eai.org/titles/deserts.2014. *Martyrs (Earth, Air, Fire, Water)*. High definition video polyptych on four plasma displays, colour, 1400 x 3380 x 100 mm; duration: 7:15 minutes; South Quire Aisle of St. Paul's Cathedral; https://www.stpauls.co.uk/history-collections/history/bill-viola.

Virilio, Paul. *The Information Bomb*. Translated by Chris Turner. London: Verso, 2000.

Wachowski, Lana, and Lilly Wachowski, dirs. *The Matrix*. Los Angeles: Warner, 1999.

Wallace, Mark I. "The Wild Bird Who Heals: Recovering the Spirit in Nature." *Theology Today* 50 (1993) 13–28.

Wallis, Brian, ed. *Andres Serrano, Body and Soul*. Hong Kong: Takarajima, 1995.

Walsh, Richard. *Reading the Gospels in the Dark: Portrayals of Jesus in Film*. Harrisburg, PA: Trinity, 2003.

Ward, Graham. "The Displaced Body of Jesus Christ." In *Radical Orthodoxy: A New Theology*, edited by John Milbank, Catherine Pickstock, and Graham Ward, 163–81. New York: Routledge, 1999.

Warner, Marina. *From the Beast to the Blonde: On Fairy Tales and Their Tellers*. New York: Farrar, Straus and Giroux, 1994.

———. *No Go the Bogeyman: Scaring, Lulling, and Making Mock*. New York: Farrar, Straus and Giroux, 1998.

Weiner, Jonah. "The New Master of Suspense." *The Wall Street Journal Magazine*, March 2019, 76–80.

Welland, Michael. *The Desert: Lands of Lost Borders*. London: Reaktion, 2015.

Wells, Liz. *Photography: A Critical Introduction*. 5th ed. New York: Routledge, 2015.

Wertheim, Margaret. *The Pearly Gates of Cyberspace: A History of Space from Dante to the Internet*. New York: Norton, 1999.

Westar Institute. "Jesus Seminar Stage Three: Profiles of Jesus." https://www.westarinstitute.org/seminars/jesus-seminar-phase-3-profiles-of-jesus.

Wiener, Norbert. *Cybernetics or Control and Communication in the Animal and the Machine*. 2nd ed. Cambridge: MIT Press, 1961.

Wilken, Robert L. *The Land Called Holy: Palestine in Christian History and Thought*. New Haven: Yale University Press, 1992.

Win, Thin Lei. "Italy's Lockdown Labour Crunch Sparks Fears of Mafia Exploitation." Thomas Reuters News Foundation, April 20, 2020. https://news.trust.org/item/20200420171731-drstc/

Wink, Walter. *Jesus and Nonviolence: A Third Way*. Minneapolis: Fortress, 2003.

Wolfreys, Julian. "Justifying the Unjustifiable: A Supplementary Introduction of Sorts." In *The Derrida Reader: Writing Performances*, edited by Julian Wolfreys, 1–49. Lincoln: University of Nebraska Press, 1988.

Wolterstorff, Nicholas. *Works and Worlds of Art*. Oxford: Clarendon, 1980.

Wood, Robin, "The American Nightmare: Horror in the 70s." In *Hollywood from Vietnam to Reagan*, 70–94. New York: Columbia University Press, 1986.

———. "An Introduction to the American Horror Film." In *Movies and Methods*, vol. 2, edited by Bill Nichols, 195–219. Berkeley: University of California Press, 1985.

———. "Return of the Repressed." *Film Comment* 14/4 (1978) 25–32.

WSR: Worker-driven Social Responsibility Network. "What Is WSR?" 2020. https://wsr-network.org/what-is-wsr/.

Wyatt, John and Stephen N. Williams, eds. *The Robot Will See You Now: Artificial Intelligence and the Christian Faith*. London: SPCK, 2021.

Yang, Wayne. *A Third University Is Possible*. Minneapolis: University of Minnesota Press, 2017.

Yarbro Collins, Adela. *Mark: A Commentary. Hermeneia: A Critical and Historical and Commentary on the Bible*. Edited by Harold W. Attridge. Philadelphia: Fortress, 2007.

Young, Matthew J. "From Aristotle to the Coalition of Immokalee Workers: Ethical Competence via Narrative Ethics Grows Food Justice." *Journal of Agriculture, Food Systems, and Community Development* 9/1 (June 1, 2019) 131–33.

Yusoff, Kathryn. *A Billion Black Anthropocenes or None*. Minneapolis: University of Minnesota Press, 2018.

Žižek, Slavoj. *Looking Awry: An Introduction to Jacques Lacan through Popular Culture*. Cambridge: MIT Press, 1991.

www.ingramcontent.com/pod-product-compliance
Lightning Source LLC
LaVergne TN
LVHW090514110826
845146LV00003B/848

* 9 7 9 8 3 8 5 2 1 7 4 1 0 *